Pro JavaScript Performance
Monitoring and Visualization

T0075810

Tom Barker

Apress®

Pro JavaScript Performance

ISBN-13 (pbk): 978-1-4302-4749-4

ISBN-13 (electronic): 978-1-4302-4750-0

President and Publisher: Paul Manning
Lead Editor: Ben Renow-Clarke
Technical Reviewer: Anirudh Prabhu
Editorial Board: Steve Anglin, Ewan Buckingham, Gary Cornell, Louise Corrigan, Morgan Ertel, Jonathan Gennick, Jonathan Hassell, Robert Hutchinson, Michelle Lowman, James Markham, Matthew Moodie, Jeff Olson, Jeffrey Pepper, Douglas Pundick, Ben Renow-Clarke, Dominic Shakeshaft, Gwenan Spearing, Matt Wade, Tom Welsh
Coordinating Editor: Katie Sullivan
Copy Editor: James Compton
Compositor: Bytheway Publishing Services
Indexer: SPi Global
Artist: SPi Global
Cover Designer: Anna Ishchenko

Distributed to the book trade worldwide by Springer Science+Business Media New York, 233 Spring Street, 6th Floor, New York, NY 10013. Phone 1-800-SPRINGER, fax (201) 348-4505, e-mail orders-ny@springer-sbm.com, or visit www.springeronline.com.

For information on translations, please e-mail rights@apress.com, or visit www.apress.com.

Apress and friends of ED books may be purchased in bulk for academic, corporate, or promotional use. eBook versions and licenses are also available for most titles. For more information, reference our Special Bulk Sales–eBook Licensing web page at www.apress.com/bulk-sales.

Any source code or other supplementary materials referenced by the author in this text is available to readers at www.apress.com. For detailed information about how to locate your book's source code, go to www.apress.com/source-code.

For my beautiful rabbit.
—Tom Barker

Contents at a Glance

Contents

About the Author

 **Tom Barker** has been a software engineer since the 90s, focusing on the full stack of web development. Currently he is the Senior Manager of Web Development at Comcast, an Adjunct Professor at Philadelphia University, a husband, a father, an amateur power lifter and an armchair philosopher. He is obsessed with elegant software solutions, continual improvement, refining processes, data analysis, and visualization.

About the Technical Reviewer

 **Anirudh Prabhu** is a software engineer at Xoriant Corporation with four years of experience in web design and development. He is responsible for JavaScript development and maintainance in his projects. His areas of expertise include HTML, CSS, JavaScript, and Jquery. When not working, Anirudh loves reading, listening to music, and photography.

Acknowledgments

I'd like to thank my wife Lynn, my son Lukas, and my daughter Paloma for their patience and love.

I'd like to thank Ben Renow-Clarke for thinking of me for this project and supporting the direction that the book went in, not just talking about performance and best practices, but also emphasizing the quantification of results and showing readers how to quantify for themselves.

I'd like to thank Katie Sullivan and Chris Nelson for staying on me and pushing for the good of the project. Several times it was their persistence that kept us going, Katie pushing me to work on chapters in tandem and Chris keeping on me to stay focused and clear with each chapter.

I'd like to thank Anirudh Prabhu for thinking of cases with the code that I didn't think about. The example code is richer because of his perspective.

And finally I'd like to thank my team at Comcast for constantly raising the bar and inspiring me to try to be as excellent as you all are.

—Tom Barker

CHAPTER 1

■ ■ ■

What is Performance

Performance refers to the speed at which an application functions. It is a multifaceted aspect of quality. When we're talking about web applications, the time it takes your application to be presented to your users is what we will call *web performance*. The speed at which your application responds to your users' interactions is what we'll call *runtime performance*. These are the two facets of performance that we will be looking at.

Performance in the context of web (and especially mobile web) development is a relatively new subject, but it is absolutely overdue for the attention it has been getting.

In this book we will explore how to quantify and optimize JavaScript performance, in the context of both web performance and runtime performance. This is vitally important because JavaScript is potentially the largest area for improvement when trying to address the total performance of your site. Steve Souders, architect of both YSlow and PageSpeed, and pioneer in the world of web performance, has demonstrated this point in an experiment where he showed an average performance improvement of 31% when removing JavaScript from a sample of web sites.[1] We can completely remove any JavaScript from our site as Steve did in his experiment, or we can refine how we write JavaScript and learn to measure the efficiencies in what we write.

It's not realistic to remove JavaScript from our front-end, so let's look at making our JavaScript more efficient. Arguably even more important, let's look at how we can create automated tools to track these efficiencies and visualize them for reporting and analysis.

Web Performance

Sitting with your laptop or holding your device, you open a web browser, type in a URL and hit Enter, and wait for the page to be delivered to and rendered by your browser. The span of time that you are waiting for the page to be usable depends on web performance. For our purposes we will define web performance as an overall indicator of the time it takes for a page to be delivered and made available to your end user.

There are many things that influence web performance, network latency being the first. How fast is your network? How many round trips and server responses are needed to serve up your content?

To better understand network latency, let's first look at the steps in an HTTP transaction (Figure 1.1).

When it requests a URL, whether the URL for a web page or a URL for each asset on a web page, the browser spins up a thread to handle the request and initiates a DNS lookup at the remote DNS server. This allows the browser to get the IP address for the URL entered.

---

1 http://www.stevesouders.com/blog/2012/01/13/javascript-performance/

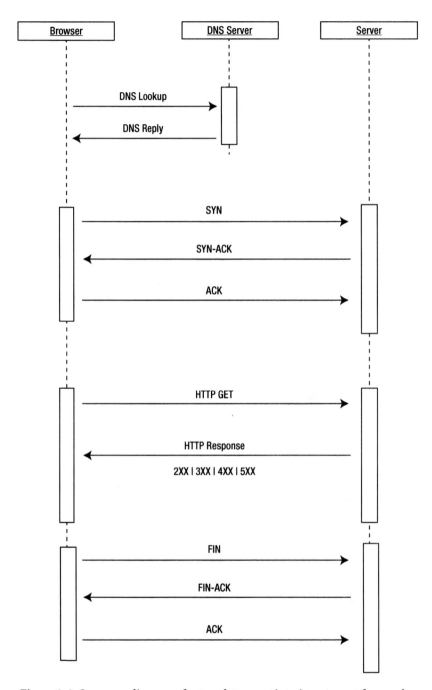

Figure 1-1. Sequence diagram of network transactions in a request for a web page and repeated for each remote -object included in a web page

---

■ **Note** *Threads* are sequential units of controlled execution for applications. Whenever an application performs any operation, it uses a thread. Some applications are multithreaded, which means that they can do multiple things at once. Generally browsers use at least one thread per tab. That means that the steps that the thread executes—the steps that we outline as part of the connection, download and rendering process—are handled sequentially.

Next the browser negotiates a TCP three-way handshake with the remote web server to set up a TCP/IP connection. This handshake consists of a Synchronize, Synchronize-Acknowledge, and Acknowledge message to be passed between the browser and the remote server. This handshake allows the client to attempt communication, the server to acknowledge and accept the attempt, and the client to acknowledge that the attempt has been accepted.

This handshake is much like the military voice procedure for two way radio communication. Picture two parties on either end of a two way radio—how do they know when the other party has finished their message, how do they know not to talk over each other, and how do they know that the one side understood the message from the other? These have been standardized in voice procedure, where certain key phrases have nuanced meaning; for example, Over means that one party has finished speaking and is waiting for a response, and Roger indicates that the message has been understood.

The TCP handshake, like all communication protocols, is just a standardized way to define communication between multiple parties.

THE TCP/IP MODEL

TCP stands for Transmission Control Protocol. It is the protocol that is used in the TCP/IP model that defines how communications between a client and a server are handled, specifically breaking the data into segments, and handling the handshake that we described earlier (Figure 1.1).

The TCP/IP model is a four-layer model that represents the relationship between the different protocols that define how data is shared across the Internet. The specification for the TCP/IP model is maintained by the Internet Engineering Task Force, in two RFC (Request For Comment) documents, found here: `http://tools.ietf.org/html/rfc1122` and `http://tools.ietf.org/html/rfc1123`.

The four layers in the TCP/IP model are, in order from furthest to closest to the end user, the Network Access layer, the Internet layer, the Transport layer, and the Application layer.

The Network Access layer controls the communication between the hardware in the network.

The Internet layer handles network addressing and routing, getting IP and MAC addresses.

The Transport layer is where our TCP (or UDP) communication takes place.

The Application layer handles the top-level communication that the client and servers use, like HTTP and SMTP for email clients.

If we compare the TCP/IP model to our sequence diagram, we see how the browser must traverse up and down the model to serve up our page, as shown here.

Once the TCP/IP connection has been established, the browser sends an HTTP GET request over the connection to the remote server. The remote server finds the resource and returns it in an HTTP Response, the status of which is 200 to indicate a good response. If the server cannot find the resource or generates an error when trying to interpret it, or if the request is redirected, the status of the HTTP Response will reflect these as well. The full list of status codes can be found at http://www.w3.org/Protocols/rfc2616/rfc2616-sec10.html but the most common ones are these:

- 200 indicates a successful response from the server.

- 404 means that the server could not find the resource requested.

- 500 means that there was an error when trying to fulfill the request.

It is here that the web server serves up the asset and the client begins downloading it. It is here that the total payload of your page—which includes file sizes of all images, CSS, and JavaScript—comes into play.

The total size of the page is important, not just because of the time it takes to download, but because the maximum size of an IP packet is 65535 octets for IPv4 and IPv6. If you take your total page size converted to bytes and divide it by the maximum packet size, you will get the number of server responses needed to serve up your total payload.

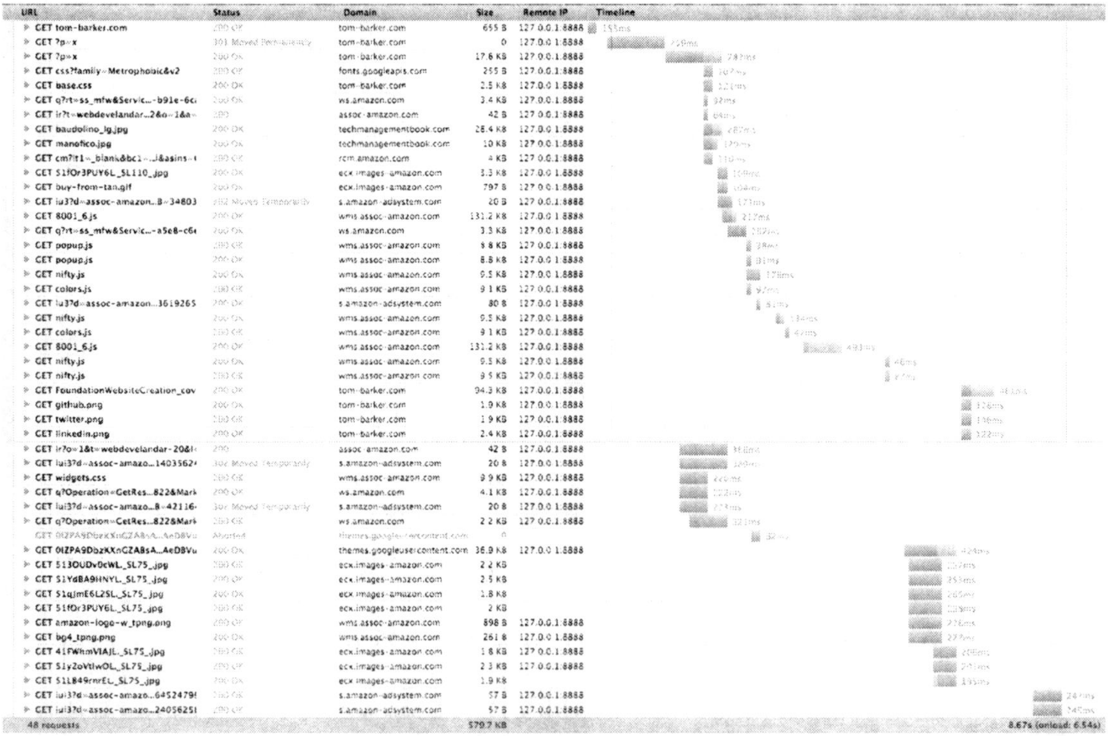

Figure 1-2. Browser architecture

Another contributor to network latency is the number of HTTP requests that your page needs to make to load all of the objects on the page. Every asset that is included on the page—each image and external JavaScript and CSS file—requires a round trip to the server. Each spins up a new thread and a new instance of the flow shown in Figure 1-1, which again includes a cost for DNS lookup, TCP connection, and HTTP request and response, plus the cost in time transmitting the sheer file size of each asset.

See Figure 1-2 for an idea of how this simple concept can exponentially grow and cause performance hits in scale.

Waterfall charts are a tool to demonstrate the time it takes to request a page and all of the assets included in the page. They show the HTTP transaction for each asset needed to construct a page, including the size of each asset, how long each one took to download, and the sequence in which they were downloaded. At a high level, each bar in the waterfall chart is a resource that we are downloading. The length of a bar corresponds to how long an item takes to connect to and download. The chart runs on a sequential timeline, so that the top bar is the first item that gets downloaded and the last bar is the final item, and the far left of the timeline is when the connections begin and the far right is when they end. We will talk much more about waterfall charts in Chapter 2, when we discuss tools for measuring and impacting performance.

Parsing and Rendering

Another influencer of web performance, outside of network concerns, is browser parsing and rendering. Browser parsing and rendering is influenced by a number of things. To better understand this concept let's first look at an overview of the browser's architecture as it pertains to parsing and rendering web pages (Figure 1-3).

Most modern browsers have the following architecture: code to handle the UI, including the location bar and the history buttons, a Rendering Engine for parsing and drawing all of the objects in the page, a JavaScript Engine for interpreting the JavaScript, and a network layer to handle the HTTP requests.

Since the browser reads content from the top down, where you place your assets impacts the perceived speed of your site. For example, if you put your JavaScript tags before HTML content, the browser will launch the JavaScript interpreter and parse the JavaScript before it finishes rendering the remainder of the HTML content, which can delay making the page usable for the end user.

Browsers are your bread and butter as a web developer, and so you should be more than familiar with each of the rendering engines and JavaScript engines. It is more than worth your time to download the

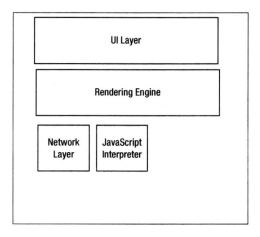

Figure 1-3. Time series of my lift log

ones that are open-source (see the next section for URLs where available) and read through some of the source code. If you are really adventurous you can put your own instrumentation or logging into the source code and automate your own performance tests running in your forked engine.

Rendering Engines

Let's take a look at some of the more widely used rendering engines out in the wild. It's important to think of the rendering engine as more than the browser. By modularizing the architecture of the browsers, the browser makers have been able to federate the components. More tools than just browsers render HTML, including email clients and web components in other applications. By having a distributable rendering engine, browser makers can reuse their own engines or license them for use by other companies. This also usually allows developers to know what to expect from a software package just by knowing which rendering engine it is using.

Firefox and all of its derivatives and cousins (like Thunderbird, Mozilla's email client) use Gecko, available at `https://developer.mozilla.org/en/Gecko`. Gecko was first developed at Netscape, before the Mozilla Project spun out as its own entity, as the successor to the original Netscape rendering engine, back in 1997.

Webkit is what Chrome and Safari use, and is your target for most mobile web development since it is used as the layout or rendering engine for Android devices as well as mobile Safari for iOS devices and the Silk browser on Kindle Fires. Webkit is available at `http://www.webkit.org/`. WebKit was started in 2001 at Apple as a fork of a previous rending engine, KHTML from KDE. WebKit was open sourced publicly in 2005.

Opera on desktop, mobile, and even all the Nintendo consoles (NDS, Wii) use Presto, which was introduced in 2003 with Opera 7. More information about Presto can be found at `http://dev.opera.com/articles/view/presto-2-1-web-standards-supported-by/`.

And finally, Internet Explorer, along with other Microsoft products like Outlook, uses MSHTML, codenamed Trident. Microsoft first introduced Trident with Internet Explorer 4 in 1997 and has been iterating on the engine since. Documentation for Trident can be found here: `http://msdn.microsoft.com/en-us/library/bb508515`.

JavaScript Engines

Next let's take a look at the JavaScript engines used by the most popular browsers. Modularizing the JavaScript interpreter makes the same kind of sense as modularizing the rendering engine, or modularizing any code for that matter. The interpreter can be shared with other properties, or embedded in other tools. The open source interpreters can even be used in your own projects, perhaps to build your own static code analysis tools, or even just to build in JavaScript support to allow your users to script certain functionality in your applications.

SpiderMonkey is the JavaScript engine made by Mozilla that is used in Firefox. Brendan Eich, creator of JavaScript, created SpiderMonkey in 1996 and it has been the JavaScript interpreter for Netscape and then Firefox ever since. The documentation for SpiderMonkey is available here: `https://developer.mozilla.org/en/SpiderMonkey`. Mozilla has provided documentation showing how to embed SpiderMonkey into our own applications here: `https://developer.mozilla.org/en/How_to_embed_the_JavaScript_engine`.

Opera uses Carakan, which was introduced in 2010. More information about Carakan can be found here: `http://my.opera.com/dragonfly/blog/index.dml/tag/Carakan`.

Google's open source JavaScript Engine used by Chrome is available here: `http://code.google.com/p/v8/`. Documentation for it is available here: `https://developers.google.com/v8/intro`.

Safari uses JavaScriptCore, sometimes called Nitro. More information about JavaScriptCore can be found here: `http://www.webkit.org/projects/javascript/index.html`.

And finally, Internet Explorer uses Chakra as their JScript engine. Remember that, as Douglas Crockford details at http://www.yuiblog.com/blog/2007/01/24/video-crockford-tjpl/, JScript started life as Microsoft's own reverse-engineered version of JavaScript. Microsoft has since gone on to give JScript its own voice in the overall ecosystem. It is a legitimate implementation of the ECMAScript spec, and Chakra even supports some aspects of the spec that most other JavaScript engines don't, specifically conditional compilation (see the accompanying discussion of conditional compilation).

All of these are nuances to consider when talking about and optimizing the overall web performance of your site.

The JavaScript team at Mozilla also maintains a site, http://arewefastyet.com/, that compares benchmarking times for V8 and SpiderMonkey, comparing the results of both engines running the benchmarking test suites of each engine.

CONDITIONAL COMPILATION

Conditional compilation is a feature of some languages that traditionally allows the language compiler to produce different executable code based on conditions specified at compile time. This is somewhat of a misnomer for JavaScript because, of course, JavaScript is interpreted, not compiled (it doesn't run at the kernel level but in the browser), but the idea translates.

Conditional compilation allows for writing JavaScript that will only be interpreted if specific conditions are met. By default conditional compilation is turned off for JScript; we need to provide an interpreter-level flag to turn it on: @cc_on. If we are going to write conditionally compiled JavaScript, we should wrap it in comments so that our code doesn't break in other JavaScript interpreters that don't support conditional compilation.

An example of JScript conditional compilation is

```
<script>
var useAX = false; //use ActiveX controls default to false
/*@cc_on
@if (@_win32)
    useAX = true;
@end
*/
</script>
```

Runtime Performance

Runtime is the duration of time that your application is executing, or running. Runtime performance speaks to how quickly your application responds to user input while it is running—for example, while saving preferences, or when accessing elements in the DOM.

Runtime performance is influenced by any number of things—from the efficiency of the algorithms employed for specific functionality, to optimizations or shortcomings of the interpreter or browser rendering engine, to effective memory management and CPU usage, to design choices between synchronous or asynchronous operations.

While runtime performance is thus a subjective perception of the overall peppiness of your application, you can build in instrumentation that will allow you to track the shape and trend of your users' overall experiences and analyze the outliers. You can also conduct multivariate testing experiments to see what approach yields the greatest performance gain at scale and with the browsers in use with your specific user base.

We will explore these ideas in Chapter 4.

Why does performance matter?

The first reason should be obvious—faster web sites mean a better overall user experience for your end user. A better experience in theory should equate to happier users.

A faster experience also means that users can access your features faster, hopefully before they abandon the session. Session or site abandonment happens for any number of reasons: pages taking too long to load, users losing interest, browsers crashing, or any other of a near-infinite number of reasons.

Figuring out your own site abandonment rate is easy. Just take the total number of users who do whatever action you want of them—purchase an item, register a new account, upsell to a service, view pages in other sections, click a given button on the homepage, whatever the high-level objective is that you have for your site. You take that number and divide it by the total number of visits. Subtract that from one and multiply that by 100 to give you the percentage of traffic that abandoned your site before fulfilling your objective:

```
[abandonment rate] = (1 - ([number of fulfilled objectives] \ [total number of visits])) * 100
```

As an example, say we have a web form, maybe a customer registration page. The whole point of that page is to get users to create accounts—once they have an account we can start tailoring things to their own personal preferences, we can target ads to their purchasing habits, and we can make recommendations to them based on past purchases and viewing history. Whatever the purpose, we want them signed in and that's how we'll measure the success of this page. Once a user hits Submit on the form, we go to a PHP script that updates a database, creates a new entry in our User table, and then directs to our homepage.

So we look at the page view metrics for this page and see that we have 100,000 unique page views; in our algorithm this is the total number of visits. If we look at the number of users created in our database, we see that we have 30,000 users. At this point we could apply the algorithm to get our abandonment rate of 70%:

```
(1 - (30,000 \ 100,000)) * 100 = 70
```

Improving performance can bring significant benefits to your bottom line by reducing your abandonment rate. There have been a number of prominent case studies where companies have demonstrated the tangible harm (seen in increased abandonment rates) caused by poor web performance.

Keynote has made available an article by Alberto Savoia, detailing the impact of performance on abandonment rates at `http://www.keynote.com/downloads/articles/tradesecrets.pdf`. In their whitepaper "Why Web Performance Matters," available at http://www.gomez.com/pdfs/wp_why_web_performance_matters.pdf, Gomez details how abandonment rates can increase from 8% up to 38% just by introducing latency in page web performance.

You can run your own experiments using the calculation just shown to quantify and extrapolate the return on investment for optimizing site performance.

Instrumentation and Visualization

A big part of this book is about putting tooling in your code and using data visualizations to demonstrate the results. In truth, that is kind of the point of this book. There is no one silver-bullet solution when it comes to performance. The results that one person sees may not be the same results that another gets, because they may have a completely different user base, using a completely different browser.

Maybe your users are locked into using Internet Explorer because of corporate policy, or maybe your audience is made up of early adopters and you have a high population of people using beta releases of browsers, which may have different optimizations in their interpreter or rendering engine, or may even have bugs in their interpreter or rendering engine.

Whatever the case, your results will vary. And they will vary at scale, because of connection speed at different times of the day (users at work versus users at home), because of their method of connecting (cable versus dial up), or any other reason.

But by measuring your own results and visualizing them to see the overall shape of what your data looks like, you'll be able to fine-tune your own site based on your own real data and trends.

Data visualization as a discipline has blossomed lately. No longer is it relegated solely to the world of mathematics, theory, or cartography. I remember when I first got an inkling of what I could do with data visualization. I was at a conference; it was Velocity in Santa Clara surrounded by my peers. I watched John Rauser give a talk about how he and his team at Amazon debug production issues by analyzing production logs. In his session he talked about sometimes needing to pull out granular data at the individual user level, lay it out in hard copy, and just squint at the data to see the overall shape of it. The shape is what was telling.

That really resonated with me, and since then I've explored that in almost every aspect of my life.

At work I use data visualizations as management tools for running my organization. Some of the charts that we will be creating in this book are derived from charts that I regularly run for my own team.

In my leisure time I trend my power lifting lift log to see my increases, my resets, and when I plateau (see Figure 1-4). I can see how other things going on in my life affect my lift increases, by cross-referencing dates in the time series. Data analysis is actually a key concept in power lifting, enabling you to manage your increases in weight by measuring your recover time. The sign that you have advanced to a higher level of experience is the time it takes to recover from heavy lifts and the increase in the amount that you are lifting. Beginners advance very quickly because they are lifting far from their potential weight ceiling, but intermediate and advanced lifters push their muscles so hard and work so close to their potential ceiling that it takes them much longer to recover and increase their lift weights.[2]

At home I also track the humidity level in each room of my house, and I play with the dials. I see what effect running the heat has on the humidity, or caulking the spaces between the floorboards and the walls, or even just having the doors open instead of closed for each room in the house. In such a way I can aspire to naturally have the lowest possible humidity level in my house without running my dehumidifier.

Visualizing my data allows me to see a larger scope of a situation and to clearly see any spikes, outliers, or trends that might not be obvious in the raw data.

---

2   See Mark Rippetoe's *Starting Strength* (Aasgard Press)

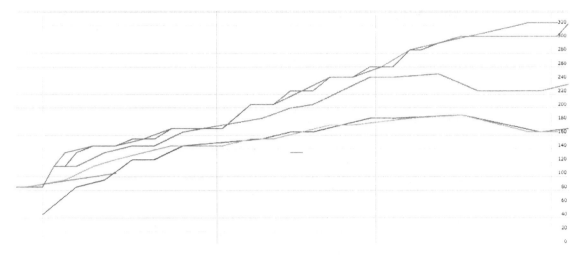

Figure 1-4 *Time series of my lift log*

The Goal of This Book

There is no shortage of information available online and in other books about current best practices for performance—but performance is a moving target. Because each browser uses a different JavaScript interpreter and rendering engine, your results will differ between browsers and browser versions. Best practices are changing or becoming redefined continually because of changes and optimizations at the interpreter level, differences in system configuration, and network speeds. This pace of change is exacerbated by the quickened release schedule that most browsers have adopted.

But just as important as following best practices is the ability to measure your own performance, so that you can adjust as times change, and so that you can note the subtle nuances in your own code and define your own best practices by your own observations.

My goal with this book is to give you the tools to observe and track over time the performance of your web applications from multiple perspectives, so that you are always aware of all aspects of your performance. And by tools, I don't just mean the code that we will develop through the course of the book or the applications available that we will talk about and even automate. I mean the insight to care about these metrics and the mental models to build such instrumentation and visualization into everything that you do.

In many ways, analyzing and optimizing the efficiency of how things operate and perform is part of reaching the next level of excellence. Any journeyman can create something to spec, but a master crafts with excellence and proves that excellence with empirical data.

Technologies Used and Further Reading

As the title suggests, we use JavaScript extensively throughout this book. We also use PHP to automate certain tools, scrape results, and format data. If you aren't already familiar with PHP, its grammar and lexicon are fairly similar to JavaScript, so you should have no problem switching context between the two languages. Extensive coverage of PHP is outside the scope of this book. If you want more of an introduction to the language you can check out *Beginning PHP and MySQL*, by W. Jason Gilmore (Apress, 2005), or if you want a deeper dive into modern PHP, check out *Pro PHP Programming*, by Peter MacIntyre, Brian Danchilla, and Mladen Gogala (Apress, 2011).

Another language we will use quite a bit is R, which is both a language and the environment that runs the language, and it is used to run statistical calculations and chart data that you import or derive. It is a very interesting language with a very specific use.

R can be daunting at first if you aren't familiar with its syntax or even things as fundamental as its different data types. Don't worry; I will explain everything that you need to know to understand the code that we will be writing in R. If you'd like a deeper dive into R—and with most statistical information from the top companies being derived in R,[3] and data science being one of the largest growth fields in the coming years,[4] why wouldn't you want to know more about R?—then I recommend *R in Action*, by Robert Kabicoff (Manning, 2011) and *The Art of R Programming: A Tour of Statistical Design*, by Norman Matloff (No Starch Press, 2011). Both books approach R as a programming language, as opposed to a mathematical environment, which makes it easier for developers to grasp.

R is amazingly useful to learn, and the more you use it the more you'll find uses for it. And it's completely extensible, with a rich plugin architecture and a huge community that builds plugins; it's rare to find something that R can't do—at least in the realm of statistics and data visualization.

As I said earlier, there are many resources available for further reading and exploration on the subject of overall web performance optimization. I've referenced Steve Souders' works already; he is a luminary in the field of web performance. His web site is http://www.stevesouders.com/ and he has written two books that go deep into many aspects of web performance. He also runs http://httparchive.org/, whose goal is to be an archive of performance metrics and statistics for the web. All manner of interesting things are to be found here, from the percentage of the web using JQuery to the overall trend of Flash usage over time. This is hugely useful for seeing overall trends as well as doing competitive analysis when developing new features or applications.

The Worldwide Web Consortium (W3C) has a working group dedicated to web performance. This group is working to create specifications and extensions to current standards to expose functionality that will give developers more control in tracking performance natively in a browser. Their charter is located here: http://www.w3.org/2010/webperf/. We will be discussing the progress and specifications that have come from this group in Chapter 5.

Since the point of this book is not just about performance but also about visualizing information, I recommend Nathan Yau's book *Visualize This: The FlowingData Guide to Design, Visualization, and Statistics* (Wiley, 2011) as a great primer for data visualization as a craft. Nathan also maintains http://flowingdata.com/.

Summary

This chapter explored some introductory concepts around performance. We defined two aspects of performance for web applications; web performance is an indication of the time it takes to serve content to our end users, and runtime performance is an indication of how responsive our applications are while our end users are using them.

We briefly explored some of the protocols that hold the web together, like the TCP/IP model, and we traced a request for content from our browser up the TCP/IP model, correlating each action along the way with where in the model it was taking place. We examined the architecture of a TCP round trip and saw the steps involved that our browsers need to take for every piece of content that we request—sometimes in the case of HTTP redirects, multiple times for each of content.

---

3 http://www.revolutionanalytics.com/what-is-open-source-r/companies-using-r.php and http://www.nytimes.com/2009/01/07/technology/business-computing/07program.html

4 http://mashable.com/2012/01/13/career-of-the-future-data-scientist-infographic/

We looked at modern browser architecture and saw that browsers are no longer huge black-box monoliths, but instead are modular and some even open source. We talked about the benefits of this modular architecture, noting that as the web becomes ubiquitous, rendering engines are being used for other applications to parse and render markup in email clients or embedded in custom applications, and that we can even embed pieces of browsers in our own applications.

We looked at why performance matters to our business, from customer happiness to looking at abandonment rates.

Finally we started to talk about gathering, analyzing, and visualizing our data. This last point is a recurring theme that we will see throughout this book—measuring and quantifying with empirical data, visualizing that data to show the overall shape of the data. The shape of the data is key; it can reveal trends and patterns that aren't obvious in the raw data. We can look at a visualization immediately and know generally what it is saying.

We'll look much deeper into these concepts in the coming chapters, and we begin in the next chapter by exploring tools that are available for us to track and improve performance.

CHAPTER 2

■ ■ ■

Tools and Technology to Measure and Impact Performance

Chapter 1 outlined the concepts of web performance and runtime performance and discussed influencing factors for each. This chapter will look at some of the tools that are available to track performance and to help improve performance.

In future chapters we will explore how to use some of these tools programmatically and combine them to create charting and reporting applications, so getting familiar with them first is essential. Other tools, like Firebug and YSlow, are just essential tools for developing and maintaining performant web sites.

Firebug

2006 was a great year for web development. First of all, Microsoft released Internet Explorer 7, which brought with it native JavaScript support for the `XMLHttpRequest` object—previously web developers had to branch their code. If a browser's JavaScript engine supported XHR we would use that; otherwise we would know that we were in an earlier version of IE and instantiate the XHR ActiveX control.

A slew of new frameworks also came out in 2006, including jQuery, MooTools, and YUI, all with the aim of speeding up and simplifying development.

Arguably the greatest milestone of the year was the release of Firebug from Joe Hewitt and the team at Mozilla. Firebug is an in-browser tool that allows web developers to do a number of tasks that were not possible previously. We can now invoke functions or run code via a console command line, alter CSS on the fly, and—the aspect that will interest us most when talking about performance—monitor network assets as they are downloaded to form a page. If you don't currently have Firebug running on your computer, take the following steps to install it.

How to Install

First let's install Firebug. You can get the latest version of Firebug here: `https://getfirebug.com/downloads/`. It was originally released as a Firefox extension, but since then there have been Firebug lite releases for most other browsers. Since Firebug lite doesn't include the Network Monitoring tab, we'll use Firefox for this section so that we have all the features of Firebug available to us.

If you navigate to the URL just shown, you come to a page presenting you with different versions of Firebug that are available for download, as shown in Figure 2-1.

13

Figure 2-1. The Firebug download screen

Once you choose the version of Firebug you want, you are taken to the download page (Figure 2-2). Click "Add to Firefox," and the extension will download and install itself. Restart the browser to complete the installation.

Once Firebug is installed, either click the Firebug icon at the top-right of the browser or at the File menu click Web Developer ➤ Firebug to open the Firebug console, as seen in Figure 2-3.

The console is beautiful and wonderfully useful. From here you can view debug messages that you put into your code, view error messages, output objects to see their structure and values, invoke functions in scope on the page, and even run ad hoc JavaScript code. If you weren't doing web development before Firebug was around, you may not be able to appreciate what a watershed it was to finally be able to do

Figure 2-2. Click the Add to Firefox button to install the plugin.

Figure 2-3. The Firebug console

those things in a browser. Back then, if you had been used to the Integrated Development Environments (IDEs) for compiled languages, and thus accustomed to memory profiling and being able to debug your code at run time and see the value inside variables and step through your logic, you would have been quite dismayed at the lack of those tools for web development.

But as beautiful and useful as the console is, our concern right now is the Net tab.

How to Use

Network Monitoring in Firebug is a passive tool; you just click on the Net tab—short for Network Monitoring— (if this is the first time you click on the tab, you'll need to enable the panel) and navigate to a web page (my tom-barker.com in the following examples). As the page loads, you see all of the network assets begin to load. This display is a waterfall chart (see Figure 2-4).

As introduced in Chapter 1, waterfall charts are a data visualization tool used to demonstrate the effects of sequentially adding and removing elements in a system. They are used in the world of web performance monitoring to demonstrate how the payload and load time of a page are influenced by the components that make up the page.

Each bar in the waterfall chart is a remote piece of content that is part of your page, whether it is an image, a JavaScript file, a SWF, or a web font. The bars are stacked in rows; sequentially top-down to indicate first to last items downloaded. This shows us where in the process each item is downloaded— image A is downloaded before image B, and our external JS files are downloaded last, and so on—and how long each piece of content takes to download. In addition to the bar of the chart, each row also has columns to indicate the URL, the HTTP status, the source domain, the file size, and the remote IP address for the corresponding piece of content. The blue vertical line indicates when the parsing of the document has completed, and the red vertical line indicates when the document has finished loading. The color coding of the vertical bars indicates where in the process of connecting the particular asset is at a given time. The blue section is for DNS lookup, the yellow section is for connecting, the red is for sending, the purple is for waiting for data, and green is for receiving data.

Below the Net tab is a sub-navigation bar that allows you to filter the results in the waterfall chart. You can show all the content, only HTML content, only JavaScript, only Ajax requests (called XHR for XML Http Request object), only images, only Flash content, or only media files. See Figure 2-5 for my results filtered by JavaScript.

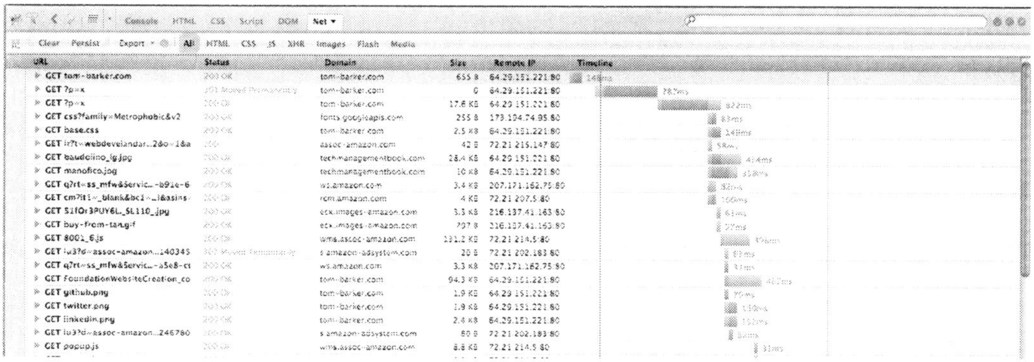

Figure 2-4. *A waterfall chart in the Network Monitoring tab*

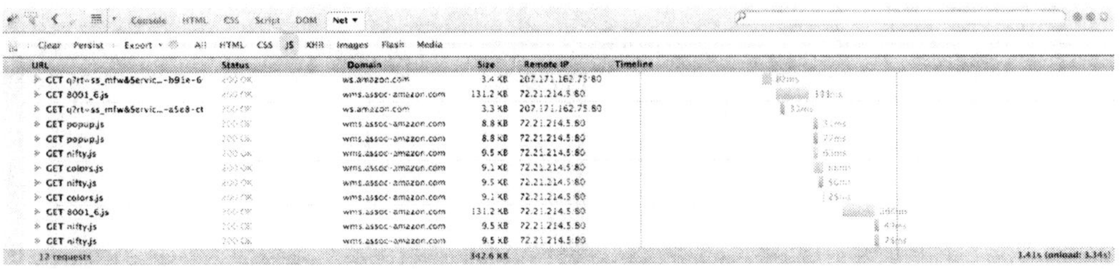

Figure 2-5. Filtering results by resource type

Generally you can use Firebug to get an idea of potential issues either during development or for production support. You can proactively monitor the size of your payloads and the general load time, and you can check to make sure that your pages aren't taking too long to load. What is the overall size of my page, what are the largest assets, and what is taking the longest to load? You can answer questions like that. You can use the filters to focus on areas of concern, like seeing how large our external JavaScript files are. Or even sort the rows by domain name to see content grouped by domain, or sort by HTTP status to quickly pick out any calls that are erroring out.

Because Firebug is a passive tool that merely reports what is happening and doesn't give recommendations for improvements, it's best suited as a development tool or for debugging issues that arise.

YSlow

For a deeper analysis of a page's web performance you can use YSlow.

Developed by Steve Souders and the team at Yahoo!, YSlow was released in 2007. It was initially released as a Firefox extension, but eventually it was ported to work with most other browsers as well. Like Firebug, YSlow is an in-browser tool, and like Firebug it does not allow much automation, but it is an invaluable tool to assess a page's web performance and get feedback on steps to take to improve performance.

The steps for improvement are what really distinguish YSlow. It uses a set of criteria to evaluate the performance of a given page and gives feedback that is specific to the needs of your site. Best of all, the criteria are a living thing, and the YSlow team updates them as best practices change and old ones become less relevant.

Let's try out YSlow.

How to Install

To install YSlow, simply navigate to http://yslow.org/ and choose the platform that you want to run it in. Figure 2-6 shows all the different browsers and platforms that are currently available on the YSlow website.

Since we are already using Firefox with Firebug, let's continue to use that browser for YSlow. Once you select the Firefox version, install the extension and restart the browser, you are ready to start using YSlow.

Availability

Figure 2-6. *Different ways to access YSlow*

How to Use

In Firefox if you open up Firebug you can see that it has a new tab called YSlow. When you click on the tab you are presented with the splash screen shown in Figure 2-7. From this screen you can run the YSlow test on the page that is currently loaded in the browser or choose to always run the test whenever a new page is loaded.

You can also choose what rule set to have the page evaluated against, As I've been saying, best practices change, and the different rule sets reflect that. There is the classic set of rules that YSlow initially launched with, an updated rule set (V2) that changed the weighting of certain rules (like making CSS and JavaScript external) and added a number of new rules, and a subset of the rules for small-scale sites and blogs where those rules would be overkill.

After running the test you'll see the results screen shown in Figure 2-8. The results screen is split into two sections: the rules with their respective ratings on the left and an explanation of the rule on the right.

For a detailed breakdown of the rules that YSlow uses, see `http://developer.yahoo.com/performance/rules.html`.

There is a sub-navigation bar that further breaks down the results, showing the page components, statistics for the page, and tools you can use for further refinement of performance.

The components section is much like the Network Monitoring tab in Firebug; it lists the individual assets in the page, and each component's file size, URL, response header, response time, expires header, and etag.

■ **Tip** Entity tags, or etags for short, are fingerprints that are generated by a web server and sent over in the HTTP transaction and stored on the client. They are a caching mechanism, by which a client can request a piece of content by sending its stored etag in the transaction, and the server can compare to see if the etag sent matches the etag that it has stored. If they match, the client uses the cached version.

Figure 2-7. *The YSlow extension*

Figure 2-8. *The YSlow results screen*

But beware; etags are unique to the server that generated them. If your content is being served by a cluster, that is an array of servers, rather than a single server. The etags won't match if a client requests the content from a different server, and you won't get the benefit of having the content cached.

The statistics section, shown in Figure 2-9, displays two pie charts that show the breakdown of page components. The left chart shows the results with no content cached, and the right shows a subsequent cached view. This is useful to identify the areas that can give the biggest improvement.

By comparing the two charts in Figure 2-9, you can see that JavaScript and images are the two largest pieces of the page before caching. Caching alleviates this for images, but I bet we can get our JavaScript footprint even lower by using a tool that we'll be talking about soon, Minify.

There are other products similar to YSlow. Google has since made available Page Speed, as a standalone site located here: `https://developers.google.com/speed/pagespeed/insights`. Page Speed is also available as a browser extension for Chrome or Firefox, available here: `https://developers.google.com/speed/pagespeed/insights_extensions`.

The differences between YSlow and Page Speed are negligible, and subject to personal preferences in style and presentation.

Figure 2-10 shows the results of a Page Speed test run in the developer tools in Chrome.

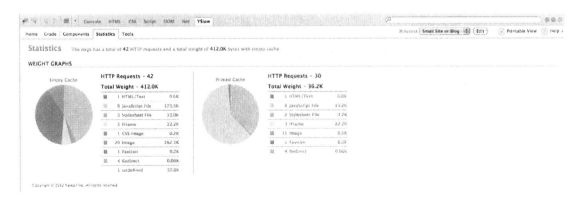

Figure 2-9. *The YSlow results screen—statistics*

Figure 2-10. *Page Speed results*

Another similar product is WebPagetest. Because of its rich feature set and potential automation, WebPagetest will be the next product that we talk about at length.

WebPagetest

WebPagetest was originally created by AOL and open sourced for public consumption and contribution in 2008. It is available as a public web site, as an open source project, or for download to run a private instance. The code repository is found at `http://code.google.com/p/webpagetest/`. The public web site is located at `http://www.webpagetest.org/` and can be seen in Figure 2-11. The public site is maintained and run by Pat Meenan, through his company WebPagetest LLC.

WebPagetest is a web application that takes a URL and a set of configuration parameters as input and runs performance tests on that URL. The number and range of parameters that we can configure for WebPagetest is extraordinarily robust.

If you want to run tests on web sites that are not publicly available—like a QA or development environment, or if you can only have your test results stored on your own servers because of legal or other reasons, then installing your own private instance of WebPagetest is the way to go.

Otherwise, there is no reason not to use the public instance.

You can choose from a set of locations from around the world where your tests can be run. Each location comes with one or more browsers that can be used for the test at that location. You can also specify the connection speed and the number of tests to run.

In the Advanced panel, you can have the test stop running at document completion. That will tell us when the `document.onload` event is fired, instead of when all assets on the page are loaded. This is useful because XHR communications that may happen after page load could register as new activity and skew the test results.

You can also have the test ignore SSL certification errors that would otherwise block the test because an interaction with the end user would be needed to either allow the transaction to proceed, view the certificate, or cancel the transaction.

19

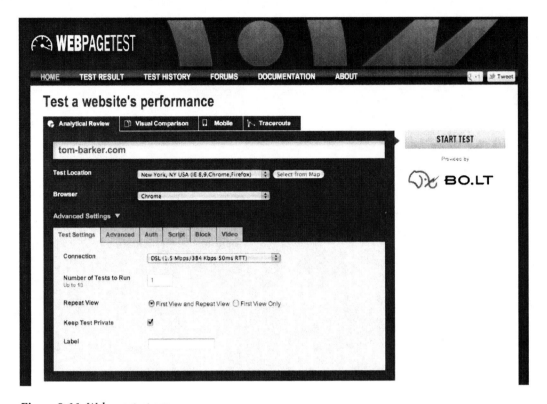

Figure 2-11. Webpagetest.org

There are a number of other options in the Advanced tab; you can have the test capture the packet trace and network log, providing the granular details of the network transactions involved in the test, or select the "Preserve original User Agent string" option to have the test keep the user agent string of the browser running the test instead of appending a string to identify the visit as a WebPagetest test.

In the Auth tab you can specify credentials to use if the web site uses HTTP authentication for access; just remember to exercise caution. Using real production usernames and passwords for tests staged and stored on public servers is never recommended. It is much more advisable to create test credentials for just this purpose, with constrained permissions.

Sometimes you need to test very specific conditions. Maybe you are running a multivariate test on a certain feature set where you are only serving specific features on specific client configurations, like iPhone specific features. Or you are targeting certain features for users that are grouped by inferred usage habits. You would want to run performance tests on these features that are only triggered by special events.

The Script tab allows you to do just that. You can run more complex tests that involve multiple steps including navigate to multiple URLs, send Click and Key events to the DOM, submit form data, execute ad hoc JavaScript, and update the DOM. You can even alter the HTTP request settings to do things like set specific cookies, set the host IP, or change the user agent.

For example, to make a client appear to be an iPhone, simply add the following script:

```
setUserAgent     Mozilla/5.0 (iPhone; U; CPU iPhone OS 4_0 like Mac OS X; en-us)
AppleWebKit/532.9 (KHTML, like Gecko) Version/4.0.5 Mobile/8A293 Safari/6531.22.7
navigate http://tom-barker.com
```

The setUserAgent command spoofs the client user agent, and the navigate command points the test to the specified URL. You can read more about the syntax and some of the great things you can do with scripting WebPagetest here: https://sites.google.com/a/webpagetest.org/docs/using-webpagetest/scripting.

The Block tab allows us to block content coming in our request. This is useful to compare results with and without ads, with or without JavaScript, and with or without images. Instead of using the block tab we could just incorporate a blocking command as part of our script in the Script tab. If we wanted to script out blocking all PNGs in a site it would look like this:

```
block .png
navigate http://www.tom-barker.com
```

And finally, the Video tab allows you to capture screen shots of your page as it loads and view them as a video. This is useful for being able to see what a page looks like as it loads, particularly when you have content loaded in asynchronously; you can see at what point in the process the page looks to be usable.

So once you've set all of the configuration choices, you can run the test. You can see my results screen in Figure 2-12.

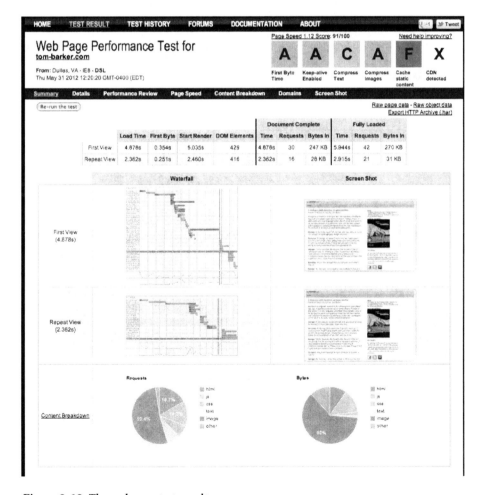

Figure 2-12. *The webpage test results page*

First the Summary screen aggregates all of the vital relevant information for you. At the top right is a summary of the Page Speed results for our page. This is a high-level representation of the same information that would be presented if we had run a test in Page Speed, but shown in YSlow's letter grading format.

Sitting in a table above the waterfall charts and screen shots are the page level metrics, numbers for the load time of the full page, how long the first byte took to load, how long until the first piece of content was drawn to the stage, how many DOM elements are on the page, the time it took for the document. onload event to fire, the time it took for all elements on the page to load, and the number of HTTP requests were needed to draw the page.

Make note of these data. They comprise the fundamental information that makes up the quantitative metrics that you will use to chart web performance in the next chapter. They are the true essence of a site's web performance.

Below this table are two columns. On the left are waterfall charts for the first-time view and the cached repeat view, and on the right are the corresponding screen shots. We've already talked at length about how useful waterfall charts are.

Below these are two pie charts. The chart on the left shows the percent of requests by content type. The chart on the right shows the percent of bytes by content type, which is useful for identifying the largest areas that can be optimized. If your JavaScript is only 5% of your overall payload but your images are 70%, you would be better served optimizing images first.

This summary page aggregates at a high level all of the data that you can find in the pages accessed by its sub-navigation bar. Click on the Details, Performance Review, Page Speed, Content Breakdown, Domains, and Screen Shot links in this bar for a deeper dive into each. The Content Breakdown section can be seen in Figure 2-13. This shows how each piece of content fares in the criteria outlined in the

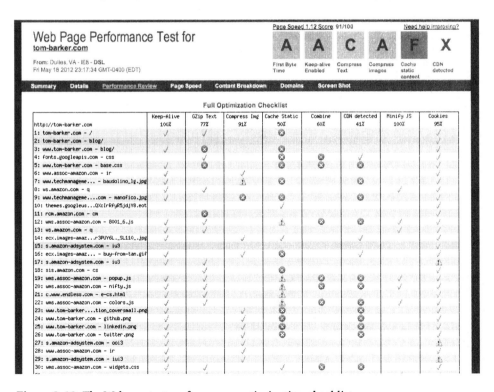

Figure 2-13. *The Webpagetest performance optimization checklist*

column names (Keep-Alive, Gzip text, Compress Images, Cache Static, Combine, CDN detected, Minify JS, and cookies). The green check marks indicate a success in the criteria, the yellow triangles with the exclamation points indicate a warning, and the red Xs indicate errors.

As you can see, WebPagetest provides a wealth of information about the web performance of a site, but best of all it's fully programmable. It provides an API that you can call to provide all of this information. Next chapter we'll explore the API and construct our own application for tracking and reporting out web performance.

Minification

In general, a good amount of energy is spent thinking about optimizing caching. This is a great thing because caching as much content as you can will both create a better user experience for subsequent visits and save on bandwidth and hits to your origin servers.

But when a user comes to a site for the first time there will be no cache. So to ensure that our first-time visits are as streamlined as possible, we need to minify our JavaScript.

Minification is originally based on the idea that the JavaScript interpreter ignores white space, line breaks, and of course comments, so we can save on total file size of our .js files if we remove those unneeded characters.

There are many products that will minify JavaScript. Some of the best ones add twists on that concept.

Minify

First we'll look at Minify, available at `http://code.google.com/p/minify/`. Minify proxies the JavaScript file; the script tag on the page points to Minify, which is a PHP file (In the following code we point to just the /min directory because the PHP file is `inde.php`). The script tag looks like this:

```
<script type="text/javascript" src="/min/?f=lib/perfLogger.js"></script>
```

▨ **Note** A web proxy is code that accepts a URL, reads in and processes the contents of the URL, and makes that content available, either as-is or decorated with additional functionality or formatting. Usually we use proxies to make content on one domain available to client-side code on another domain. Minify reads in the content, decorates it by way of removing extraneous characters, and gzips the response.

Minify reads the JavaScript file in, minifies it and when it responds it sets the accept encoding HTTP header to gzip, deflate. Effectively it has built in HTTP static compression. This is especially useful if your web host doesn't allow the gzipping of static content (like the web host I use, unfortunately). See the high level architecture of how Minify works in Figure 2-14.

To use Minify, simply download the project from `http://code.google.com/p/minify/`, place the decompressed /min folder in the root of your web site, and navigate to the Minify control panel, located at /min/builder/.

From this control panel you can add the JavaScript files you want included in the minified result, and the page generates the script tag that you can use to link to this result. Fairly simple.

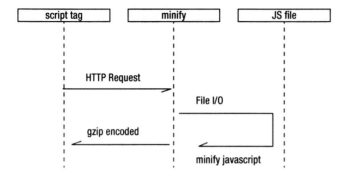

Figure 2-14. Sequence diagram for Minify. The script tag points to Minify, passing in the URL of the JavaScript file. Minify strips out unneeded characters, sets the response header to be gzip-encoded, and returns the result to the script tag, which loads in the browser.

YUI Compressor

Another minification tool is Yahoo's YUI Compressor, available here: `http://yuilibrary.com/download/yuicompressor/`. YUI Compressor is a jar file and runs from the command line. Because of this it is easily integrated into a build process. It looks like this:

```
java -jar yuicompressor-[version].jar [options] [file name]
```

Just like Minify, YUI Compressor strips out all of the unnecessary characters from your JavaScript, including spaces, line breaks, and comments. For a more detailed look at the options available for YUI Compressor, see `http://developer.yahoo.com/yui/compressor`.

Closure Compiler

Finally we'll look at Google's Closure Compiler, available at `https://developers.google.com/closure/compiler/`. Closure Compiler can also run from the command line and be built into an automated process, but it takes minification one step further by rewriting as well as minifying the JavaScript. To rewrite our JavaScript, Closure Compiler runs through a number of "scorched-earth" optimizations—it unfurls functions, rewrites variable names, and removes functions that are never called (as far as it can tell). These are considered "scorched-earth" optimizations because they strip everything out, including best practices, in search of the leanest payload possible. And the approach succeeds. We would never write our code in this way, so we keep our originals, and run them through Closure Compiler to "compile" them into the most optimized code possible. We keep this "compiled" code as a separate file, so that we have our originals to update.

To get an idea of how Closure Compiler rewrites our JavaScript, let's look at some code before and after running Closure Compiler. For the "before" we're using a small code example that we will be using in Chapter 7.

```
<script src="/lib/perfLogger.js"></script>
<script>
    function populateArray(len){
        var retArray = new Array(len)
        for(var i = 0; i < len; i++){
            retArray[i] = 1;
        }
```

```
        return retArray
    }
perfLogger.startTimeLogging("page_render", "timing page render", true, true)
/* ***


7.1
Compare timing for loop against for in loop
****/

var stepTest = populateArray(40);

perfLogger.startTimeLogging("for_loop", "timing for loop", true,true, true)
for(var x = 0; x < stepTest.length; x++){
}
perfLogger.stopTimeLogging("for_loop");

perfLogger.startTimeLogging("for_in_loop", "timing for in loop", true, true)
for(ind in stepTest){

}
perfLogger.stopTimeLogging("for_in_loop")

/** end 7.1 ***/

/* ***


7.1.1
Benchmark for loop and for in loop

****/
function useForLoop(){
    var stepTest = populateArray(40);
    for(var x = 0; x < stepTest.length; x++){
    }
}

function useForInLoop(){
    var stepTest = populateArray(40);
    for(ind in stepTest){
    }
}

perfLogger.logBenchmark("f", 1, useForLoop, true, true);
perfLogger.logBenchmark("fi", 1, useForInLoop, true, true);

perfLogger.stopTimeLogging("page_render")
</script>
```

Closure Compiler takes that code and rewrites it as this:

```
<script>
```

```
var b=[];function e(a,c){b[a]={};b[a].id=a;b[a].startTime=new Date;b[a].description=c;b[a].a=!0}
function f(a){b[a].d=new Date;b[a].c=b[a].d-b[a].startTime;b[a].url=window.location;b[a].
e=navigator.userAgent;b[a].a&&g(a)}function h(a,c){for(var d=0,j=0;10>j;j++)e(a,"benchmarking
"+c),c(),f(a),d+=b[a].c;b[a].a=drawToPage;b[a].b=d/10;b[a].a&&g(a)}
function g(a){var c=document.getElementById("debug"),d="<p><strong>"+b[a].description+"</strong>
<br/>",d=b[a].b?d+("average run time: "+b[a].b+"ms<br/>"):d+("run time: "+b[a].
c+"ms<br/>"),d=d+("path: "+b[a].url+"<br/>"),d=d+("useragent: "+b[a].e+"<br/>"),a=d+"</p>";c?c.
innerHTML+=a:(c=document.createElement("div"),c.id="debug",c.innerHTML=a,document.body.
appendChild(c))}function i(){for(var a=Array(4E4),c=0;4E4>c;c++)a[c]=1;return a}e("page_
render","timing page render");var k=i();e("for_loop","timing for loop");
for(var l=0;l<k.length;l++);f("for_loop");e("for_in_loop","timing for in loop");for(ind in
k);f("for_in_loop");h("f",function(){for(var a=i(),c=0;c<a.length;c++);});h("fi",function(){var
a=i();for(ind in a);});f("page_render");
</script>
```

It's a significant improvement in all performance metrics, but at the cost of readability, and abstraction from the original code.

Comparison of Results

To determine the best tool to use for a given situation, we'll take the scientific approach! Let's implement the tools just discussed and run a multivariate test to see for ourselves which will give us the best results.

First we'll look at a waterfall chart of a sample of unminified code, as seen in Figure 2-15.

We see that uncompressed and unminified our JavaScript file is 2.1 KB and our total page size is 3.3KB. This sample can be found at http://tom-barker.com/lab/perfLogger_example.html.

Now let's use Minify and test those results. You can see in the waterfall chart from Figure 2-16 that the JavaScript served from Minify (both minified and gzipped) is only 573 bytes, and the total page size is 1.9 KB.

When I use YUI Compressor and Closure Compiler (with simple options chosen, so the file is only minified, not rewritten) on these same files I get the same result; the JavaScript file is reduced to 1.6 KB for each and the total page size is 2.9 KB. See Figure 2-17.

Remember, the web host that I am using does not support HTTP compression at a global scale, so these results are simply minified, not gzipped. Thus these are not apples-to-apples comparison of the minification algorithm, just a comparison of using the products out of the box.

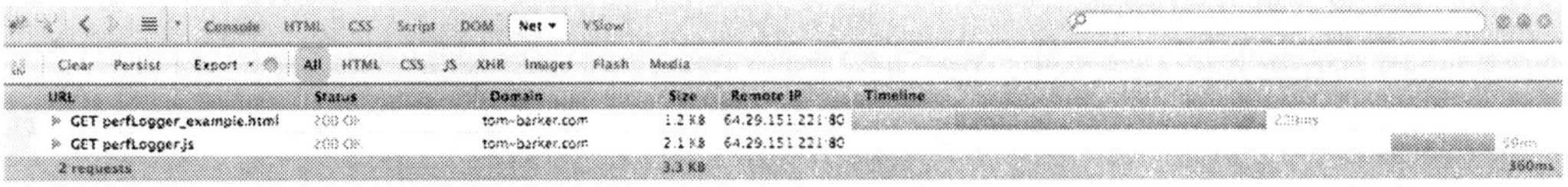

Figure 2-15. *Waterfall chart with uncompressed JavaScript, our baseline*

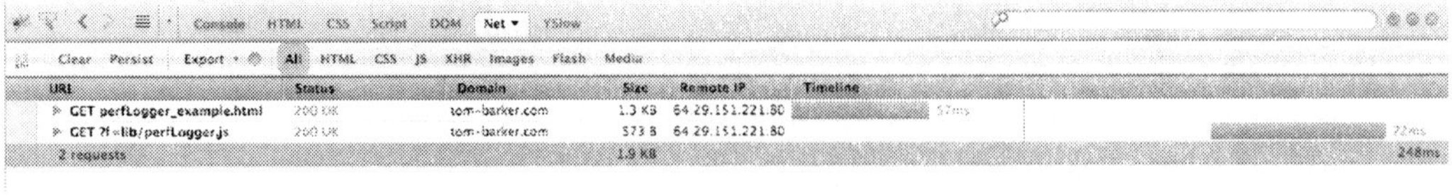

Figure 2-16. *The page compressed with Minify*

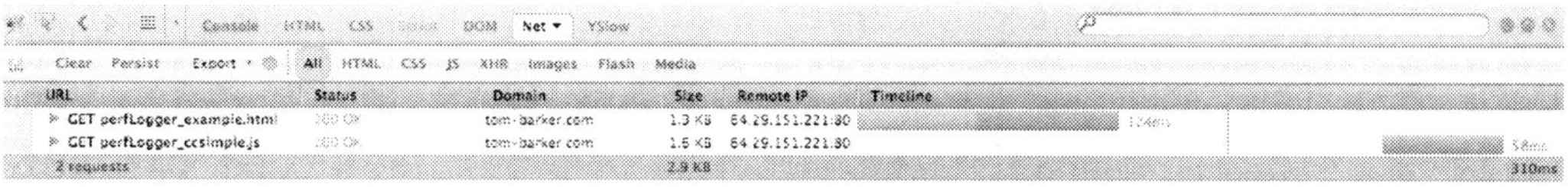

Figure 2-17. The page compressed with Closure Compiler (simple)

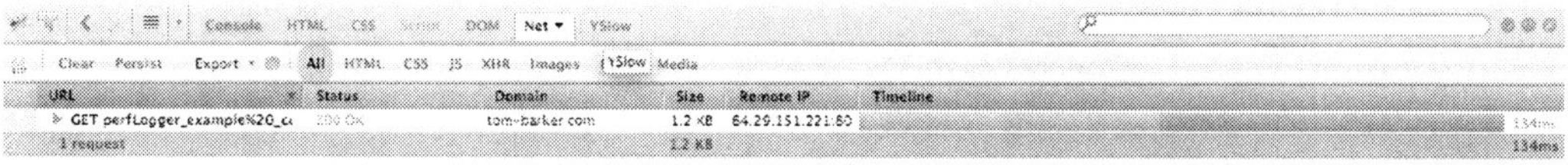

Figure 2-18. The page compressed and included in-line with Closure Compiler (advanced)

The final comparison is to take the original JavaScript file and run it through Closure Compiler with the Advanced option enabled, so it rewrites the code to be as streamlined as possible. When you do this, make sure you include all JavaScript on the page; that is, not just the remote js file, but also the JavaScript on the page that instantiates the objects. It's necessary to do this because Closure Compiler will eliminate all code that it does not see executed. So if you have a namespaced object in a remote JS file but code to instantiate it on the HTML page, you need to include the code that instantiates the object in the same file so Closure Compiler can see that it's used and include it in its output.

The final output from Closure Compiler I will embed on the HTML page instead of linking to it externally. You can see the results in Figure 2-18.

Now that we have some data, let's visualize it and evaluate.

Analysis and Visualization

We'll open up R and pour in our minification results, the tool names, the new file size for each tool's output, and the percent difference for each. We'll then code some R to create a horizontal bar chart to compare the difference.

Don't worry, to do this we'll explore R in depth, and when we do I'll explain what each line does. For now let's roll with it and look at the chart you'll ultimately generate, shown in Figure 2-19.

You can see from Figure 2-19 that Closure Compiler gives the greatest reduction in size right out of the box, but Minify's combination of minification and gzipping brings it in to a close second. YUI and the simple minification that Closure Compiler provide come in tied a distant third.

Again this comparison is performance out of the box—if we had gzipped our results at third place they would have had comparable results to Minify's, but Minify supplies gzipping out of the box.

Sheer file size reduction is only one aspect of our overall determination. As you saw in the example earlier, Closure Compiler's advanced output is far different from the code that originally went into it. If issues were to arise in production they could be difficult to debug, especially if there is third-party code on your pages interacting with your own code.

Does your site have third-party code, like ad code? Are you hosting your own servers or beholden to a web host? How important is production support to you, compared to having the absolute fastest experience possible? When determining your own preferred tool, it is best to evaluate as we just did and see what works best for your own situation, environment, and business rules. For example, do you have a build environment where you can integrate this tool and have control over configuring your web host? If so, then YUI or Closure Compiler might be your best choices. Are you comfortable with the scorched-earth approach of Closure Compiler's advanced setting? If so, that gives the greatest performance boost – but good luck trying to debug its output in production.

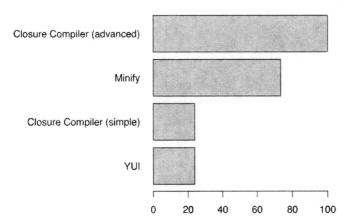

Figure 2-19. Comparison chart generated in R to show percent of file reduction by product

Getting Started with R

R was created in 1993 by Ross Ihaka and Robert Gentleman. It is an extension of and successor to the S language, which was itself a statistical language created in 1976 by John Chambers while at Bell Labs.

R is both an open source environment and the language that runs in that environment, for doing statistical computing. That's a very general description. I'm not a statistician, nor am I a data analyst. I'm a web developer and I run a department of web developers, if you are reading this, chances are you are a web developer. So what do we, as web developers, do with R?

Generally I use R to suck in data, parse it, process it, and then visualize it for reporting purposes. Figure 2-20 illustrates this workflow. It's not the only language I use in this workflow, but it is my new favorite. I need other languages usually to access a data source or scrape another application. In the next chapter we use PHP for this, our glue language, but we could use almost any other language—Ruby, shell script, Perl, Python, and so on.

After I use a glue language to collect the data, I write the data out as a comma-separated file, and read it into R. Within R I process the data, splitting it, averaging it, aggregating it, overlaying two or more data sets, and then from within R I chart the data out to tell the story that I see in it.

Once I have a chart created, generally as a PDF so that it maintains its vectors and fonts, from R I import the chart into Adobe Illustrator, or any other such program, where I can clean up things like font consistency and make sure axis labels with long names are visible.

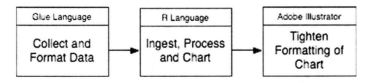

Figure 2-20. Workflow for preparing data visualizations with R

What kinds of data do I run in R? All kinds. In this book we look at visualizing performance data in R, but I also report on my departmental metrics using R, things like defect density, or code coverage for my code repositories.

As a language it is small, self-contained, extensible, and just fun to use. That said, it does have its own philosophy, and quirks, some of which we'll look at here.

Installing and Running R

To install R, you first need to download a precompiled R binary, from http://cran.r-project.org/. For Mac and PC, this is a standard installer that walks you through the installation process. The PC installer comes in three flavors: Base is the base install, Contrib comes with compiled third-party packages, and Rtools comes with tools to build your own R packages. For our purposes we'll stick with the base install. See Figure 2-21 for a screen shot of the R installer.

Instead of a compiled installer, Linux users get the command sequence to install for their particular Linux flavor.

Once R is installed, you can open the R Console, the environment from which we will run the R language. The console can be seen in Figure 2-22.

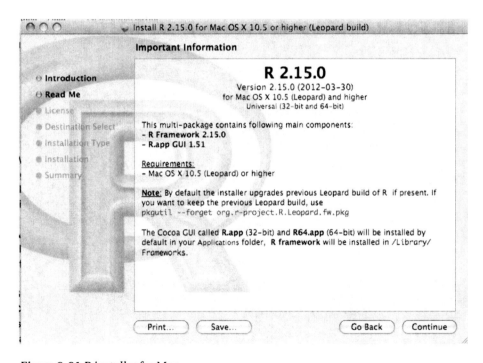

Figure 2-21. R installer for Mac

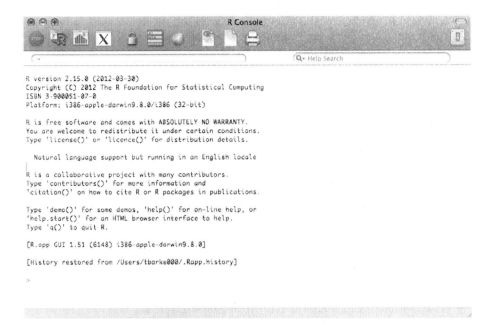

Figure 2-22. *The R console*

The console's toolbar allows us to do tasks like interrupt the execution of running R processes, run stand-alone .R files, adjust the look and feel of the console, create new stand-alone .R files, and so on.

The R Console is a command-line environment for running ad hoc R commands. Usually I use the console to flesh out ideas, and tweak them until they produce what I am looking for, and then I move those functioning expressions to a standalone R file.

You can create external files to hold your R code, generally they have the extension .R.

R is also highly extensible and has a robust community that builds packages that extend what can be done with R. That said, for all of the R code in this book we will not be using any packages, sticking only to the base install of R.

An R Primer

Now that you understand what R is, how do you use R? The first things to note are that at any time you can type ?[keyword] to open the help window for a particular subject. If you aren't sure that what you are looking for has a topic, simply type ??[keyword] to do a more extensive search. For example, type ?hist to search for help on creating histograms.

```
> ?hist
starting httpd help server ... done
```

Also important to note is that R supports single-line comments, but not multiline comments. The hash symbol starts a comment, and the R interpreter ignores everything after the hash symbol to the line break.

```
#this is a comment
```

Variables and Data Types

To declare a variable you simply assign value to it. The assignment operator is a left-pointing arrow, so creating and declaring variables looks like this:

```
foo <- bar
```

R is loosely typed, and it supports all of the scalar data types you would expect: string, numbers, and booleans.

```
myString <- "This is a string"
myNumber <- 23
myBool <- TRUE
```

It also supports lists, but here is one of the quirks of the language. R has a data type called vector that functions almost like a strictly typed single-dimensional array. It is a list whose items are the same data type, either strings, numbers, or booleans. To declare vectors use the combine function c(), and you add to vectors with the c() function as well. You access elements in vectors using square brackets. Unlike arrays in most languages, vectors are not zero based; the first element is referenced as element [1].

```
myVector <- c(12,343,564) #declare a vector
myVector <- c(myVector, 545) # appends the number 545 to myVector
myVector[3] # returns 564
```

R also has another list type, called matrix. Matrices are like strictly typed two dimensional arrays. You create a matrix using the matrix function, which accepts five parameters: a vector to use as the content, the number of rows to shape the content into, the number of columns to shape the content into, an optional boolean value to indicate whether the content should be shaped by row or by column (the default is FALSE for by column), and a list that contains vectors for row names and column names:

```
matrix([content vector], nrow=[number of rows], ncol=[number of columns], byrow=[how to sort],
dimnames=[vector of row names, vector of column names])
```

You access indexes in a matrix with square brackets as well, you we must specify the column and the row in the square brackets.

```
m <- matrix(c(11,12,13,14,15,16,17,18), nrow=4, ncol=2, dimnames=list(c("row1", "row2", "row3",
"row4"), c("col1", "col2")))

> m
     col1 col2
row1   11   15
row2   12   16
row3   13   17
row4   14   18

>m[1,1]  #will return 11
[1]11

> m[4,2]   #will return 18
[1] 18
```

So far both matrices and vectors can only contain a single data type. R supports another list type, called a data frame. Data frames are multidimensional lists that can contain multiple data types—sort of.

It is easier to think of data frames as collections of vectors. Vectors still have to hold only one data type, but a data frame can hold multiple types of vectors.

You create data frames using the data.frame() function, which accepts a number of vectors as content, and then the following parameters: row.names to specify the vector to use as row identifiers, check.rows to check consistency of row data, and check.names to check for duplicates among other syntactical checks.

```
userid <- c(1,2,3,4,5,6,7,8,9)
    username <- c("user1", "user2", "user3", "user4", "user5", "user6", "user7", "user8",
"user9")
    admin <- c(FALSE, FALSE, TRUE, FALSE, TRUE, FALSE, FALSE, TRUE, TRUE)

users <- data.frame(username, admin, row.names=userid)
> users
 username admin
1    user1 FALSE
2    user2 FALSE
3    user3  TRUE
4    user4 FALSE
5    user5  TRUE
6    user6 FALSE
7    user7 FALSE
8    user8  TRUE
9    user9  TRUE
```

Use square brackets to access individual vectors within data frames:

```
> users[1]
 Username
1    user1
2    user2
3    user3
4    user4
5    user5
6    user6
7    user7
8    user8
9    user9
```

Use the $ notation to isolate columns, and the square bracket for individual indexes of those columns. The $ in R is much like dot notation in most other languages.

```
> users$admin[3]
[1] TRUE
```

Importing External Data

Now that you've seen how to hold data, let's look at how to import data. You can read data in from a flat file using the read.table() function. This function accepts four parameters: the path to the flat file to read in, a boolean to indicate whether the first row of the flat file contains header names or not, the character to treat as the column delimiter, and the column to treat as the row identifier. The read.table() function returns a data frame.

```
read.table([path to file], [treat first row as headers],[character to treat as delimiter],[column
to make row identifier])
```

For example, suppose you have the following flat file, which has a breakdown of a bug backlog:

```
Section,Resolved,UnResolved,Total
Regression,71,32,103
Compliance,4,2,6
Development,19,8,27
```

You would read this in with the following code:

```
bugData <- read.table("/bugsbyUS.txt", header=TRUE, sep=",", row.names="Section")
```

If you examine the resulting bugData object, you should see the following:

```
> bugData
            Resolved UnResolved Total
Regression        71         32   103
Compliance         4          2     6
Development        19          8    27
```

Loops

R supports both for loops and while loops, and they are structured much as you would expect them to be:

```
for(n in list){}
while ([condition is true]){}
```

To loop through the users data frame, you can simply do the following:

```
for(i in users){
print(users$admin[i])
}
[1] FALSE FALSE   TRUE FALSE FALSE
[1] TRUE
```

The same applies for the bug data:

```
> for(x in bugData$UnResolved){
+       print(x)
+ }
32
2
8
```

Functions

Functions in R also work as you would expect; we can pass in arguments, and the function accepts them as parameters and can return data out of the function. Note that all data is passed by value in R.

We construct functions in this way:

```
functionName <- function([parameters]){

}
```

Simple Charting with R

Now here is where things start to get really fun with R. You know how to import data, store data, and iterate through data; let's visualize data!

R natively supports several charting functions. The first we will look at is plot().

The plot() function will display a different type of chart depending on the arguments that you pass in to it. It accepts the following parameters: an R object that supports the plotting function, an optional parameter that will supplement as a y axis value in case the first parameter does not include it, the number of named graphical parameters, a string to determine the type of plot to draw (more on this in a second), the title of the chart, a subtitle of the chart, the label for the x-axis, the label for the y-axis, and finally a number to indicate the aspect ratio for the chart (the aspect ratio is the numeric result of y/x).

Let's take a look at how some of the plot type options are reflected in the display of the chart. Note that when you plot the users data frame, you get a numeric representation of the user names column on the x-axis and the y-axis is the admin column, but shown in a range from 0 to 1 (instead of TRUE and FALSE). Figure 2-23 shows the results.

```
plot(users, main="plotting user data frame\nno type specified")
plot(users, type="p", main="plotting user data frame\ntype=p for points")
plot(users, type="l", main="plotting user data frame\ntype=l for lines")
plot(users, type="b", main="plotting user data frame\ntype=b for both")
plot(users, type="c", main="plotting user data frame\ntype=c for lines minus points")
plot(users, type="o", main="plotting user data frame\ntype=o for overplotting")
plot(users, type="h", main="plotting user data frame\ntype=h for histogram")
plot(users, type="s", main="plotting user data frame\ntype=s for stair steps")
plot(users, type="n", main="plotting user data frame\ntype=n for no plotting")
```

Bar charts are also supported in the base installation of R, with the barplot() function. Some of the most useful parameters that the barplot() function accepts are a vector or matrix to model the height of the bars, an optional width parameter, the amount of space that will precede each bar, a vector to list as the names for each bar, the text to use as the legend, a boolean value named beside that signifies whether the bar chart is stacked, another boolean value set to true if the bars should be horizontal instead of vertical, a vector of colors to use to color the bars, a vector of colors to use as the border color for each bar, and the header and sub header for the chart. For the full list simply type ?barplot in the console.

Figure 2-24 shows what the users data frame looks like as a bar chart.

```
barplot(users$admin, names.arg=users$username, main="Bar chart of users that are admins")
```

You can also create bubble charts natively in R. To do this, use the symbols() function, pass in the R object that you want to represent, and set the circles parameter to a column that represents the radius of each circle.

▨ **Note:** Bubble charts are used to represent three-dimensional data. They are much like a scatter plot, with the placement of the dots on the x-axis and the y-axis denoting value, but in the case of bubble charts the radius of the dots also denotes value.

Figure 2-25 shows the result.

```
symbols(users, circles=users$admin, bg="red", main="Bubble chart of users that are admins")
```

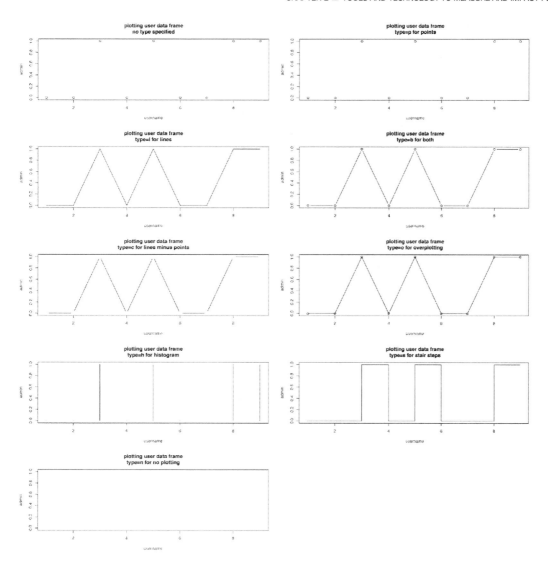

Figure 2-23. The different types of chart with the plot function

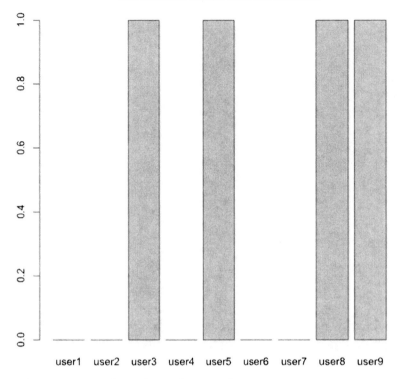

Figure 2-24. Bar chart of users that are admins

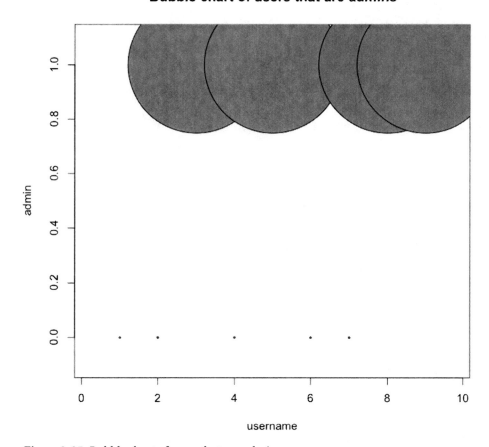

Bubble chart of users that are admins

Figure 2-25. Bubble chart of users that are admins

The symbols() function can be used to draw other shapes on a plot; for more information about this type ?symbols at the R console.

You can save the charts that you generate by calling the appropriate function for the file type you want to save. Note that you need to call dev.off after you are done outputting. So, for example, to create a JPEG of the barplot you would call:

```
jpeg("test.jpg")
barplot(users$admin)
dev.off()
```

The functions available are these:

```
pdf([filename]) #saves chart as a pdf
win.metafile([filename]) #saves chart as a Windows metafile
png([filename]) #saves chart as a png file
jpeg([filename]) #saves chart as a jpg file
bmp([filename]) #saves chart as a bmp file
postscript([filename]) #saves chart as a ps file
```

A Practical Example of R

This has been just the barest taste of R, but now that you understand its basic building blocks, let's construct the chart that you saw in Figure 2-19 earlier.

First you'll create four variables, one a number to hold the value of the uncompressed JavaScript file, one a vector to hold the names of the tools, one a vector to hold the file size of the JavaScript files after they have been run through the tools, and a final vector to hold the percentage difference between the minified size and the original size.

You'll be refactoring that last variable soon, but for now leave it hard-coded so you can see the pattern that we are applying to gather the percentage—100 minus the result of the new size divided by the total size multiplied by 100.

```
originalSize <- 2150
tool <- c("YUI", "Closure Compiler (simple)", "Minify", "Closure Compiler (advanced)")
size <- c(1638, 1638, 573, 0)
diff <- c((100 - (1638  / 2150)*100), (100 - (1638 / 2150)*100), (100 - (573 / 2150)*100), (100
- (0 / 2150)*100))
```

Next create a data frame from those vectors, and make the row identifier the vector of tool names.

```
mincompare <- data.frame(diff, size, row.names=tool)
```

If you type **mincompare** in the console, you'll see that it is structured like this:

```
>mincompare
                               diff size

YUI                         23.81395 1638
Closure Compiler (simple)   23.81395 1638
Minify                      73.34884  573
Closure Compiler (advanced) 100.00000   0
```

Perfect! From here you can start to construct the chart. Use the barplot function to plot the diff column. Make the chart horizontal, explicitly set the y-axis names to the row names of the data frame, and give the chart a title of "Percent of file size reduction by product":

```
barplot(mincompare$diff, horiz=TRUE, names.arg =row.names(mincompare), main="Percent of file size
reduction by product")
```

If you run this in the console you'll see that we're almost there. It should look like Figure 2-26.

You can see that the first and third y-axis names are missing; that's because the copy is too large to fit vertically as it is now. You can correct this by making the text horizontal just like the bars are.

To do this, set the graphical parameters of the chart using the par function. But first, save the existing parameters so that you can revert back to them after creating the chart:

```
opar <- par(no.readonly=TRUE)
```

This saves the existing parameters in a variable called opar so you can retrieve them after you are done.

Next you can make the text horizontal, with the par() function:

```
par(las=1, mar=c(10,10,10,10))
```

Percent of file size reduction by product

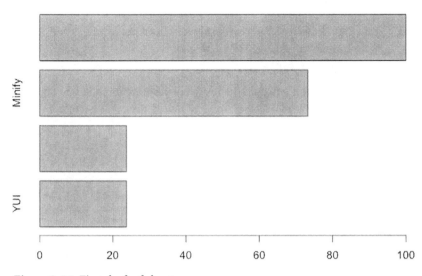

Figure 2-26. *First draft of chart*

The par() function accepts several parameters. This code passes in the las parameter (to alter the axis label style) and sets it to 1, which makes the axis labels always horizontal, and passes in the mar parameter to set the margins for the chart.

After you call barplot to draw the chart, you can then revert to the original graphical parameters, with this code:

```
par(opar)
```

To save this chart you need to export it. You can wrap the barplot and par calls in a call to the pdf function, passing in the file name to save the chart with. This example will export as a PDF to retain the vector lines and raw text so that we can edit and refine those things in post-production using Illustrator or some other such program:

```
pdf("Figure 2-19.pdf")
```

After restoring the graphical parameters, close the file by calling dev.off()

So far the code should look like this:

```
originalSize <- 2150
tool <- c("YUI", "Closure Compiler (simple)", "Minify", "Closure Compiler (advanced)")
size <- c(1638, 1638, 573, 0)
diff <- c((100 - (1638  / 2150)*100), (100 - (1638 / 2150)*100), (100 - (573 / 2150)*100), (100
- (0 / 2150)*100))
mincompare <- data.frame(diff, size, row.names=tool)

pdf("Figure 2-19.pdf")
opar <- par(no.readonly=TRUE)
    par(las=1, mar=c(10,10,10,10))
    barplot(mincompare$diff, horiz=TRUE, names.arg =row.names(mincompare), main="Percent of file
size reduction by product")
par(opar)
```

```
dev.off()
```

But something about this bothers me. I don't like having our `diff` variable hard-coded, and we're repeating the algorithm over and over again to set the values. Let's abstract that out into a function.

Call the function `getPercentImproved` and have it accept two parameters, a vector of values and a number value:

```
getPercentImproved <- function(sourceVector, totalSize){}
```

Within the function, create an empty vector; this will hold the results of our function and we will return this vector at the end of the function:

```
percentVector <- c()
```

Then loop through the passed-in vector:

```
for(i in sourceVector){}
```

Within the iteration we run our algorithm to get the difference between the numbers in each element. Remember, it's

(100–([new file size] /[original file size])*100)

Save the result of this in our new vector `percentVector`:

```
percentVector <- c(percentVector,(100 - (i  / totalSize)*100))
```
And after the loop completes we'll return the new vector.
```
return(percentVector)
```
Our final function should look like this:
```
getPercentImproved <- function(sourceVector, totalSize){
    percentVector <- c()
    for(i in sourceVector){
        percentVector <- c(percentVector,(100 - (i  / totalSize)*100))
    }
    return(percentVector)
}
```

Finally, set the vector `diff` to be the result of `getPercentImproved`, and pass in the vector called `size` and the variable `originalSize`;

```
diff <- getPercentImproved(size, originalSize)
```

Your final code should look like this:

```
getPercentImproved <- function(sourceVector, totalSize){
    percentVector <- c()
    for(i in sourceVector){
        percentVector <- c(percentVector,(100 - (i  / totalSize)*100))
    }
    return(percentVector)
}

originalSize <- 2150
tool <- c("YUI", "Closure Compiler (simple)", "Minify", "Closure Compiler (advanced)")
size <- c(1638, 1638, 573, 0)
diff <- getPercentImproved(size, originalSize)
```

```
mincompare <- data.frame(tool,diff, size, row.names=tool)

pdf("Figure 2-19.pdf")
opar <- par(no.readonly=TRUE)
    par(las=1, mar=c(10,10,10,10))
    barplot(mincompare$diff, horiz=TRUE, names.arg =row.names(mincompare), main="Percent of file
size reduction by product")
par(opar)
dev.off()
```

There are many ways to further refine this if you wanted. You could abstract the generating and exporting of the chart to a function.

Or you could use a native function of R called apply() to derive the difference instead of looping through the vector. Let's take a look at that right now.

Using apply()

The apply() function allows us to apply a function to elements in a list. It takes several parameters; first is a list of values, next a number vector to indicate how we apply the function through the list (1 is for rows, 2 is for columns, and c(1,2) indicates both rows and columns), and finally the function to apply to the list:

```
apply([list], [how to apply function], [function to apply])
```

We could eliminate the getPercentImproved function and instead use the following:

```
diff <- apply(as.matrix(size), 1, function(x)100 - (x  / 2150)*100)
```

Note that this converts the size variable into a matrix as we pass it to apply(). This is because apply() expects matrices, arrays, or data frames. The apply() function has a derivative lapply() that you could use as well.

When using apply your code is smaller, and it uses the language as it was intended, it adheres to the philosophy of the language, meaning that it is more about logical programming with statistical analysis than imperative programming. The updated code should now look like this:

```
originalSize <- 2150
tool <- c("YUI", "Closure Compiler (simple)", "Minify", "Closure Compiler (advanced)")
size <- c(1638, 1638, 573, 0)
diff <- apply(as.matrix(size), 1, function(x)100 - (x  / originalSize)*100)
mincompare <- data.frame(diff, size, row.names=tool)

pdf("Figure 2-19.pdf")
opar <- par(no.readonly=TRUE)
    par(las=1, mar=c(10,10,10,10))
    barplot(mincompare$diff, horiz=TRUE, names.arg =row.names(mincompare), main="Percent of file
size reduction by product")
par(opar)
dev.off()
```

The final step to constructing the chart would be to bring it into Adobe Illustrator or some other vector painting program to refine it, for example adjusting the alignment of text or the size of fonts. While this kind of formatting is possible within R, it is much more robust in a dedicated application.

Summary

In this chapter we learned about several tools that are invaluable to us in our goal to create and maintain performant web sites. We saw how Firebug's Network Monitoring tab is a great tool to keep track of the network dependencies that make up our pages and the impacts that they have on our page speed. Its passive nature makes Network Monitoring a great tool to use as we develop pages or debug known issues.

We used the different filters with YSlow to test the current performance of our sites, but also to get customized tips to better optimize the web performance of these sites.

With Webpagetest we were also able to see the impact of external assets and get performance tips, but we were then able to see the results of repeat viewing, and get high level aggregate data for several different aspects of data as well. We saw the robust configuration set that WebPagetest sports, including scripting capabilities to test more complex scenarios. We also saw that WebPagetest exposes an API, we will use that next chapter to automate performance monitoring.

We explored several tools for minifying our JavaScript. We implemented each tool and compared the results by visualizing the differences in file size that each tool gave us. We also started to look at some of the abstract details that make performance about more than just the numbers.

We then dipped our toes in the R language. We installed the R console, explored some introductory concepts in R, and coded our first chart in R—the same chart that we used to compare the results of the minification tool comparison.

In the coming chapters we will use and expand on our knowledge of R, as well as make use of many of the tools and concepts that we explored this chapter.

■ ■ ■

CHAPTER 3

WPTRunner—Automated Performance Monitoring and Visualization with WebPagetest

The last chapter laid a good amount of ground work that we will be building upon throughout the rest of the book. We looked at how to generate waterfall charts with Firebug and YSlow, and use them as debugging tools. We explored some of the extensive features and functionality of WebPagetest. We talked about the concept of minifying JavaScript and ran a multivariate test to compare the results of several minifying tools. We closed the chapter by learning about R and writing a script to visualize the results of our multivariate test.

This chapter expands on those concepts. You will be hooking into the API provided by WebPagetest to automate monitoring of a number of URLs, and using R to visualize those results.

You will essentially create a framework that will allow you to monitor the web performance of your sites. By also plugging in specific URLs, you can run multivariate test across URLs, and compare the impact to performance that feature updates or ad choices may have on our sites.

Architecture

Let's start by fleshing out an architecture. I usually start a project by standing in front of a whiteboard and working out high-level concepts and use cases using UML. Or I'll open up Omnigraffle or Visio or some other flow-charting application and work on an architecture document. For this you will create a UML sequence diagram to show the interactions between the objects or processes in the system.

As you saw in the last chapter, WebPagetest is a robust web application that will provide detailed web performance information. It also exposes an API that you can invoke to fire off a test. With this in mind you know that you'll need something to call the API, and get the response back.

You also know that you will need to parse the response that comes back from WebPagetest, so let's create three processes in the architecture document: one to represent WebPagetest, one to call the API, and one to process the response.

Let's call the process that calls the pagetest API `run_wpt` and the process that handles the result, `process_wpt_response`. So far our sequence diagram should look like Figure 3-1.

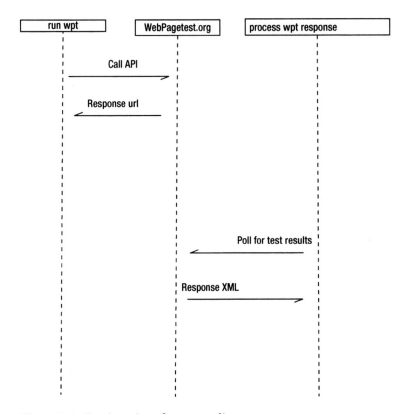

Figure 3-1. *First iteration of sequence diagram*

This is a great start. You know from our experience with WebPagetest last chapter that tests run in WPT are not usually run instantaneously. You have to get into a queue, and even when you are in the front of the queue the test itself takes a little while. This is to be expected because the test isn't simulating the experience; it is really loading the site in the agent that you choose.

What this means tactically is that when you call the API, it returns a URL that you can poll that will indicate when the test is complete. This is important to note because you'll want to save the returned URLs that you get and be able to reference them again and again, until the test is complete, so you'll want to store them in a flat file. You'll tail the values to the flat file; that is, you'll append the newest values to the end of the file. To keep it simple you can use a flat file that you'll call webpagetest_responses.txt.

You'll also use a flat file to store the test results once the tests complete. You will call this flat file wpo_log.txt. The final piece you'll need is an R script to read wpo_log.txt and generate the chart.

If you add these additional parts to the sequence diagram, your finished architecture document should look like Figure 3-2.

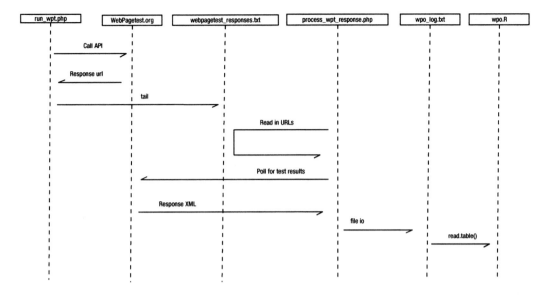

Figure 3-2. *Finished WPTRunner sequence diagram*

For this example you will create PHP files to automate the run_wpt and process_wpt_response processes, but realistically you could have used almost any language.

For this project create the following directory structure:

```
/data - to hold our flat files
/util - to hold our shared files and utilities
/charts - to hold the charts that we generate in R
```

Creating a Shared Configuration File

Before you begin, you need a key to access the WebPagetest API. Per the API documentation at https://sites.google.com/a/webpagetest.org/docs/advanced-features/webpagetest-restful-apis, you can obtain a key by emailing the site owner, Pat Meenan, at pmeenan@webpagetest.org. It may take a day or two or longer to receive your key. Once you have an API key you should create a separate file to hold all of the configuration information that you will need to share between processes.

The key you will store as a string:

```
$key = "[your key here]";
```

You know that you'll want to store the API key in this shared file, but there are also some other things you'll want to store.

Since the point of this framework is to programmatically test a series of URLs over time, you should create a mechanism for storing URLs. Be they URLs that hold experimental features or configurations, or just regular site monitoring, you will store all of the URLs in an array:

```
$urls_to_benchmark = array("tom-barker.com", "apress.com/", "amazon.com", "apple.com", "google.com");
```

Finally you want to store paths to all of the flat files that you will need to reference:

```
$csvFiles = "/WPTRunner/data/webpagetest_responses.txt";
$wpologfile = "/WPTRunner/data/wpo_log.txt
```

You can call this shared file wpt_credentials_urls.php. It should live in the /util directory, and it should look like this:

```
<?php
$key = "xxxx"; // our API key
$urls_to_benchmark = array("tom-barker.com", "apress.com/", "amazon.com", "apple.com", "google.
com"); // our list of URLs to monitor
$csvFiles = "/WPTRunner/data/webpagetest_responses.txt";   // flat file to store response URLs
$wpologfile = "/WPTRunner/data/wpo_log.txt"; // flat file to store test results
?>
```

From the architecture document you also know that you will need to be writing to a couple of flat files. It may be a good idea to make another shared file to handle at a minimum, file writing. So let's create a file called fileio.php, also in the /util directory.

In fileio.php you will make a function called appendToFile() that you pass a file path and data into. The function will check if the passed in file exists, if it does it will append the passed in data to the file, if it does not exist it will create the file and write the passed in data to it.

```
<?php
function appendToFile($data, $file){
    echo "writing to file $file\n";
  $writeFlag = "w";
  if(file_exists($file)){
      $writeFlag = "a";
  }
  $fh = fopen($file, $writeFlag) or die("can't open file");
  fwrite($fh, $data . "\n");
  fclose($fh);
}

?>
```

So far you've laid out the architecture of the system and created external files to hold configuration information and common functionality. Let's start to flesh out the system itself.

Accessing the WebPagetest API

OK, let's start out by coding the initial test request. The URL to access the WebPagetest is http://www.webpagetest.org/runtest.php. The API accepts a number of parameters, among them are:

url: The URL that you want to test.

location: This specifies the agent location, speed and browser to use for the test, formatted as *location.browser:location*. For example, the Dulles location with Chrome would be Dulles.Chrome. IE is a little different, and IE 8, for instance, would be formatted Dulles_IE8.

■ **Note**   The documentation is unclear on why Internet Explorer uses the underscore character, but this variation is good to keep in mind.

runs: This specifies the number of tests to run.

fvonly: If you set fvonly to 1, you get results only for the first view, and do not run the repeat view test.

private: Setting the private flag to 1 will make sure that the test is not displayed in the public list of tests.

block: This parameter allows you to set a comma separated list of block options. Remember from last chapter that you can specify URLs as well as types of files.

f: This specifies the format that the test result will be. It accepts xml and json.

k: This is where you specify the public API key.

A sample call to the API would look like this:

```
http://www.webpagetest.org/runtest.php?f=xml&private=1&k=111 &url=tom-barker.com
```

You'll create a new PHP file named run_wpt.php. The first thing you'll do is to form the URL. You'll import the shared configuration file to make sure you have access to the API key as well as the array of URLs:

```
require("util/wpt_credentials_urls.php");
```

Then you'll create some variables to hold the API parameters. For this example you only care about the output format, which you'll set to XML, and to make sure that our tests are kept private.

```
$outputformat = "xml";
$private = 1;
```

And finally you'll create a new variable $wpt_url to store the API URL with the parameters concatenated to it, all except the URL parameter. You'll get to the URL parameter next:

```
$wpt_url = "http://www.webpagetest.org/runtest.php?f=$outputformat&private=private&k=$key&url=";
```

To set the URL parameter you'll need to iterate through the URL array that you set in wpt_credentials_urls.php.

```
for($x=0;$x<count($urls_to_benchmark); $x++){
}
```

As you step through this loop you'll pull out each element one at a time, and concatenate it to $wpt_url. You'll use PHP's native function file_get_contents() to hit the URL and read the server's response into a variable $wpt_response:

```
$wpt_response = file_get_contents($wpt_url . $urls_to_benchmark[$x]);
```

Remember, the API will return an XML structure that you will need to parse. The XML looks like this:

```
<response>
<statusCode>200</statusCode>
<statusText>Ok</statusText>
<data>
<testId></testId>
<ownerKey></ownerKey>
<xmlUrl></xmlUrl>
<userUrl></userUrl>
<summaryCSV></summaryCSV>
<detailCSV></detailCSV>
</data>
</response>
```

So you'll convert the string that the API returns into an XML object using `SimpleXMLElement()` and store the result in $xml.

```php
$wpt_response = file_get_contents($wpt_url . $urls_to_benchmark[$x]);
$xml = new SimpleXMLElement($wpt_response);
```

That will allow you to parse the result and pull out the necessary data. The first piece of data that you want to check is the `statusCode` node. That holds the HTTP status of the response. If that is a 200 to signify a good response you then pull get the xmlURL node value, which contains the URL of the test results once the test is complete, and write that to the flat file `webpagetest_responses.txt`.

```php
if($xml->statusCode == 200){
    appendToFile($xml->data->xmlUrl, $csvFiles);
}
```

Your completed `run_wpt.php` file should look like this:

```php
<?php
require("util/wpt_credentials_urls.php");
require("util/fileio.php");
$outputformat = "xml";
$private = 1;
$wpt_url = "http://www.webpagetest.org/runtest.php?f=$outputformat&private=private&k=$key&url=";

for($x=0;$x<count($urls_to_benchmark); $x++){
    $wpt_response = file_get_contents($wpt_url . $urls_to_benchmark[$x]);
    $xml = new SimpleXMLElement($wpt_response);
    if($xml->statusCode == 200){
        appendToFile($xml->data->xmlUrl, $csvFiles);
    }
}
?>
```

■ **Note** Be sure to run run_wpt.php from the command line, not from a browser. To run PHP files from the command line you simply invoke the PHP binary and specify the –f option along with the path to the file. The –f option tells the interpreter to read in the file, parse it and execute it. So to run run_wpt.php, type into the console:

```
>php -f run_wpt.php
```

And it should produce a flat file formatted like the following:

```
http://www.webpagetest.org/xmlResult/120528_SK_db5196c3143a1b81aacc30b2426cec71/
http://www.webpagetest.org/xmlResult/120528_TB_0ca4cfaa17613b0c2213b4e701c5a9dd/
http://www.webpagetest.org/xmlResult/120529_TN_8c20efe8c82a663917456f56aae7c235/
http://www.webpagetest.org/xmlResult/120529_6P_253e58b1cda284b9cf9a80becd19ef9f/
```

Parsing the Test Results

So far you have a flat file with a list of URLs that point to WebPagetest test results. These tests are not instantaneous, so you need to wait for them to complete before beginning to parse the results.

You can begin polling the test result URLs to see if they have completed. The test results are formatted as such:

```
<response>
<statusCode></statusCode>
<statusText></statusText>
<data>
<startTime></startTime>
</data>
</response>
```

To see if the test is complete, you check the statusCode node. A 100 status means that the test is pending, a 101 means that the test has started, and a 200 means the test is complete. Any 400 status code indicates an error.

With this in mind let's start parsing the results!

First you'll need to include the shared files so you have access to the fileio() function and the paths to the flat files:

```
require("util/wpt_credentials_urls.php");
require("util/fileio.php");
```

Next you'll need to create a function to check the test results. Name the function readCSVurls() and have it accept two parameters: $csvFiles, which will reference the flat file webpagetest_responses.txt, which in turn holds the test result URLs, and $file, which will reference the flat file wpo_log.txt that will hold the values that you pull from the test results:

```
function readCSVurls($csvFiles, $file){
}
```

Within the function you'll delete wpo_log if it exists. This is just for housekeeping purposes, since it is easier and less error-prone to simply rewrite your results than to check to see where you left off and insert there. Then check to make sure webpagetest_responses exists, and that it is readable. If it is, open the file and begin to loop through it:

```
unlink($file); //delete wpo_log
if (file_exists($csvFiles) && is_readable ($csvFiles)) { //if the file is there and readable
    $fh = fopen($csvFiles, "r") or die("\n can't open file $csvFiles");
    while (!feof($fh)) {}
}
```

So within this while loop, which is looping until it reaches the end of file, you will pull out each line of the file, which contains the test result URL. Take the URL and get the response from the server and store it in $tailEntry:

```
$line = fgets($fh);
$tailEntry = file_get_contents(trim($line));
```

If you get a response back, you convert it from a string value to an XML object named $xml:

```
if($tailEntry){
$xml = new SimpleXMLElement($tailEntry);
```

The response XML is structured like so:

```
<response>
    <statusCode></statusCode>
    <statusText></statusText>
    <requestId></requestId>
    <data>
        <runs></runs>
        <average>
            <firstView>
            </firstView>
            <repeatView>
            </repeatView>
        </average>
        <run>
            <id></id>
            <firstView>
                <results>
                </results>
                <pages>
                </pages>
                <thumbnails>
                </thumbnails>
                <images>
                </images>
                <rawData>
                </rawData>
            </firstView>
            <repeatView>
                <results>
                </results>
                <pages>
                </pages>
                <thumbnails>
                </thumbnails>
```

```
            <images>
            </images>
            <rawData>
            </rawData>
        </repeatView>
    </run>
</data>
</response>
```

From this structure the first thing that concerns you is the statusCode node. If the statusCode is equal to 200, you know you have a good response and you can begin parsing up the XML. If it is not 200 you know the test is not complete and you should stop any further processing:

```
if($xml->statusCode == 200){

}else{
die("report not ready at webpagetest yet.\n");
}
```

Out of this XML object you will pull the URL for the page that the test was run against, so you can use that as the row identifier. Then you will pull out the date the test was completed, the load time of the page, the total file size of the page, and the number of HTTP requests needed to form the page.

Then concatenate all these values into a single string, separated by commas, called $newline:

```
$url = $xml->data->run->firstView->results->URL;
$date = $xml->data->completed;
$loadtime = $xml->data->run->firstView->results->loadTime;
$bytes = $xml->data->run->firstView->results->bytesInDoc;
$httprequests = $xml->data->run->firstView->results->requests;
$newline = "$url, $date, $loadtime, $bytes, $httprequests";
```

Note   You are pulling the result data out of the firstView node. This is so that you can test the page uncached. If you want to test the cache version of the page, pull the data out of the repeatView node.

You then check to see if wpo_log exists. If it doesn't exist—and the first time through the loop it won't exist, because you delete it at the beginning of the function—you'll need to format the flat file to have the necessary headers.

Let's abstract that out to a function. For now you can put a stub function call in there called formatWPOLog(). After you finish the current function you'll go back and define the implementation.

You then pass the $newline variable and the path to wpo_log to the shared function appendToFile:

```
if(!file_exists($file)){
formatWPOLog($file);
}
appendToFile($newline, $file);
```

Finally, once you are done pulling each line from webpagetest_responses, close the file:

```php
fclose($fh);
```

There is only one thing left to do — define the implementation for the `formatWPOLog()` function. It should accept a path to a file, and append as the first line the text "url,day,date,loadtime,bytes,httprequests." This first line will be the column headers:

```php
function formatWPOLog($file){
    $headerline = "url, day, date, loadtime, bytes, httprequests";
    appendToFile($headerline, $file);
}
```

Complete Example

Your completed process_wpt_response file should look like this:

```php
<?php

require("util/wpt_credentials_urls.php");
require("util/fileio.php");


function readCSVurls($csvFiles, $file){
    unlink($file);
    if (file_exists($csvFiles) && is_readable ($csvFiles)) {
        $fh = fopen($csvFiles, "r") or die("\n can't open file $csvFiles");
        while (!feof($fh)) {
            $line = fgets($fh);
            $tailEntry = file_get_contents(trim($line));
            if($tailEntry){
                $xml = new SimpleXMLElement($tailEntry);
                if($xml->statusCode == 200){
                    $url = $xml->data->run->firstView->results->URL;
                    $date = $xml->data->completed;
                    $loadtime = $xml->data->run->firstView->results->loadTime;
                    $bytes = $xml->data->run->firstView->results->bytesInDoc;
                    $httprequests = $xml->data->run->firstView->results->requests;
                    $newline = "$url, $date, $loadtime, $bytes, $httprequests";
                    if(!file_exists($file)){
                        formatWPOLog($file);
                    }
                    appendToFile($newline, $file);
                }else{
                    die("report not ready at webpagetest yet.\n");
                }
            }
        }
    }
    fclose($fh);
}

function formatWPOLog($file){
```

```
    $headerline = "url, day, date, loadtime, bytes, httprequests";
    appendToFile($headerline, $file);
}


readCSVurls($csvFiles, $wpologfile);

?>
```

The output of process_wpt_response is the flat file wpo_log, which should now look something like this:

```
url, day, date, loadtime, bytes, httprequests
http://tom-barker.com, Tue, 29 May 2012 20:12:21 +0000, 10786, 255329, 42
http://apress.com/, Tue, 29 May 2012 20:12:47 +0000, 4761, 714655, 57
http://amazon.com, Tue, 29 May 2012 20:13:07 +0000, 2504, 268549, 94
http://apple.com, Tue, 29 May 2012 20:12:41 +0000, 3436, 473678, 38
http://google.com, Tue, 29 May 2012 20:12:50 +0000, 763, 182802, 13
```

Charting with R

Running run_wpt daily gives you a daily log, a comma-separated list of the load time, total payload, and number of HTTP requests for each URL that you want to track. That's great, but it's only part of the story. You can't distribute that data and expect your audience to get the full story. It is up to you to represent that data visually.

So let's use R to build a time series chart to show the change in performance. First let's create a new R file. From the architecture diagram, you can see that it should be called wpo.R.

First create variables to hold the path to the data and chart directories:

```
dataDirectory <- "/Users/tbarke000/WPTRunner/data/"
chartDirectory <- "/Users/tbarke000/WPTRunner/charts/"
```

Then read in the contents of wpo_log and store it as a data frame named wpologs:

```
wpologs <- read.table(paste(dataDirectory, "wpo_log.txt", sep=""), header=TRUE, sep=",")
```

■ **Note** This code uses the paste() function to concatenate the stored data directory to the file name to construct the full path to the file. In R there is no string concatenation operator as in most other languages. You must use the paste() function instead. This function accepts N number of strings to concatenate and a sep parameter that specifies a string to paste between the strings—for example, if you wanted to insert commas between each string, or some other sort of separator. In the example you specify an empty string.

In much the same way, you should create a variable to hold the path to the file that you will create for our chart. Call this variable wpochart, and also convert the data in the bytes column from bytes to kilobytes.

```
wpochart <- paste(chartDirectory, "WPO_timeseries.pdf", sep="")
wpologs$bytes <- wpologs$bytes / 1000 #convert bytes to KB
```

Parsing the Data

At this point you have the data loaded in, and you have paths set up to the chart you want to draw. Let's take a look at the structure of the data. Type `wpologs` into the console and the data should be structured like so:

```
> wpologs
                    url  day                          date loadtime  bytes httprequests
1   http://tom-barker.com  Tue  29 May 2012 20:12:21 +0000    10786 255.329           42
2       http://apress.com/  Tue  29 May 2012 20:12:47 +0000     4761 714.655           57
3       http://amazon.com  Tue  29 May 2012 20:13:07 +0000     2504 268.549           94
4        http://apple.com  Tue  29 May 2012 20:12:41 +0000     3436 473.678           38
5       http://google.com  Tue  29 May 2012 20:12:50 +0000      763 182.802           13
6   http://tom-barker.com  Wed  30 May 2012 16:28:09 +0000     5890 256.169           42
7       http://apress.com/  Wed  30 May 2012 16:27:56 +0000     4854 708.577           57
8       http://amazon.com  Wed  30 May 2012 16:28:14 +0000     3045 338.276          112
9        http://apple.com  Wed  30 May 2012 16:27:58 +0000     3810 472.700           38
10      http://google.com  Wed  30 May 2012 16:28:09 +0000     1524 253.984           15
```

Think about what a time series chart is—you want to draw the performance metrics for each URL as a line over time. That means you will need to isolate the data for each URL. To do this, create a function called `createDataFrameByURL()`. You can pass in the `wpologs` data and the URL that you want to isolate:

```
createDataFrameByURL <- function(wpologs, url){
}
```

In this function you'll create an empty data frame; this will be the data frame that you populate and return from the function:

```
df <- data.frame()
```

Next you will loop through the passed in `wpologs` data:

```
for (i in 1:nrow(wpologs)){}
```

Within the loop you will check the `url` column to see if it matches the passed-in URL value. If it does, add it to the new data frame that you made at the beginning of the function:

```
if(wpologs$url[i] == url){
    df <- rbind(df , wpologs[i,])
}
```

Then set the row name of the new data frame and return it from the function:

```
row.names(df) <- df$date
return(df)
```

Now that you have the function to isolate the WebPagetest results by URL, you will create new data frames for each unique URL that you want to chart.

```
tbdotcom <- createDataFrameByURL(wpologs, "http://tom-barker.com")
apr <- createDataFrameByURL(wpologs, "http://apress.com/")
amz <- createDataFrameByURL(wpologs, "http://amazon.com")
aapl <- createDataFrameByURL(wpologs, "http://apple.com")
ggl <- createDataFrameByURL(wpologs, "http://google.com")
```

If you inspect one of these new data frames in the console, you should see:

```
> tbdotcom
                                              url  day        date  loadtime    bytes
httprequests
29 May 2012 20:12:21 +0000 http://tom-barker.com  Tue  29 May 2012     10786  255.329
42
30 May 2012 16:28:09 +0000 http://tom-barker.com  Wed  30 May 2012      5890  256.169
42
31 May 2012 12:33:52 +0000 http://tom-barker.com  Thu  31 May 2012      5877  249.528
42
01 Jun 2012 17:58:19 +0000 http://tom-barker.com  Fri  01 Jun 2012      3671  255.337
42
03 Jun 2012 14:41:38 +0000 http://tom-barker.com  Sun  03 Jun 2012      5729  249.590
42
```

Plotting Load Time

Excellent! Let's plot one of those columns now. The most important column is the page load time, so let's do that one first. You'll use the plot() function and pass in tbdotcom$loadtime. You'll set the following options for plot():

```
type="l" so that we are drawing lines
xaxt="n" to not draw an x-axis
col="#ff0000" to make the line color red
ylab = "Load Time in Milliseconds" to set that as the label displayed on the y axis.
```

The call to the plot() function should look like this:

```
plot(tbdotcom$loadtime, ylim=c(2000,10000), type="l", xaxt="n", xlab="", col="#ff0000",
ylab="Load Time in Milliseconds")
```

If you hadn't hidden the x axis, it would have appeared as a series of numbers since R defaults to displaying x-axis names as incrementing integers when it identifies the values as nominal ordinal factors. To get the dates to show up in the x axis, you need to draw a custom axis. Use the axis() function to do this. The first parameter that the axis function accepts is a number that indicates which axis to draw: 1 for the bottom, 2 for the left, 3 for the top, and 4 for the right side. The rest of the parameters are named values, including these:

> at: The points where tick marks should be drawn

> lab: The values to show as the axis labels, either a boolean or a vector of strings

> tick: A boolean value to show or hide checkmarks

> lty: The line type

> lwd: The line width

You can also pass in graphical parameters. For more details, type ?axis or ?par at the console. So you'll use the axis() function to draw an x axis to show all of the dates, like so:

```
axis(1, at=1: length(row.names(tbdotcom)), lab= rownames(tbdotcom), cex.axis=0.3)
```

See Figure 3-3 for what the chart looks like so far.

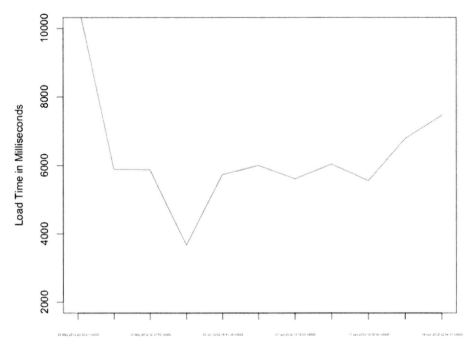

Figure 3-3. Load time over time for tom-barker.com

This is excellent! Now let's layer in the load time for the other URLs. You can draw lines using the line() function. It works very similar to the plot() function; you pass in an R object to plot, and choose the line type and color.

Let's draw lines for the load time for each additional URL that you have been tracking.

```
lines(apr$loadtime, type="l", lty = 2, col="#0000ff")
lines(amz$loadtime, type="l", col="#00ff00")
lines(aapl$loadtime, type="l", col="#ffff00")
lines(ggl$loadtime, type="l", col="#ff6600")
```

Putting this together, the load time plot should now look like Figure 3-4.

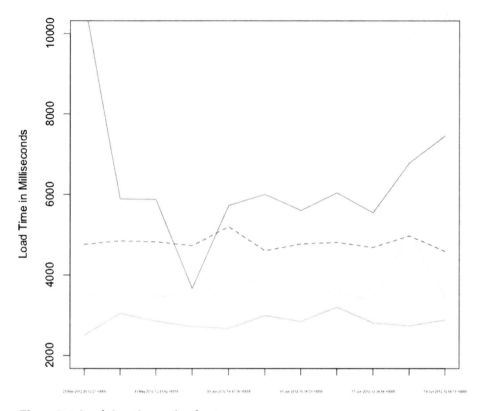

Figure 3-4. *Load time time series chart*

This is exciting, and ultimately the most important part of the data that you get from WebPagetest. But you want to also chart the other aspects of performance that you pulled from the test result, because they are contributors to the ultimate page load time. If you chart out the page size and the number of HTTP requests, you will paint a larger picture that shows indicators of page speed.

Plotting Payload and Number of HTTP Requests

The next chart adds those elements. The scales are different between each metric — page speed is in the thousands of milliseconds, the number of HTTP requests is in the tens, and file size is in the hundreds of bytes. You could normalize all of this data and show it in terms of standard deviations, but that would abstract the data from the actual numbers, and you need those numbers to debug any issues.

Instead, you'll create a time series chart for each aspect of quality. BUT you'll include these time series charts on one single graphic. The reason for this is to adhere to one of Edward Tufte's principals of good data design—to make our graphic as dense with data as possible.

This code charts the remaining columns in our data frames, the bytes and httprequests columns, much the same way you charted the loadtime column:

```
plot(tbdotcom$bytes, ylim=c(0, 1000), type ="l", col="#ff0000", ylab="Page Size in KB", xlab="",
xaxt="n")
axis(1, at=1: length(row.names(tbdotcom)), lab= rownames(tbdotcom), cex.axis=0.3)
```

```
lines(apr$bytes, type="l", lty = 2, col="#0000ff")
lines(amz$bytes, type="l", col="#00ff00")
lines(aapl$bytes, type="l", col="#ffff00")
lines(ggl$bytes, type="l", col="#ff6600")

plot(tbdotcom$httprequests, ylim=c(10, 150), type ="l", col="#ff0000", ylab="HTTP Requests",
xlab="", xaxt="n")
axis(1, at=1: length(row.names(tbdotcom)), lab= rownames(tbdotcom), cex.axis=0.3)
lines(apr$httprequests, type="l", lty = 2, col="#0000ff")
lines(amz$httprequests, type="l", col="#00ff00")
lines(aapl$httprequests, type="l", col="#ffff00")
lines(ggl$httprequests, type="l", col="#ff6600")
```

Now add a legend so that you know what colors correspond to what URLS. First you'll create vectors to hold the labels that you'll use for each URL, and the corresponding colors.

```
WebSites <- c("tom-barker.com", "apress.com/", "amazon.com", "apple.com", "google.com")
WebSiteColors <- c("#ff0000", "#0000ff", "#00ff00", "#ffff00", "#ff6600")
```

Then create a new chart using plot, but pass "n" to the type parameter so that no line is drawn to the chart, and xaxt and yaxt to "n" so that no axes are drawn. But to this plot you'll add a legend using the legend() function and pass in the label and color vectors just created:

```
plot(tbdotcom$httprequests, type ="n", xlab="", ylab="", xaxt="n", yaxt="n", frame=FALSE)
legend("topright", inset=.05, title="Legend", WebSites, lty=c(1,2,1,1,1,1,1,1,1,1,1,1,1,1,1,2),
col= WebSiteColors)
```

To draw all of these charts to the same graphic, wrap all of these calls to the plot() function in a call to par() that you pass in the named parameter mfrow. The mfrow parameter accepts a vector that specifies how many rows and columns should be drawn, so pass in c(2,2) to indicate two rows and two columns:

```
par(mfrow=c(2,2))
```

This should produce the graphic shown in Figure 3-5.

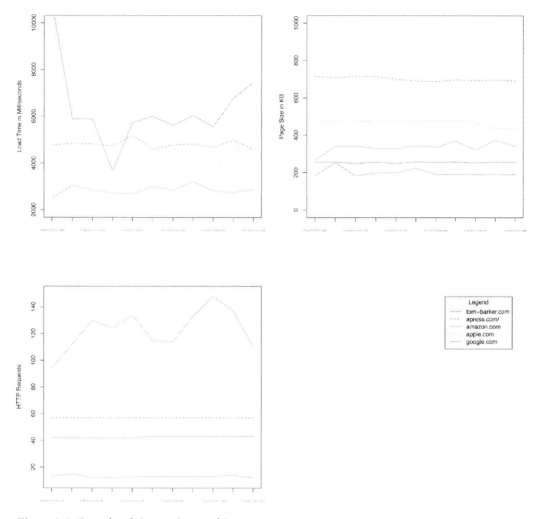

Figure 3-5. *Completed time series graphic*

Your completed R code should look like this:

```
dataDirectory <- "/Users/tbarke000/WPTRunner/data/"
chartDirectory <- "/Users/tbarke000/WPTRunner/charts/"
wpologs <- read.table(paste(dataDirectory, "wpo_log.txt", sep=""), header=TRUE, sep=",")
wpochart <- paste(chartDirectory, "WPO_timeseries.pdf", sep="")


createDataFrameByURL <- function(wpologs, url){
df <- data.frame()
for (i in 1:nrow(wpologs)){
    if(wpologs$url[i] == url){
        df <- rbind(df , wpologs[i,])
    }
```

```
}
row.names(df) <- df$date
return(df)
}

wpologs$bytes <- wpologs$bytes / 1000 #convert bytes to KB

tbdotcom <- createDataFrameByURL(wpologs, "http://tom-barker.com")
apr <- createDataFrameByURL(wpologs, "http://apress.com/")
amz <- createDataFrameByURL(wpologs, "http://amazon.com")
aapl <- createDataFrameByURL(wpologs, "http://apple.com")
ggl <- createDataFrameByURL(wpologs, "http://google.com")

WebSites <- c("tom-barker.com", "apress.com/", "amazon.com", "apple.com", "google.com")
WebSiteColors <- c("#ff0000", "#0000ff", "#00ff00", "#ffff00", "#ff6600")

pdf(wpochart, height=12, width=12)
par(mfrow=c(2,2))
plot(tbdotcom$loadtime, ylim=c(2000,10000), type="l", xaxt="n", xlab="", col="#ff0000",
ylab="Load Time in Milliseconds")
axis(1, at=1: length(row.names(tbdotcom)), lab= rownames(tbdotcom), cex.axis=0.3)
lines(apr$loadtime, type="l", lty = 2, col="#0000ff")
lines(amz$loadtime, type="l", col="#00ff00")
lines(aapl$loadtime, type="l", col="#ffff00")
lines(ggl$loadtime, type="l", col="#ff6600")

plot(tbdotcom$bytes, ylim=c(0, 1000), type ="l", col="#ff0000", ylab="Page Size in KB", xlab="",
xaxt="n")
axis(1, at=1: length(row.names(tbdotcom)), lab= rownames(tbdotcom), cex.axis=0.3)
lines(apr$bytes, type="l", lty = 2, col="#0000ff")
lines(amz$bytes, type="l", col="#00ff00")
lines(aapl$bytes, type="l", col="#ffff00")
lines(ggl$bytes, type="l", col="#ff6600")


plot(tbdotcom$httprequests, ylim=c(10, 150), type ="l", col="#ff0000", ylab="HTTP Requests",
xlab="", xaxt="n")
axis(1, at=1: length(row.names(tbdotcom)), lab= rownames(tbdotcom), cex.axis=0.3)
lines(apr$httprequests, type="l", lty = 2, col="#0000ff")
lines(amz$httprequests, type="l", col="#00ff00")
lines(aapl$httprequests, type="l", col="#ffff00")
lines(ggl$httprequests, type="l", col="#ff6600")


plot(tbdotcom$httprequests, type ="n", xlab="", ylab="", xaxt="n", yaxt="n", frame=FALSE)
legend("topright", inset=.05, title="Legend", WebSites, lty=c(1,2,1,1,1,1,1,1,1,1,1,1,1,1,1,1,2),
col= WebSiteColors)
dev.off()
```

As always, there are numerous ways to refactor and refine this code. You could abstract the plotting of the time series data into a single function to reduce the amount of duplicate code. I left them as is to reinforce what you are doing to create the time series. You could use R's native `apply()` function instead of looping through the data in the `createDataFrameByURL()` function. I left it as is to be as descriptive as possible about what the code was doing with the data.

Open Source

I've named this project WPTRunner and put the source code for it in its own open source project up on Github, the URL is `https://github.com/tomjbarker/WPTRunner` and I welcome you to grab it and use it for your own purposes, fork it to start your own projects, or contribute back to make it a better project for everyone's benefit.

Summary

This chapter explored an automated way to track the web performance of a set of URLs using WebPagetest, PHP, and R. There are so many things you could use this for. Of course you could track the performance of your sites over time, but you could also track the performance of experimental features that you want to add to your sites, or even track the performance of pages while they are in development before they go to production.

You could use the results of this report to form a standard of what you expect your performance to be and create process to make sure new features don't impact that performance. You can generate internal, external and executive level reports where you tie this data with other data, like release dates, user visits, or any other number of related and pertinent data.

Next chapter you will create a JavaScript library to benchmark the run time performance of your JavaScript, and chart that data as well to extract useful metrics that you can use to form not only your own code standards, but to influence product decisions and browser support matrices. As an added bonus, we'll close this chapter with an interview with Patrick Meenan, creator of WebPagetest, about the tool and its future.

Interview with Patrick Meenan of WebPagetest

Patrick Meenan was kind enough to answer a wide range of questions about WebPagetest for *Pro JavaScript Performance* readers.

What was the original inspiration for creating WebPagetest?

There were a couple of situations that we were having difficulty with back in 2006–2007 when it was created:

1. Most of our developers were using Firefox (because of Firebug).

2. Our office was across the street from the data center, so developers had high-bandwidth/low-latency connections to the server.

As a result, pages always felt fast to the developers, and it was very difficult to start a conversation about speeding things up. Our monitoring services were all testing from backbone locations, so those weren't much better. So we had a need for a tool that would let developers see what the performance looked like for our users (on more representative browsers with more realistic connections).

Was it tough getting the project open sourced?

Not at all. AOL was very supportive and really understood the benefit of opening the tool to the community, particularly since it wasn't specifically strategic to the business.

What were some of the challenges that you ran into while working on the project?

Getting access to the interfaces in the browsers to get useful information has been the biggest challenge. Some of the newer browsers (now) make the information a lot more accessible but there were no extension or browser APIs for getting access to the request chain inside of IE. I tried a lot of different techniques and API interception points before getting to a useful place (and it's still evolving, as even the current injection points still have caveats, particularly around HTTPS).

The other big challenge was just finding the time to work on it. It wasn't actually part of my day job at AOL to develop it so it was largely built as I got cycles to work on it. I'm extremely grateful to Google for letting me work on it full-time now (though the work always seems to outstrip available time).

What is the goal of WebPagetest LLC?

It was originally created as a shell to hold on to the WebPagetest assets and give it a place to live. In early 2012 I worked with several other web performance developers and formed the WPO Foundation. We're still in the process of filing for nonprofit status, but the goal is to have a foundation that will invest in open source web performance efforts and freely available data research. WebPagetest is being moved into the WPO Foundation and will help fund some of the efforts.

How long are test results stored?

Theoretically forever. I still have the test data on the server from when it initially launched in 2008. It's somewhere around 2TB right now, but with how storage systems are growing I don't see a problem for the foreseeable future. WebPagetest has some auto-archiving support built-in where it can archive test data to external storage or to the cloud after a period of time and it knows how to automatically restore the archive when a test is accessed so long-term storage isn't much of a problem. That said, I don't currently maintain offsite backups so if there is a disaster at the site then the data will be gone (I do maintain redundant copies on-site).

How long do tests take to run on average?

I'm not sure that there IS an average time— it really depends on how many runs and if a test will include first and repeat view data. Each run has a forced time limit of 60 seconds (on the public instance), so worst-case with 10 runs it could take 20 minutes to complete a single test. Since only one test can run at a time on a given test machine, it makes it really expensive to scale (which is why there isn't broad support for a lot of testing through the API).

Do you recommend a different approach than polling for test complete when using the API?

The API supports a callback method where the server will make a request to a beacon URL that you provide (see the pingback test parameter) but you're still going to want to poll anyway in case the callback gets missed for some reason so you can do it for efficiency but it won't make the code any easier.

What is the process for tests going through your queue?

Each location has a separate queue, so they are independent, but here is the basic flow:

1. `runtest.php` writes a job file to the queue directory for the given location and adds it to an in-memory queue (to make sure tests are done in order). There are actually 10 different priority queues for a given location, so tests are dropped into the appropriate queue (user-initiated tests get top priority, API tests get medium priority, and there are a few other explicit classes).

2. The test agents poll the server for work, specifying their location as part of the request (`work/getwork.php`).

3. The server picks goes through the priority queues in order and returns the first job it finds for the given location.

4. The test agent parses the test request and runs the tests specified (all of the runs, first and repeat view).

5. As each run completes, the test agent uploads the results for that run to `work/workdone.php`.

6. When the test is fully complete the test agent sends a "done" flag along with the test data.

What are some of the most interesting things you have heard that people are doing with WebPagetest?

I'm excited to see the systems that people built on top of it. The HTTP Archive (`httparchive.org`) is a great public example, but a lot of companies have integrated it into their internal systems using the API.

Could you talk a little bit about the agent architecture?

These days there are actually several different agents. There is the legacy IE agent, the newer Windows agent that supports Chrome and Firefox, and there are the iOS and Android agents that Akamai open-sourced. There is also an experimental WebDriver/NodeJS agent that we are working with that provides cross-platform support for testing in Chrome. WebPagetest has a standard API for test agents, which makes it easy to roll a new agent and plug it in.

The Windows agents are probably some of the more interesting ones architecturally because they do some crazy things to get access to the data they need. The new Windows agent, for example:

- Launches the given browser process (Chrome, Firefox or IE).

- Uses code injection techniques to inject and run code in the context of the browser.

- The injected code installs API intercepts for the winsock, wininet, and SSL API functions and intercepts all of the API calls to record the waterfall data.

- The injected code also runs a web server on localhost (inside of the browser) for our browser extensions to communicate with.

- Our browser extensions (one for each supported browser) poll localhost over Ajax for any commands they need to execute (navigating the browser for example).

- The browser extensions also post events as they happen to the injected browser code (onload for example).

It's quite a bizarre setup to think that all of that is going on inside of the browser just to control the browser and record the network activity.

How do you use WebPagetest with the applications that you develop?

WebPagetest IS the application that I develop ;-). I use it a lot when working with developers on website issues, though, so I get to see it from both a user and developer perspective. The main thing I do is look at waterfalls. I can't stress strongly enough that I feel all web developers should know how to interpret a waterfall and not to rely on checklists or scores. Seeing how a website actually loads is critical.

What features are in the near and longer term for WebPagetest? Personally I'd love a memory profiler.

Mobile is probably the biggest focus area right now. The tooling there is really primitive and it's a lot harder to get access to the kind of data we can get on the desktop, but we're getting there. Getting more information from browsers is always high on the list as well. We recently added support for capturing the Chrome dev tools timeline data from Chrome agents, and we're looking at what other options are available.

CHAPTER 4

▨ ▨ ▨

perfLogger—JavaScript Benchmarking and Logging

Last chapter we coded an automated solution to track and visualize the web performance of URLs over time. We used WebPagetest to generate our metrics, PHP to aggregate and scrub the numbers, and R to create data visualizations from those numbers. We called this project WPTRunner, and we can use it to test the efficacy of future optimizations that we would want to implement and the performance of new features that we will develop.

WPTRunner covered the tracking of web performance; in this chapter we'll create a tool to track runtime performance.

We are going to create a JavaScript library to benchmark the runtime performance of almost anything—from ad hoc pieces of code, to functions, to the render time of modules. Following our running theme, we will then visualize the results of these tests.

We'll be using these tools to analyze the results of some performance best practices that we will be going over in later chapters, but more than anything I hope that you take these tools and the thirst to quantify results with empirical data with you in everything that you do.

Architecture

Once again we start out with the architecture phase. Before starting any endeavor, think about all of the pieces involved, and how they should interact.

There are a couple of ways to benchmark code—either by timing it or by calculating the number of operations performed during execution. For our example, and to be sure that we minimize the observer effect as much as possible,[1] we'll calculate the time in milliseconds during code execution. To do this we'll capture a time stamp right before we begin to run the code and a time stamp right after we run the code, and call the difference our run time results.

```
[end time] - [start time] = [run time]
```

This is a great starting point. A flowchart of what we have so far looks like the diagram in Figure 4-1.

---

1 The *observer effect* says that simply observing an act influences its outcome. For our tests, performing additional operations during the operation that we are timing could add latency in the code that we are benchmarking.

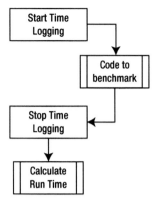

Figure 4-1. Workflow to calculate run time

Results can vary for a number of different reasons, among them client machine resources available, JavaScript engine, and browser render engine, and so what we'll want to do is benchmark by averaging multiple executions at scale across our entire user base. To do this we'll put our benchmarking code out in production and log all of our results where we can analyze and chart it out.

So the next step is to expose our data. We have fleshed out a workflow that has us calculating running time; let's expand that by either displaying that runtime information to the end user, or logging it to a server.

Let's assume there will be times that we don't want to expose the data so we should have this hinge on a decision tree. The addition of this logic is reflected in the flowchart in Figure 4-2.

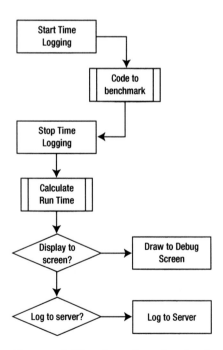

Figure 4-2. Flowchart of runtime logging

At this pointwe have a high level description of how our benchmarking engine will work. Let's call this functionality perfLogger. We still need to interact with other processes in order to save our data and visualize it, so let's create a sequence diagram to flesh out the interactions of these processes.

Our benchmarking process, perfLogger, will call an external process, savePerfData. We'll use the XHR object to post the data to savePerfData. The process savePerfData should in turn save the results of the test in a flat file. We'll call the flat file runtimeperf_results.

It is this flat file that we will read in from R and generate our chart or charts with. The diagram of this work flow can be seen in Figure 4-3.

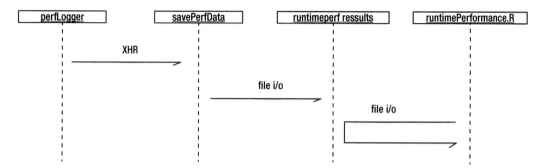

Figure 4-3. *High-level sequence diagram*

So far you've seen how we are going to generate the runtime numbers for the code that we want to benchmark, as well as the flow for how we will save the data. Let's now think about the API for our library.

Ultimately perfLogger is meant to be used by external code, so make sure you give thought to what the public signature will be, what methods and attributes it will have, and which of them to expose publicly.

Based on Figure 4-2, we know that we want startTimeLogging() and stopTimeLogging() functions. These we will invoke before ad hoc code and after to get the start and stop times. Figure 4-2 also demonstrates a need for a drawToDebugScreen() function to draw the test results to the page and a logToServer() function to send the test results to savePerfData.

But as I've said, this logic just captures the running time of ad hoc code. Benchmarking is more than just capturing runtime, it's getting the mean of multiple executions since system variance can introduce deviations in a resultset. So let's create a logBenchmark() function that will average the results of multiple calls to startTimeLogging() and stopTimeLogging().

We should also expose a property that will hold the URL to the savePerfData, which we'll call serverLogURL.

And finally we need a way to be able to run multiple tests on a single page. To do that we'll create an associative array that will hold a collection of tests with a string as the identifier. We'll call this associative array loggerPool.

Out of all these methods and properties, which ones will we want to expose publicly? We don't want to expose any of the properties publicly; if we do that, there is a possibility of external code altering them. If we do want to allow them to be set externally we should make a setter function, but for our purposes right now we won't.

The functions drawToDebugScreen(), logToServer(), and calculateResults() also shouldn't be exposed publicly. Based on the flowchart we will pass in boolean values to determine if a test should be displayed or saved, so most likely we'll have our stopTimeLogging() function call these based on properties of our test result object.

So the only functions that we will expose as our API will be startTimeLogging(), stopTimeLogging(), and logBenchmark(). Using startTimeLogging() and stopTimeLogging() will allow users to get the runtime for ad hoc code, and using `logBenchmark()` will allow for real benchmarking—averaging of multiple executions of passed in functions.

The object diagram from this architecture can be seen in Figure 4-4. We'll list all properties and methods, but bold only the public ones.

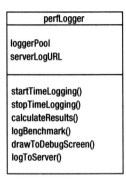

Figure 4-4. *perfLogger object diagram*

Speaking of using loggerPool to keep a dictionary or list of tests, we'll need to spec out a test object, to hold all of the information related to a test. It should have a `startTime`, `endTime`, and boolean values for `drawToPage` and `logtoserver`. We should also give it an identifier so we can retrieve it from the dictionary, a variable to hold the runtime so that we don't need to calculate it each time we want to reference it.

For our own tracking purposes we'll include the URL for the page that the test was run on and a user agent string. This metadata will be useful for running reports on our collected data. Think about it—with this structure we'll be able to report performance for each test by user agent, or any other metadata we may want to add later.

With this in mind we should refactor our perfLogger diagram to include another private function, `setResultsMetaData()`.

The object diagram for our test result object can be seen in Figure 4-5.

Figure 4-5. *TestResults object diagram*

Let's Code!

Start by creating the perfLogger object. Since we'll be keeping certain properties and methods private, we'll return the perfLogger object as an object literal from a self-executing function, and declare our private variables within the self-executing function:

```
var perfLogger = function(){
    var serverLogURL = "savePerfData.php",
    loggerPool = [];

    return {};
}()
```

Next let's begin coding the private functions. Since we sketched out the functions we would need, and the structure of the object that we will be using for test results, we can start to code against those. Let's start with calculateResults().

Calculating Test Results

We know that we will be referencing test result objects by their IDs, so we'll have calculateResults() accept an ID:

```
function calculateResults(id){
}
```

Within calculateResults() we'll reference the test result in loggerPool by the passed-in ID and perform the calculation that we discussed in the architecture phase, end time minus start time:

```
function calculateResults(id){
loggerPool[id].runtime = loggerPool[id].stopTime - loggerPool[id].startTime;
}
```

Setting Test Result Metadata

While you're at it, do the same for setResultsMetaData(). Pass in an ID and reference that test in loggerPool. Set the url property to the current window location and the useragent property to the navigator object's userAgent property. These will give us interesting metrics to compare results against, specifically comparing to see how each rendering engine and JavaScript interpreter differs in its handling of certain functionality.

```
function setResultsMetaData(id){
loggerPool[id].url = window.location.href;
    loggerPool[id].useragent = navigator.userAgent;
}
```

Displaying Test Results

Next add the drawToDebugScreen() private function. To draw to a debug screen you will need to have a named div on the page to write to. So first create a reference to an element on the page with the ID of "debug" and store that reference in a variable named debug.

Then format the debug information—but to keep the format modular, let's abstract that to its own function and just stub in a function call for now. Store the formatted output in a variable named output:

```
function drawToDebugScreen(id){
var debug = document.getElementById("debug")
    var output = formatDebugInfo(id)
}
```

Now it gets a little interesting. You'll test whether the debug variable has any value; this tells you if you already have a named element on the page to write to. If debug has no value, create a new div, give it an ID of "debug", set its innerHTML to our formatted output, and append it to the page.

But if debug already exists, simply append the current formatted output information to its innerHTML.

```
function drawToDebugScreen(id){
var debug = document.getElementById("debug")
   var output = formatDebugInfo(id)
   if(!debug){
      var divTag = document.createElement("div");
      divTag.id = "debug";
      divTag.innerHTML = output
      document.body.appendChild(divTag);
   }else{
      debug.innerHTML += output
   }
}
```

Now flesh out the formatDebugInfo() function. For our purposes, keep it simple. Simply format a string in a paragraph, with the description in bold, and runtime and useragent on their own lines below it. The only complication— benchmarks will have average runtimes, but ad hoc tests will simply have runtimes, so you need to check to see if the test result object has an avgRunTime property and use that; if it doesn't, you'll default to using the runtime property:

```
function formatDebugInfo(id){
var debuginfo = "<p><strong>" + loggerPool[id].description + "</strong><br/>";
   if(loggerPool[id].avgRunTime){
      debuginfo += "average run time: " + loggerPool[id].avgRunTime + "ms<br/>";
   }else{
      debuginfo += "run time: " + loggerPool[id].runtime + "ms<br/>";
   }
   debuginfo += "path: " + loggerPool[id].url + "<br/>";
   debuginfo += "useragent: " +  loggerPool[id].useragent + "<br/>";
   debuginfo += "</p>";
   return debuginfo
}
```

Saving the Data

The final private function is logToServer(). Once again you'll pass in an ID to reference the results object in our loggerPool array. But this time use the native function JSON.stringify() to serialize the object literal to a string value. Prefix that string value with "data=" to encapsulate the data in a name that you can pull out of the POST variables on the server side:

```
function logToServer(id){
   var params = "data=" + (JSON.stringify(loggerPool[id]));
}
```

Next the function creates a new XHR object, sets the delivery method to POST and points to our saved serverLogURL variable (which points to savePerfData). Since this data isn't mission critical, logToServer() doesn't process the readystatechange event, and simply POSTs our data to our script waiting for it:

```
function logToServer(id){
```

```
    var params = "data=" + (JSON.stringify(loggerPool[id]));
    var xhr = new XMLHttpRequest();
    xhr.open("POST", serverLogURL, true);
    xhr.setRequestHeader("Content-type", "application/x-www-form-urlencoded");
    xhr.setRequestHeader("Content-length", params.length);
    xhr.setRequestHeader("Connection", "close");
    xhr.onreadystatechange = function(){};
    xhr.send(params);
}
```

Crafting the Public API

Now you'll start creating the public functions in the returned object literal. First tackle startTimeLogging(). We'll have it accept an ID that we'll use as the ID for the test results, a description of the test, and a boolean value for drawToPage and logToServer. Within the function you'll create a new object in loggerPool and set the passed-in properties, as well as the startTime value, which is just a new Date object.

```
startTimeLogging: function(id, descr,drawToPage,logToServer){
    loggerPool[id] = {};
    loggerPool[id].id = id;
    loggerPool[id].startTime = new Date;
    loggerPool[id].description = descr;
    loggerPool[id].drawtopage = drawToPage;
    loggerPool[id].logtoserver = logToServer
}
```

If you wanted to refine that further, you could create a constructor and simply invoke the constructor here. That would encapsulate the functionality already here and allow you to reuse it in other places without having to rewrite it.

Next code the implementation for the stopTimeLogging() function. Once again you can rely on the architecture outlined above, so stopTimeLogging()simply sets the stop time, and then calls the private functions to calculate the runtime and set the metadata for the test results:

```
loggerPool[id].stopTime = new Date;
calculateResults(id);
setResultsMetaData(id);
```

Finally stopTimeLogging() checks the boolean values to see if the test should be drawn to the screen and if it should be logged to the server:

```
if(loggerPool[id].drawtopage){
    drawToDebugScreen(id);
}
if(loggerPool[id].logtoserver){
    logToServer(id);
}
```

The complete function should look like this:

```
stopTimeLogging: function(id){
    loggerPool[id].stopTime = new Date;
    calculateResults(id);
    setResultsMetaData(id);
```

```
    if(loggerPool[id].drawtopage){
        drawToDebugScreen(id);
    }
    if(loggerPool[id].logtoserver){
        logToServer(id);
    }
}
```

The last function you will need to implement is logBenchmark(). This is the most complicated function in the library so far. At a high level, this function will use startTimeLogging() and stopTimeLogging() a set number of times on a function that is passed in, and then get the average of the results.

Let's take this one step at a time. First you'll need to pass in an ID to use, the number of times to run the test, the function to test, and whether to draw the results to the page and log them to the server:

```
logBenchmark: function(id, timestoIterate, func, debug, log){
}
```

Next create a variable to hold the sum of each test run and begin iterating based on the timestoIterate variable:

```
var timeSum = 0;
for(var x = 0; x < timestoIterate; x++){
}
```

Within that loop call startTimeLogging(),invoke the passed-in function , call stopTimeLogging(), and finally add the running time of each iteration to the timeSum variable:

```
for(var x = 0; x < timestoIterate; x++){
    perfLogger.startTimeLogging(id, "benchmarking "+ func, false, false);
    func();
    perfLogger.stopTimeLogging(id)
    timeSum += loggerPool[id].runtime
}
```

Notice that each iteration in the loop uses the same ID for the test that it is running; you are just overwriting the test results each time. Also notice that the code passes in false to avoid drawing to the debug screen or logging each individual test.

After looping is done you calculate the average runtime by dividing the summed runtimes by the number:

```
loggerPool[id].avgRunTime = timeSum/timestoIterate
if(debug){
    drawToDebugScreen(id)
}
if(log){
    logToServer(id)
}
```

The finished function should now look like this:

```
logBenchmark: function(id, timestoIterate, func, debug, log){
    var timeSum = 0;
    for(var x = 0; x < timestoIterate; x++){
        perfLogger.startTimeLogging(id, "benchmarking "+ func, false, false);
        func();
```

```
        perfLogger.stopTimeLogging(id)
        timeSum += loggerPool[id].runtime
    }
    loggerPool[id].avgRunTime = timeSum/timestoIterate
    if(debug){
        drawToDebugScreen(id)
    }
    if(log){
        logToServer(id)
    }
}
```

Your finished library should look like this:

```
var perfLogger = function(){
    var serverLogURL = "savePerfData.php",
        loggerPool = [];

        function calculateResults(id){
            loggerPool[id].runtime = loggerPool[id].stopTime - loggerPool[id].startTime;
        }

        function setResultsMetaData(id){
            loggerPool[id].url = window.location.href;
            loggerPool[id].useragent = navigator.userAgent;
        }

        function drawToDebugScreen(id){
            var debug = document.getElementById("debug")
            var output = formatDebugInfo(id)
            if(!debug){
                var divTag = document.createElement("div");
                divTag.id = "debug";
                divTag.innerHTML = output
                document.body.appendChild(divTag);
            }else{
                debug.innerHTML += output
            }
        }

        function logToServer(id){
            var params = "data=" + (JSON.stringify(loggerPool[id]));
            var xhr = new XMLHttpRequest();
            xhr.open("POST", serverLogURL, true);
            xhr.setRequestHeader("Content-type", "application/x-www-form-urlencoded");
            xhr.setRequestHeader("Content-length", params.length);
            xhr.setRequestHeader("Connection", "close");
            xhr.onreadystatechange = function(){};
            xhr.send(params);
        }
```

```
    function formatDebugInfo(id){
        var debuginfo = "<p><strong>" + loggerPool[id].description + "</strong><br/>";
        if(loggerPool[id].avgRunTime){
            debuginfo += "average run time: " + loggerPool[id].avgRunTime + "ms<br/>";
        }else{
            debuginfo += "run time: " + loggerPool[id].runtime + "ms<br/>";
        }
        debuginfo += "path: " + loggerPool[id].url + "<br/>";
        debuginfo += "useragent: " +  loggerPool[id].useragent + "<br/>";
        debuginfo += "</p>";
        return debuginfo
    }


return {
startTimeLogging: function(id, descr,drawToPage,logToServer){
    loggerPool[id] = {};
    loggerPool[id].id = id;
    loggerPool[id].startTime = new Date;
    loggerPool[id].description = descr;
    loggerPool[id].drawtopage = drawToPage;
    loggerPool[id].logtoserver = logToServer
},

stopTimeLogging: function(id){
    loggerPool[id].stopTime = new Date;
    calculateResults(id);
    setResultsMetaData(id);
    if(loggerPool[id].drawtopage){
        drawToDebugScreen(id);
    }
    if(loggerPool[id].logtoserver){
        logToServer(id);
    }
},


logBenchmark: function(id, timestoIterate, func, debug, log){
    var timeSum = 0;
    for(var x = 0; x < timestoIterate; x++){
        perfLogger.startTimeLogging(id, "benchmarking "+ func, false, false);
        func();
        perfLogger.stopTimeLogging(id)
        timeSum += loggerPool[id].runtime
    }
    loggerPool[id].avgRunTime = timeSum/timestoIterate
    if(debug){
        drawToDebugScreen(id)
    }
    if(log){
        logToServer(id)
```

```
        }
    }

}
}();
```

■ **Note**   Because of the speed of modern interpreters and systems, smaller ad hoc tests may yield a 0 millisecond result. When benchmarking, make sure you are testing a large enough block of functionality to yield results. This means that if you want to benchmark looping over an array, you'll need to make the array large enough that it takes more than a millisecond to step through it. I'll talk more about this in later chapters when we are benchmarking small snippets of ad hoc code; we'll run tests at large enough scales to see what the implied benefit actually is. We'll also explore the concept of High Resolution Time in next chapter, a feature that gives us access to time measurements in sub-milliseconds.

Remote Logging

OK, so perfLogger.js is calling savePerfData with the test results serialized to string form. Let's flesh out what we do with savePerfData.

You can reuse the fileio.php shared file from last chapter's WPTRunner example, and create two variables, $logfile to hold the path to the flat file, and $benchmarkResults to hold the test results. Pull the results out of the $_POST array; remember that you prefixed the serialized object with "data=", so now refer to it with the string "data". Stub out a function call to formatResults, pass in a reference to $_POST, and return that to $benchmarkResults. Finally, pass $benchmarkResults and $logfile to a stubbed out function saveLog():

```php
<?php
require("util/fileio.php");

$logfile = "log/runtimeperf_results.txt";
$benchmarkResults = formatResults($_POST["data"]);

saveLog($benchmarkResults, $logfile);
?>
```

Now let's flesh out formatResults().It should accept an object, in the parameter $r:

```php
function formatResults($r){}
```

Keep in mind that because it was serialized and encoded to pass over HTTP, the data will look something like this:

```
{\"id\":\"fi\",\"startTime\":59,\"description\":\"benchmarking function useForInLoop() {\\n var
stepTest = populateArray(4);\\n for (ind in stepTest) {\\n
}\\n}\",\"drawtopage\":false,\"logtoserver\":false,\"stopTime\":59,\"runtime\":0,\"url\":\"ht
tp://localhost:8888/lab/perfLogger_example.html\",\"useragent\":\"Mozilla/5.0 (Macintosh; Intel
Mac OS X 10.5; rv:13.0) Gecko/20100101 Firefox/13.0.1\",\"avgRunTime\":0}
```

So within the function you need to strip out all preceding slashes and use the native json_decode() to take the serialized data and convert it to a native JSON object:

```
$r = stripcslashes($r);
$r = json_decode($r);
```

To make sure that the value was properly converted, check the value of json_last_error(). From the PHP manual, at http://php.net/manual/en/function.json-last-error.php, you can see that the potential values in json_last_error are :

```
0 - JSON_ERROR_NONE
1 - JSON_ERROR_DEPTH
2 - JSON_ERROR_STATE_MISMATCH
3 - JSON_ERROR_CTRL_CHAR
4 - JSON_ERROR_SYNTAX
5 - JSON_ERROR_UTF8
```

▪ **Note** json_last_error is supported in PHP versions 5.3 and above. If you are running an older version of PHP, remove the check to json_last_error or you will get an error.

If any errors are found, you should exit the application completely. And finally, the function returns $r:

```
f(json_last_error() > 0){
    die("invalid json");
}
return($r);
```

Your completed function should look like this:

```
function formatResults($r){
    $r = stripcslashes($r);
    $r = json_decode($r);
    if(json_last_error() > 0){
        die("invalid json");
    }
    return($r);
}
```

Saving the Test Results

Next let's flesh out the saveLog() function. It, of course, accepts a string that is the path to our log file. As in the previous chapter, it should check whether the file exists, and if it doesn't, create and format a new log file. Stub out a function called formatNewLog() for this for now.

```
function saveLog($obj, $file){
    if(!file_exists($file)){
        formatNewLog($file);
    }
}
```

Some user agent strings contain commas. Since the delimiter that you will use to separate fields in our flat file will be a comma, you'll need to strip commas out of the user agent. Abstract that functionality into its own function called cleanCommas() and stub out a call to it for now:

```
$obj->useragent = cleanCommas($obj->useragent);
```

Next, you'll construct a comma-separated string from all of the property values and pass that to the appendToFile() function from the shared file, fileio.php. For an extra dimension of data, also prepend an IP address to that file. Adding this data will allow you to extrapolate information and categorize the results in all sorts of interesting ways; for example, converting IP address to geographical information and sorting the results by region, or by ISP.

```
$newLine = $_SERVER["REMOTE_ADDR"] . "," . $obj->id .",". $obj->startTime . "," . $obj->stopTime
. "," . $obj->runtime . "," . $obj->url . "," . $obj->useragent;
appendToFile($newLine, $file);
```

Your complete function should look like this:

```
function saveLog($obj, $file){
    if(!file_exists($file)){
        formatNewLog($file);
    }
    $obj->useragent = cleanCommas($obj->useragent);
    $newLine = $_SERVER["REMOTE_ADDR"] . "," . $obj->id .",". $obj->startTime . "," . $obj-
>stopTime . "," . $obj->runtime . "," . $obj->url . "," . $obj->useragent;
    appendToFile($newLine, $file);
}
```

Let's quickly flesh out the stubbed out cleanCommas() function. The function will accept a parameter $data. You'll use a little trick, calling the explode() function—PHP's equivalent to the split() function, which splits a string at a defined delimiter (in this case a comma)and returns an array with each string part as a separate element. Pass that array to the implode() function; it is PHP's equivalent to the join() function, which accepts an array and concatenates all elements into a single string. By using the two functions in conjunction you create a single-line find-and-replace function.

```
function cleanCommas($data){
    return implode("", explode(",", $data));
}
```

■ **Note** Let's linger on this find-and-replace trick for a minute. Think about how it's working. Exploding on the delimiter splits the string at each instance of the delimiter. So if we take the string "the quick brown fox jumps over the lazy dog" and explode it on the delimiter "the," it becomes the array

```
["quick", "brown", "fox", "jumps", "over", "lazy", "dog"]
```

If we then implode that array and pass in the string "a" to use to glue the array together, we get the following result:

```
"a quick brown fox jumps over a lazy dog"
```

And finally let's quickly flesh out our formatNewLog() function. This function will add the first line to a new log file, containing all of the headers for the file:

```php
function formatNewLog($file){
    $headerline = "IP, TestID, StartTime, StopTime, RunTime, URL, UserAgent";
    appendToFile($headerline, $file);
}
```

The completed savePerfData.php file should look like the following.

```php
<?php
require("util/fileio.php");

$logfile = "log/runtimeperf_results.txt";
$benchmarkResults = formatResults($_POST["data"]);

saveLog($benchmarkResults, $logfile);

function formatResults($r){
    $r = stripcslashes($r);
    $r = json_decode($r);
    if(json_last_error() > 0){
        die("invalid json");
    }
    return($r);
}

function formatNewLog($file){
    $headerline = "IP, TestID, StartTime, StopTime, RunTime, URL, UserAgent";
    appendToFile($headerline, $file);
}

function saveLog($obj, $file){
    if(!file_exists($file)){
        formatNewLog($file);
    }
$obj->useragent = cleanCommas($obj->useragent);
$newLine = $_SERVER["REMOTE_ADDR"] . "," . $obj->id .",". $obj->startTime . "," . $obj->stopTime
. "," . $obj->runtime . "," . $obj->url . "," . $obj->useragent;
    appendToFile($newLine, $file);
}

function cleanCommas($data){
    return implode("", explode(",", $data));
}

?>
```

An Example Page

Excellent! Now you can make a quick page that uses the library to get some data. Create the skeletal structure of an HTML page, give it a title of perfLogger Example, and link to perfLogger.js in the head section of the page. Then, also in the head of the page, put another script tag invoking perfLogger. startTimeLogging(). Pass in an ID of "page_render", a description of "timing page render", and true so that the results are displayed to the page, and true so that the results are also logged server side:

```
<!DOCTYPE html>
<html>
<head>
    <title>perfLogger Example</title>
    <script src="perfLogger.js"></script>
    <script>
    perfLogger.startTimeLogging("page_render", "timing page render", true, true)
    </script>
</head>
<body>
<script>
perfLogger.stopTimeLogging("page_render")
</script>
</body>
</html>
```

You're putting this function invocation in the head section so that it begins counting before the visible section of the page starts rendering. In the body section, we will put a new script tag with a call to perfLogger.stopTimeLogging("page_render").

Save this file as perfLogger_example.html. If you view it in a browser, it should look like Figure 4-6.

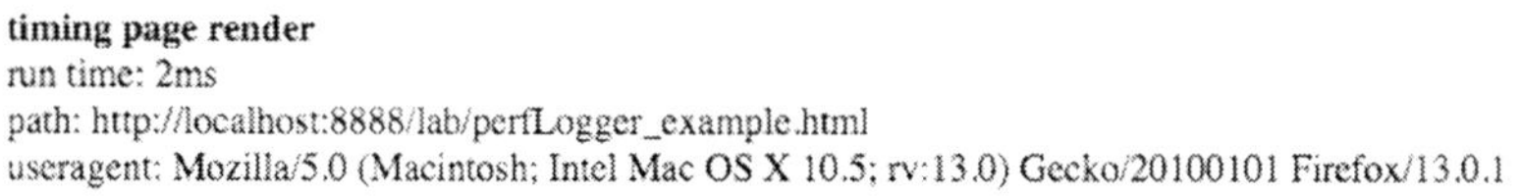

timing page render
run time: 2ms
path: http://localhost:8888/lab/perfLogger_example.html
useragent: Mozilla/5.0 (Macintosh; Intel Mac OS X 10.5; rv:13.0) Gecko/20100101 Firefox/13.0.1

Figure 4-6. Screen shot of perfLogger_example.html

And the runtimeperf_results.txt file should look like the following:

```
IP, TestID, StartTime, StopTime, RunTime, URL, UserAgent
71.225.152.145,page_render,2012-06-19T23:52:52.448Z,2012-06-19T23:52:52.448Z,0,http://tom-
barker.com/lab/perfLogger_example.html,Mozilla/5.0 (Macintosh; Intel Mac OS X 10_5_8)
AppleWebKit/536.5 (KHTML like Gecko) Chrome/19.0.1084.52 Safari/536.5
71.225.152.145,page_render,2012-06-19T23:52:52.452Z,2012-06-19T23:52:52.452Z,0,http://tom-
barker.com/lab/perfLogger_example.html,Mozilla/5.0 (Macintosh; Intel Mac OS X 10_5_8)
AppleWebKit/536.5 (KHTML like Gecko) Chrome/19.0.1084.52 Safari/536.5
```

■ **Note** Depending on the browser, you may get 0 millisecond results for this test, because there is nothing on the page. Real tests will have content. Or you could build your own test suite to benchmark, much like SunSpider, at http://www.webkit.org/perf/sunspider/sunspider.html.

We'll put this page in production to gather metrics for all of our users that hit it. You can see this page at http://tom-barker.com/lab/perfLogger_example.html.

Charting the Results

Now that we've got some data, let's take a stab at visualizing it. We'll look at the page_render test results runtime by user agent. Create a new R document called runtimePerformance.R and create the following variables: dataDirectory to hold the path to the log directory, chartDirectory to hold the path to the directory where you will write the charts, and testname to hold the name of the test that you will be charting:

```
dataDirectory <- "/Applications/MAMP/htdocs/lab/log/"
chartDirectory <- "/Applications/MAMP/htdocs/lab/charts/"
testname = "page_render"
```

Read in the log file and store it as a data frame in the variable perflogs, and create a path to the chart that you want to draw in the variable perfchart:

```
perflogs <- read.table(paste(dataDirectory, "runtimeperf_results.txt", sep=""), header=TRUE,
sep=",")
perfchart <- paste(chartDirectory, "runtime_",testname, ".pdf", sep="")
```

Next you'll do a bit of analysis. Right now you only have results for the page_render test in the log, but eventually as you run different tests you'll have differently named results, so pull only the results that have a column TestID whose value is "page_render":

```
pagerender <- perflogs[perflogs$TestID == "page_render",]
```

Then create a new data frame made up only of the columns that we want to chart the UserAgent column and the RunTime column.

```
df <- data.frame(pagerender$UserAgent, pagerender$RunTime)
```

Next you'll use the by() function of R. This function applies another function to a data frame and groups by a passed-in factor. For our example we'll group by the UserAgent column and apply the mean() function to each element.

```
df <- by(df$pagerender.RunTime, df$pagerender.UserAgent, mean)
```

If you type df at the console again, you'll see this:

```
> df
df$pagerender.UserAgent
Mozilla/5.0 (Macintosh; U; Intel Mac OS X 10_5_8; en-us) AppleWebKit/533.21.1 (KHTML like Gecko)
Version/5.0.5 Safari/533.21.1

6.00000
Mozilla/5.0 (Macintosh; Intel Mac OS X 10_5_8) AppleWebKit/536.5 (KHTML like Gecko)
Chrome/19.0.1084.52 Safari/536.5

20.75000
Mozilla/5.0 (Macintosh; Intel Mac OS X 10.5; rv:13.0) Gecko/20100101 Firefox/13.0.1

55.63158
```

```
Mozilla/5.0 (Macintosh; Intel Mac OS X 10.5; rv:13.0) Gecko/20100101 Firefox/13.0
```

```
144.00000
Mozilla/4.0 (compatible; MSIE 8.0; Windows NT 5.1; Trident/4.0; .NET CLR 2.0.50727; .NET CLR
3.0.4506.2152; .NET CLR 3.5.30729)
```

```
511.00000
```

This data frame now holds the average run time grouped by raw user agent. It is the mathematical mean of the run time result of each test, by user agent.

And finally we'll order the data frame and generate the chart as a bar chart.

```
df <- df[order(df)]
pdf(perfchart, width=10, height=10)
opar <- par(no.readonly=TRUE)
    par(las=1, mar=c(10,10,10,10))
    barplot(df, horiz=TRUE, main="Page Render Runtime Performance in Milliseconds\nBy User
Agent")
par(opar)
dev.off()
```

See Figure 4-7 for the resulting chart.

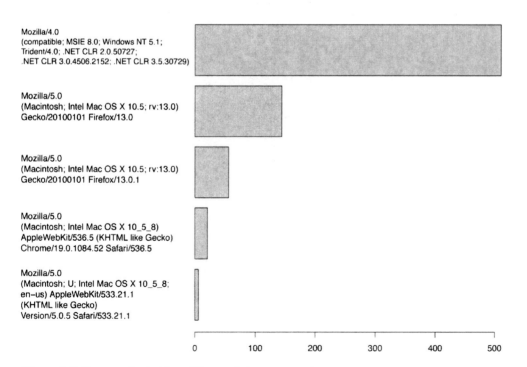

Figure 4-7. Page render test in milliseconds by user agent

The complete R script should look like this:

```
dataDirectory <- "/Applications/MAMP/htdocs/lab/log/"
chartDirectory <- "/Applications/MAMP/htdocs/lab/charts/"
testname = "page_render"

perflogs <- read.table(paste(dataDirectory, "runtimeperf_results.txt", sep=""), header=TRUE,
sep=",")
perfchart <- paste(chartDirectory, "runtime_",testname, ".pdf", sep="")

pagerender <- perflogs[perflogs$TestID == "page_render",]
df <- data.frame(pagerender$UserAgent, pagerender$RunTime)
df <- by(df$pagerender.RunTime, df$pagerender.UserAgent, mean)
df <- df[order(df)]

pdf(perfchart, width=10, height=10)
opar <- par(no.readonly=TRUE)
   par(las=1, mar=c(10,10,10,10))
   barplot(df, horiz=TRUE)
par(opar)
dev.off()
```

Open Source

Just as I did with WPTRunner, I've put the source code for perfLogger up on Github, available here:
https://github.com/tomjbarker/perfLogger.

Summary

In this chapter you created a tool to gather the running time of ad hoc blocks of code, or benchmark passed-in functions through aggregating the running time of multiple iterations of that code. You created a server-side script in PHP to which our library can send the results of these tests. Finally, you created an R script to pull out and chart our test results.

In the coming chapters we will be exploring a number of performance best practices. To demonstrate why these practices are more performant, we will be using these tools that you just developed to back these claims up with empirical data, and visualize our results for mass consumption.

But first Chapter 5 will look at the future of performance in the browser, the coming of Web Performance Standards.

CHAPTER 5

■ ■ ■

Looking Forward, a Standard for Performance

In Chapter 4 we built a JavaScript library to track ad hoc code and benchmark functions. This is a great tool to gather timing metrics and extrapolate performance gains through coding styles, as you'll see in the coming chapters.

So far we've seen how to build our own tools, or use existing tools to gather the data that we need in order to measure performance, but now we will look at the work that the W3C has been doing to craft a standard for tracking performance metrics in browsers.

Note that some of these features are just now starting to be supported in modern browsers; some features are only available in beta and pre-beta versions of the browsers. For this reason I will identify the release version used in all of the examples in this chapter when relevant. It is also for this reason that I may show screen shots of the same thing but in different browsers, to illustrate the differing levels of support for these features.

W3C Web Performance Working Group

In late 2010 the W3C created a new working group, the Web Performance Working Group. The mission for this working group, as stated on its mission page, is *to provide methods to measure aspects of application performance of user agent features and APIs.* What that means in a very practical sense is that the working group has developed an API that browsers can and will expose to JavaScript that holds key performance metrics.

This is implemented in a new performance object that is part of the native window object:

```
>>window.performance
```

The Performance Object

If you type window.performance in a JavaScript console, you'll see that it returns an object of type Performance with potentially several objects and methods that it exposes. Figure 5-1 shows the Performance object structure in Chrome 20 beta.

memory	MemoryInfo { jsHeapSizeLimit=0, totalJSHeapSize=0, ... }
jsHeapSizeLimit	0
totalJSHeapSize	0
usedJSHeapSize	0
navigation	PerformanceNavigation { redirectCount=0, type=0, ... }
TYPE_BACK_FORWARD	2
TYPE_NAVIGATE	0
TYPE_RELOAD	1
TYPE_RESERVED	255
redirectCount	0
type	0
timing	PerformanceTiming { fetchStart=1340762919512, ... }
connectEnd	1340762919514
connectStart	1340762919514
domComplete	1340762920145
domContentLoadedEventEnd	1340762919698
domContentLoadedEventStart	1340762919698
domInteractive	1340762919698
domLoading	1340762919582
domainLookupEnd	1340762919512
domainLookupStart	1340762919512
fetchStart	1340762919512
loadEventEnd	1340762920150
loadEventStart	1340762920145
navigationStart	1340762919512
redirectEnd	0
redirectStart	0
requestStart	1340762919514
responseEnd	1340762919696
responseStart	1340762919579
secureConnectionStart	0
unloadEventEnd	0
unloadEventStart	0
webkitNow	webkitNow()

Figure 5-1. Window.performance in Chrome 20 beta

If we type this into Chrome we see that it supports a navigation object, of type PerformanceNavigation, and a timing object, of type PerformanceTiming. Chrome also supports a memory object, and webkitNow— a browser-specific version of High Resolution Time (I'll cover high-resolution time towards the end of this chapter).

Let's take a look at each object and see how we can make use of these for our own performance tracking.

Performance Timing

The timing object has the following properties, all of which contain millisecond snapshots of when these events occur, much like our own startTimeLogging() function from last chapter. See Figure 5-2 for a flowchart of each timing metric in sequential order.

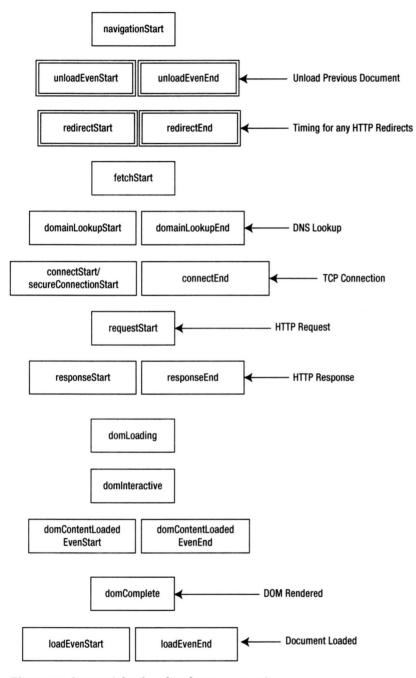

Figure 5-2. Sequential order of Performance metrics

navigationStart: This is the time snapshot for when navigation begins, either
when the browser starts to unload the previous page if there is one, or if not,
when it begins to fetch the content. It will either contain the unloadEventStart

data or the `fetchStart` data. If we want to track end-to-end time we will often start with this value.

`unloadEventStart`: This is the time snapshot for when the browser begins to unload the previous page, if there is a previous page at the same domain to unload.

`unloadEventEnd`: This is the time snapshot for when the browser completes unloading the previous page.

`redirectStart`: This is the time snapshot for when the browser begins any HTTP redirects.

`redirectEnd`: This is the time snapshot for when all HTTP redirects are complete.

To calculate total time spent on HTTP redirects, simply subtract `redirectStart` from `redirectEnd`:

```
<script>
var http_redirect_time = performance.timing.redirectEnd - performance.timing.redirectStart;
</script>
```

`fetchStart`: This is the time snapshot for when the browser first begins to check the cache for the requested resource.

To calculate the total time spent loading cache, subtract `fetchStart` from `domainLookupStart`:

```
<script>
var cache_time = performance.timing.domainLookupStart - performance.timing.fetchStart;
</script>
```

`domainLookupStart`: This is the time snapshot for when the browser begins the DNS lookup for the requested content.

`domainLookupEnd`: This is the time snapshot for when the browser completes the DNS lookup for the requested content.

To calculate the total time spent on a DNS lookup, subtract the `domainLookupStart` from the `domainLookupEnd`:

```
<script>
var dns_time = performance.timing.domainLookupEnd - performance.timing.domainLookupStart;
</script>
```

`connectStart`: This is the time snapshot for when the browser begins establishing the TCP connection to the remote server for the current page.

`secureConnectionStart`: When the page is loaded over HTTPS, this property captures the time snapshot for when the HTTPS communication begins.

`connectEnd`: This is the time snapshot for when the browser finishes establishing the TCP connection to the remote server for the current page.

To calculate the total time spent establishing the TCP connection, subtract `connectStart` from `connectEnd`:

```
<script>
var tcp_connection_time = performance.timing.connectEnd - performance.timing.connectStart;
</script>
```

> requestStart: This is the time snapshot for when the browser sends the HTTP request.

> responseStart: This is the time snapshot for when the browser first registers the server response.

> responseEnd: This is the time snapshot for when the browser finishes receiving the server response.

To calculate the total time spent on the complete HTTP roundtrip, including establishing the TCP connection, we can subtract connectStart from responseEnd:

```
<script>
var roundtrip_time = performance.timing.responseEnd - performance.timing.connectStart;
</script>
```

> domLoading: This is the time snapshot for when the document begins loading.

> domComplete: This is the time snapshot for when the document is finished loading.

To calculate the time spent rendering the page, we just subtract the domLoading from the domComplete:

```
<script>
var page_render_time = performance.timing.domComplete - performance.timing.domLoading;
</script>
```

To calculate the time spent loading the page, from the first request to when it is fully loaded, subtract navigationStart from domComplete:

```
<script>
var full_load_time = performance.timing.domComplete - performance.timing.navigationStart
</script>
```

> domContentLoadedEventEnd: This is fired when the DOMContentLoaded event completes.

> domContentLoadedEventStart: This is fired when the DOMContentLoaded event begins.

The DOMContentLoaded event is fired when the browser completes parsing the document. For more information about this event, see the W3C's documentation for the steps that happen at the end of the document parsing, located at http://www.w3.org/TR/html5/the-end.html.

> domInteractive: This is fired when the document's readyState property is set to interactive, indicating that the user can now interact with the page.

> loadEventEnd: This is fired when the load event of the document is finished.

> loadEventStart: This is fired when the load even of the document starts.

Let's update perfLogger to use this new-found wealth of performance data! We'll add read-only public properties that will return calculated values that we want to record. We'll also update the prototype of the

Test Result object so that each result we send to the server automatically has these performance metrics built in.

Let's get started!

Integrating the Performance Object with perfLogger

First, you need to create private variables in the self-executing function of perfLogger. Create values for perceived time, redirect time, cache time, DNS lookup time, TCP connection time, total round trip time, and page render time:

```
var perfLogger = function(){
    var serverLogURL = "savePerfData.php",
    loggerPool = [];
    if(window.performance){
    var _pTime = Date.now() - performance.timing.navigationStart || 0,
    _redirTime = performance.timing.redirectEnd - performance.timing.redirectStart || 0,
    _cacheTime = performance.timing.domainLookupStart - performance.timing.fetchStart || 0,
    _dnsTime = performance.timing.domainLookupEnd - performance.timing.domainLookupStart || 0,
    _tcpTime = performance.timing.connectEnd - performance.timing.connectStart || 0,
    _roundtripTime = performance.timing.responseEnd - performance.timing.connectStart || 0,
    _renderTime = performance.timing.domComplete - performance.timing.domLoading || 0;
    }
}
```

First this code wraps our variable assignments in an `if` statement to make sure we only invoke `window. performance` if the current browser supports it. Then note that we are using short circuit evaluation when assigning these variables. This technique uses a logic operator—in this case a logical OR—in the variable assignments. If the first value is unavailable, null or undefined, then the second value is used in the assignment.

Next, still within the self-executing function, you'll explicitly create a `TestResults` constructor. Remember that we architected the `TestResults` object last chapter, but we never ended up using it, instead we had `loggerPool` hold general objects. You're going to use `TestResults` now, and take advantage of prototypal inheritance to make sure each `TestResults` object has our new performance metrics built in.

First create the `TestResults` constructor.

```
function TestResults(){};
```

Then add a property to the prototype of `TestResults` for each of our `window.performance` metrics:

```
TestResults.prototype.perceivedTime = _pTime;
TestResults.prototype.redirectTime = _redirTime;
TestResults.prototype.cacheTime = _cacheTime;
TestResults.prototype.dnsLookupTime = _dnsTime;
TestResults.prototype.tcpConnectionTime = _tcpTime;
TestResults.prototype.roundTripTime = _roundtripTime;
TestResults.prototype.pageRenderTime = _renderTime;
```

Excellent! Now let's go and edit our public method `startTimeLogging()`. Right now the first line of the function assigns an empty object to `loggerPool`:

```
loggerPool[id] = {};
```

Change that to instead instantiate a new instance of `TestResults`:

```
loggerPool[id] = new TestResults();
```

At this point if you console.log a TestResults object, it should look like Figure 5-3.

Figure 5-3. TestResults object

You can see that we now have cacheTime, dnsLookupTime, pageRenderTime, perceivedTime, redirectTime, roundTripTime, and tcpConnectionTime properties for each TestResults object that we create. You can also see that these properties exist on the prototype.

This is an important point, because if you console.log the serialized object in logToServer() you will see that those properties are not serialized with the rest of the object. This is because JSON.stringify does not serialize undefined values or functions within an object.

That's not a problem, though. To solve this, you just need to make a small private function to concatenate two objects. So go back to the self-executing function at the top, where you'll add a new function jsonConcat() and have it accept two objects:

```
function jsonConcat(object1, object2) {}
```

Next loop through each property in the second object and add the properties to the first object. Finally, return the first object:

```
for (var key in object2) {
object1[key] = object2[key];
}
return object1;
```

Note that this will also overwrite the values of any properties in the first object that the two objects may have in common.

The finished function should look like this.

```
function jsonConcat(object1, object2) {
for (var key in object2) {
object1[key] = object2[key];
    }
```

```
    return object1;
}
```

Now to make this work, go back to logToServer(). Recall that in the beginning of the function we serialize our TestResults object this way:

```
var params = "data=" + (JSON.stringify(loggerPool[id]));
```

Change that to pass the TestResults object and its prototype into jsonConcat(), and pass the returned object to JSON.stringify:

```
var params = "data=" + JSON.stringify(jsonConcat(loggerPool[id],TestResults.prototype));
```

If you console.log the params variable, it should look like this:

data={"id":"page_render","startTime":1341152573075,"description":"timing page render","drawtopage":true,"logtoserver":true,"stopTime":1341152573077,"runtime":2,"url":"http://localhost:8888/lab/perfLogger_example.html","useragent":"Mozilla/5.0 (Macintosh; Intel Mac OS X 10.5; rv:13.0) Gecko/20100101 Firefox/13.0.1","perceivedTime":78,"redirectTime":0,"cacheTime":-2,"dnsLookupTime":0,"tcpConnectionTime":0,"roundTripTime":2,"pageRenderTime":72}

Next you'll expose these private performance variables via public methods in order to expose them via the perfLogger namespace without needing to run any tests. If you didn't expose the variables at the object level, you would need to create a test and pull them from the test object; recall that we added these Performance object numbers to the prototype of every test object.

```
//expose derived performance data
perceivedTime: function(){
return _pTime;
},
redirectTime: function(){
    _redirTime;
},
cacheTime: function(){
    return _cacheTime;
},
dnsLookupTime: function(){
    return _dnsTime;
},
tcpConnectionTime: function(){
    return _tcpTime;
},
roundTripTime: function(){
    return _roundtripTime;
},
pageRenderTime: function(){
    return _renderTime;
}
```

Excellent! These public functions expose the data from the perfLogger object like so:

```
>>> perfLogger.perceivedTime()
78
```

So now your updated perfLogger.js should look like this:

```javascript
var perfLogger = function(){
var serverLogURL = "savePerfData.php",
    loggerPool = [],
    _pTime = Date.now() - performance.timing.navigationStart || 0,
    _redirTime = performance.timing.redirectEnd - performance.timing.redirectStart || 0,
    _cacheTime = performance.timing.domainLookupStart - performance.timing.fetchStart || 0,
    _dnsTime = performance.timing.domainLookupEnd - performance.timing.domainLookupStart || 0,
    _tcpTime = performance.timing.connectEnd - performance.timing.connectStart || 0,
    _roundtripTime = performance.timing.responseEnd - performance.timing.connectStart || 0,
    _renderTime = Date.now() - performance.timing.domLoading || 0;

function TestResults(){};
TestResults.prototype.perceivedTime = _pTime;
TestResults.prototype.redirectTime = _redirTime;
TestResults.prototype.cacheTime = _cacheTime;
TestResults.prototype.dnsLookupTime = _dnsTime;
TestResults.prototype.tcpConnectionTime = _tcpTime;
TestResults.prototype.roundTripTime = _roundtripTime;
TestResults.prototype.pageRenderTime = _renderTime;

function jsonConcat(object1, object2) {
for (var key in object2) {
    object1[key] = object2[key];
}
return object1;
}

function calculateResults(id){
    loggerPool[id].runtime = loggerPool[id].stopTime - loggerPool[id].startTime;
}

function setResultsMetaData(id){
    loggerPool[id].url = window.location.href;
    loggerPool[id].useragent = navigator.userAgent;
}

function drawToDebugScreen(id){
    var debug = document.getElementById("debug")
    var output = formatDebugInfo(id)
    if(!debug){
        var divTag = document.createElement("div");
        divTag.id = "debug";
        divTag.innerHTML = output
        document.body.appendChild(divTag);
    }else{
        debug.innerHTML += output
    }
}

function logToServer(id){
    var params = "data=" + JSON.stringify(jsonConcat(loggerPool[id],TestResults.prototype));
```

```
        var xhr = new XMLHttpRequest();
        xhr.open("POST", serverLogURL, true);
        xhr.setRequestHeader("Content-type", "application/x-www-form-urlencoded");
        xhr.setRequestHeader("Content-length", params.length);
        xhr.setRequestHeader("Connection", "close");
        xhr.onreadystatechange = function()
         {
         if (xhr.readyState==4 && xhr.status==200)
           {}
         };
        xhr.send(params);
    }

    function formatDebugInfo(id){
        var debuginfo = "<p><strong>" + loggerPool[id].description + "</strong><br/>";
        if(loggerPool[id].avgRunTime){
            debuginfo += "average run time: " + loggerPool[id].avgRunTime + "ms<br/>";
        }else{
            debuginfo += "run time: " + loggerPool[id].runtime + "ms<br/>";
        }
        debuginfo += "path: " + loggerPool[id].url + "<br/>";
        debuginfo += "useragent: " + loggerPool[id].useragent + "<br/>";
        debuginfo += "</p>";
        return debuginfo
    }

    return {

    startTimeLogging: function(id, descr,drawToPage,logToServer){
    loggerPool[id] = new TestResults();
        loggerPool[id].id = id;
        loggerPool[id].startTime =  Date.now();
        loggerPool[id].description = descr;
        loggerPool[id].drawtopage = drawToPage;
        loggerPool[id].logtoserver = logToServer
    },

    stopTimeLogging: function(id){
    loggerPool[id].stopTime =  Date.now();
        calculateResults(id);
        setResultsMetaData(id);
        if(loggerPool[id].drawtopage){
            drawToDebugScreen(id);
        }
        if(loggerPool[id].logtoserver){
            logToServer(id);
        }
    },

    logBenchmark: function(id, timestoIterate, func, debug, log){
        var timeSum = 0;
```

```
        for(var x = 0; x < timestoIterate; x++){
            perfLogger.startTimeLogging(id, "benchmarking "+ func, false, false);
            func();
            perfLogger.stopTimeLogging(id)
            timeSum += loggerPool[id].runtime
        }
        loggerPool[id].avgRunTime = timeSum/timestoIterate
        if(debug){
            drawToDebugScreen(id)
        }
        if(log){
            logToServer(id)
        }
    },

    //expose derived performance data
    perceivedTime: function(){
    return _pTime;
    },
    redirectTime: function(){
        _redirTime;
    },
    cacheTime: function(){
        return _cacheTime;
    },
    dnsLookupTime: function(){
        return _dnsTime;
    },
    tcpConnectionTime: function(){
        return _tcpTime;
    },
    roundTripTime: function(){
        return _roundtripTime;
    },
    pageRenderTime: function(){
        return _renderTime;
    }
    }
}();
```

Updating the Logging Functionality

Let's next update our savePerfData.php file. Start by adding new headers to the formatNewLog() function, so that each new log file to be created has column headers for our new data points:

```
function formatNewLog($file){
    $headerline = "IP, TestID, StartTime, StopTime, RunTime, URL, UserAgent, PerceivedLoadTime,
PageRenderTime, RoundTripTime, TCPConnectionTime, DNSLookupTime, CacheTime, RedirectTime";
    appendToFile($headerline, $file);
}
```

Then update saveLog() to include the additional values that we are now passing in:

```
function saveLog($obj, $file){
    if(!file_exists($file)){
        formatNewLog($file);
    }
    $obj->useragent = cleanCommas($obj->useragent);
    $newLine = $_SERVER["REMOTE_ADDR"] . "," . $obj->id .",". $obj->startTime . "," . $obj-
>stopTime . "," . $obj->runtime . "," . $obj->url . "," . $obj->useragent . "," . $obj-
>perceivedTime . "," . $obj->pageRenderTime . "," . $obj->roundTripTime . "," . $obj-
>tcpConnectionTime . "," . $obj->dnsLookupTime . "," . $obj->cacheTime . "," . $obj-
>redirectTime;
    appendToFile($newLine, $file);
}
```

The updated log file should now look like this:

```
IP, TestID, StartTime, StopTime, RunTime, URL, UserAgent, PerceivedLoadTime, PageRenderTime,
RoundTripTime, TCPConnectionTime, DNSLookupTime, CacheTime, RedirectTime
127.0.0.1,page_render,1.34116648339,1.3411664834,2,http://localhost:8888/lab/perfLogger_example.
html,Mozilla/5.0 (Macintosh; Intel Mac OS X 10.5; rv:13.0) Gecko/20100101 Firef
ox/13.0.1115,86,21,1,1,-4,0
127.0.0.1,page_render,345.173000009,345.331000019,0.158000009833,http://localhost:8888/lab/
perfLogger_example.html,Mozilla/5.0 (Macintosh; Intel Mac OS X 10_5_8) AppleWebKit/536.11 (KHTML
like Gecko) Chrome/20.0.1132.43 Safari/536.11495,261,79,0,0,0,0
```

Performance Navigation

Let's now take a look at the Performance Navigation object. If you type `performance.navigation` into your console, you'll see something like Figure 5-4.

⊞ memory	MemoryInfo { jsHeapSizeLimit=0, totalJSHeapSize=0, ... }
⊟ navigation	PerformanceNavigation { redirectCount=0, type=0, ... }
TYPE_BACK_FORWARD	2
TYPE_NAVIGATE	0
TYPE_RELOAD	1
TYPE_RESERVED	255
redirectCount	0
type	0
⊞ timing	PerformanceTiming { fetchStart=1341159869669, ... }
webkitNow	webkitNow()

Figure 5-4. Performance Navigation object

Note that the navigation object has two read-only attributes: redirectCount and type. The redirectCount attribute is exactly what it sounds like, the number of HTTP redirects that the browser follows to get to the current page.

■ **Note** HTTP redirects are significant because they cause a complete roundtrip for each redirect. The original request is returned from the web server as either a 301 or a 302 with the path to the new location. The browser must then initialize a new TCP connection and send a new request for the new location. See Figure 5-5 for a sequence diagram of a single HTTP redirect. Note how the DNS lookup, the TCP handshake, and the HTTP request are all repeated for the redirected asset. This repetition doubles the network connection time for a single redirect.

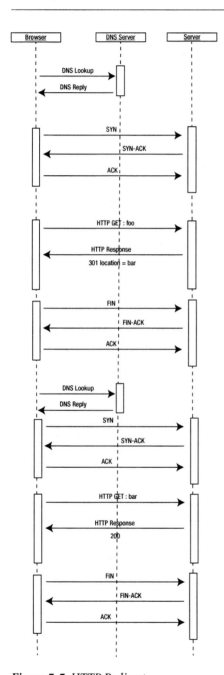

Figure 5-5. HTTP Redirect

We can access the redirectCount property like so:

```
>>> performance.navigation.redirectCount
0
```

The other attribute of the navigation object is type. The navigation.type attribute will be one of four values represented by the following constants:

TYPE_NAVIGATE: Has the value of 0, which indicates that the current page was navigated to by clicking on a link, submitting a form, or entering the URL directly in the address bar.

TYPE_RELOAD: Has the value of 1, indicating that the current page was arrived at via a reload operation.

TYPE_BACK_FORWARD: Has the value of 2, indicating that the page was navigated to via the browser history, either using the back or forward buttons or programmatically through the browser's history object.

TYPE_RESERVED: Has the value of 255 and is a catch-all for any navigation type not defined above.

Performance Memory

The memory object is a feature of Chrome that allows us to see the memory usage that Chrome is taking up while running our page. Notice in Figure 5-1 earlier that all of the values return 0—that is because we need to enable the memory info flag before we can take advantage of this capability.

The way to do this is slightly platform dependent, but essentially you need to pass the --enable-memory-info command-line parameter into Chrome. To do this on a Windows platform, right-click the Chrome icon, go to Properties, and at the end of the path to the executable, append the flag --enable-memory-info. The executable should look like this:

```
[path to exe]\chrome.exe --enable-memory-info
```

For the Mac OS, instead of updating a shortcut, go into Terminal and invoke the Chrome application like so:

```
/Applications/Google\ Chrome.app/Contents/MacOS/Google\ Chrome --enable-memory-info
```

For more information, see http://www.chromium.org/developers/how-tos/run-chromium-with-flags.

Once you launch Chrome with the flag enabled, you should see data now in the memory object, as in Figure 5-6.

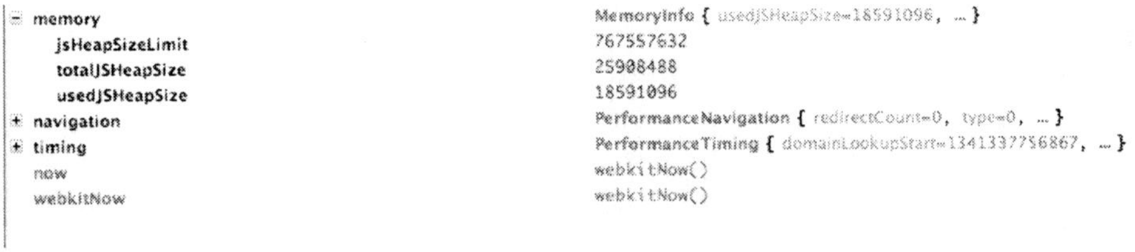

Figure 5-6. Performance Memory object with data

```
>>> performance.memory. jsHeapSizeLimit
767557632
```

For reference, the *heap* is the collection of JavaScript objects that the interpreter keeps in resident memory. In the heap each object is an interconnected node, connected via properties, like the prototype chain, or composed objects. JavaScript running in the browser references the objects in the heap via object references, as diagrammed in Figure 5-7. When we destroy an object in JavaScript, what we are really doing is destroying the object reference. When the interpreter sees an object in the heap with no object references, it removes that object from the heap. This is called *garbage collection*.

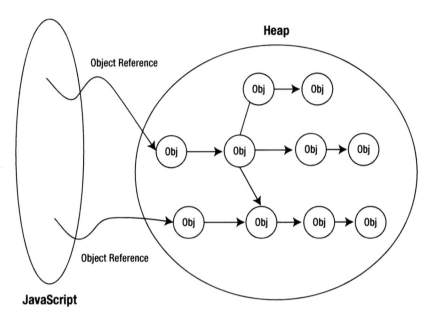

Figure 5-7. the JavaScript Heap

The usedJsHeapSize property shown in Figure 5-6 is the amount of memory that all of the current objects in the heap are using. The totalJsHeapSize is size of the heap including free space not used by objects.

Because we need to launch the browser with command-line parameters to get these properties, this isn't something that we can include in our library and put out in our production environment and hope to get real data from it. Instead it is a tool we can monitor and run in our own lab for profiling purposes.

■ **Note** Profiling allows us to monitor our memory usage. This is useful for detecting memory leaks, the creation of objects that never get destroyed. Usually in JavaScript this occurs when we programmatically assign event handlers to DOM objects and forget to remove the event handlers. More nuanced than just detecting leakages, profiling is also useful for optimizing the memory usage of our applications over time. We should intelligently create, destroy, or re-use objects and always be mindful of scope to avoid profiling charts that trend upward in an ever-growing series of spikes. A much better profile chart shows a controlled rise and plateau.

Firefox has started allowing insight into its memory usage as well. Typing about:memory into the location bar brings up a page that gives a high-level breakdown of memory usage; to get a more granular insight, type about:memory?verbose. See Figure 5-8 for the resulting granular breakdown of memory usage in Firefox.

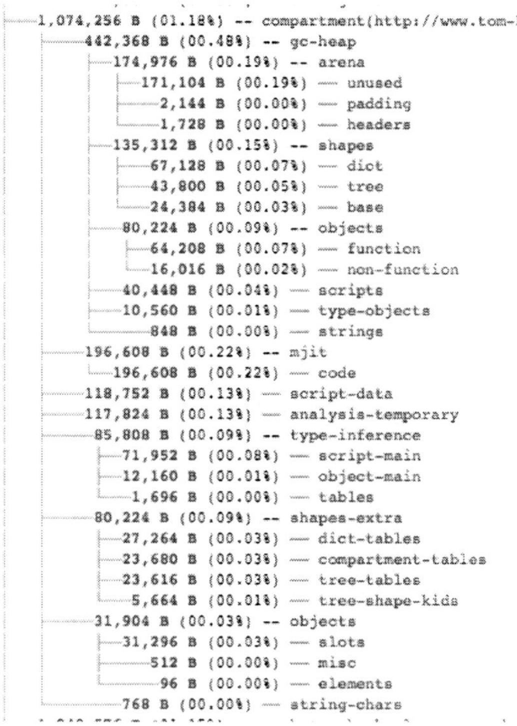

```
──1,074,256 B (01.18%) -- compartment(http://www.tom-barker.com/blog/?p=x)
    ├───442,368 B (00.48%) -- gc-heap
    │   ├───174,976 B (00.19%) -- arena
    │   │   ├───171,104 B (00.19%) ── unused
    │   │   ├─────2,144 B (00.00%) ── padding
    │   │   └─────1,728 B (00.00%) ── headers
    │   ├───135,312 B (00.15%) -- shapes
    │   │   ├────67,128 B (00.07%) ── dict
    │   │   ├────43,800 B (00.05%) ── tree
    │   │   └────24,384 B (00.03%) ── base
    │   ├────80,224 B (00.09%) -- objects
    │   │   ├────64,208 B (00.07%) ── function
    │   │   └────16,016 B (00.02%) ── non-function
    │   ├────40,448 B (00.04%) ── scripts
    │   ├────10,560 B (00.01%) ── type-objects
    │   └───────848 B (00.00%) ── strings
    ├───196,608 B (00.22%) -- mjit
    │   └───196,608 B (00.22%) ── code
    ├───118,752 B (00.13%) ── script-data
    ├───117,824 B (00.13%) ── analysis-temporary
    ├────85,808 B (00.09%) -- type-inference
    │   ├────71,952 B (00.08%) ── script-main
    │   ├────12,160 B (00.01%) ── object-main
    │   └─────1,696 B (00.00%) ── tables
    ├────80,224 B (00.09%) -- shapes-extra
    │   ├────27,264 B (00.03%) ── dict-tables
    │   ├────23,680 B (00.03%) ── compartment-tables
    │   ├────23,616 B (00.03%) ── tree-tables
    │   └─────5,664 B (00.01%) ── tree-shape-kids
    ├────31,904 B (00.03%) -- objects
    │   ├────31,296 B (00.03%) ── slots
    │   ├───────512 B (00.00%) ── misc
    │   └────────96 B (00.00%) ── elements
    └───────768 B (00.00%) ── string-chars
```

Figure 5-8. *Firefox memory window*

High-Resolution Time

The next change we will look at is a feature called *high-resolution time*— time recorded in sub-millisecond values. This is useful for capturing timing data that happens in less than 1 millisecond. We'll make extensive use of high-resolution time in the next chapter to capture run time performance metrics.

The Web Performance Working Group has detailed a public method of the performance object, performance.now().

As you saw in the previous chapter, when timing code execution we ran into cases where we had 0 millisecond results. That is because the values that are returned from the Date() object only had precision to up to 1 millisecond. Type the following into a JavaScript console to see the Date() object:

```
>>> new Date().getMilliseconds()
603

>>> Date.now()
1340722684122
```

Because of refinements in the performance of JavaScript interpreters and browser rendering engines, some of our operations may complete within microseconds. That's when we get 0 millisecond results for our tests.

A more subtle danger with this sort of test is that the value in the Date object is based on system date, which theoretically can be changed during a test, and would skew the results. Any number of things could change the system date without our input, from daylight savings time adherence, to corporate policy synchronizing system times. And any of these would change our timed results, even to potentially negative results.

The `performance.now()` method returns results in fractions of milliseconds. It also is relative to the `navigationStart` event, not the system date, so it will not be impacted by changing system time. Chrome started supporting high-resolution time with Chrome 20 via the browser-specific prefixed `webkitNow()` function, which looks like this:

```
Google Chrome 20
>>> performance.webkitNow()
290117.4699999974
```

And Firefox began supporting high-resolution time with Firefox 15 Aurora release:

```
Firefox 15 aurora
>>> performance.now()
56491.447434
```

This is great, but how do we start to use this now, and how do we make sure the code that we write now will be relevant once this is supported in all browsers? To future-proof our perfLogger library, we can code against the `performance.now()` method and build in a shim for a fallback if the browser does not yet support it.

■ **Note** A shim is an abstraction layer that intercepts API calls or events and either changes the signature of the call and passes on the call to fit an updated API signature, or handles the functionality of the API itself. Figure 5-9 diagrams a shim intercepting an event or message dispatch, presumably to perform some logic, before republishing out the message. Figure 5-10 diagrams a shim that is overriding a function or an object, processes the information, and then either passes data to, or invokes via composition, the original object or function.

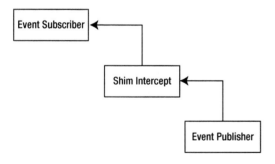

Figure 5-9. Intercept

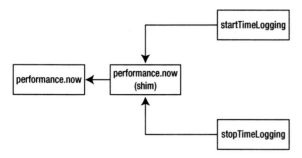

Figure 5-10. *Override*

In this case you will override the performance.now() function call and add a layer of functionality before passing it on or handling it ourselves.

In perfLogger.js, after the perfLogger self-executing function, add a function declaration to override the native call to performance.now:

```
performance.now = (function() {
})();
```

This function should return performance.now if it is supported; if it is not, the code iterates through the potential browser-specific implementations, and if none of those are supported it defaults to the old Date() functionality.

```
performance.now = (function() {
 return performance.now         ||
         performance.webkitNow ||
       function() { return new Date().getTime(); };
})();
```

Next update perfLogger's startTimeLogging() and stopTimeLogging() functions to use performance.now():

```
startTimeLogging: function(id, descr,drawToPage,logToServer){
loggerPool[id] = {};
    loggerPool[id].id = id;
    loggerPool[id].startTime =  performance.now(); // high resolution time support
    loggerPool[id].description = descr;
    loggerPool[id].drawtopage = drawToPage;
    loggerPool[id].logtoserver = logToServer
}

stopTimeLogging: function(id){
loggerPool[id].stopTime =  performance.now(); //high resolution time support
    calculateResults(id);
    setResultsMetaData(id);
    if(loggerPool[id].drawtopage){
        drawToDebugScreen(id);
    }
    if(loggerPool[id].logtoserver){
        logToServer(id);
    }
```

}

Now let's take a look at what the page render benchmarking results from last chapter look like with browsers that support high-resolution time. In Figure 5-11, we'll look at our results in Chrome 19 to see how the browser reacts without the support of high-resolution time. In Figure 5-12, we'll see our results in Firefox 15 Aurora release; and in Figure 5-13, we'll see our results in Chrome 20, as both browsers support high-resolution time.

timing page render
run time: 1ms
path: http://localhost:8888/lab/perfLogger_example.html
useragent: Mozilla/5.0 (Macintosh; Intel Mac OS X 10_5_8) AppleWebKit/536.5 (KHTML, like Gecko) Chrome/19.0.1084.56 Safari/536.5

Figure 5-11. Chrome 19 defaulting to Date object

timing page render
run time: 2.5096750000000156ms
path: http://localhost:8888/lab/perfLogger_example.html
useragent: Mozilla/5.0 (Macintosh; Intel Mac OS X 10.5; rv:15.0) Gecko/20120626 Firefox/15.0a2

Figure 5-12. Firefox 15 Aurora release supports performance.now

timing page render
run time: 0.1919999995152466ms
path: http://localhost:8888/lab/perfLogger_example.html
useragent: Mozilla/5.0 (Macintosh; Intel Mac OS X 10_5_8) AppleWebKit/536.11 (KHTML, like Gecko) Chrome/20.0.1132.43 Safari/536.11

Figure 5-13. Chrome 20 supports performance.webkitNow

At this point you've integrated the new `Performance` object into the perfLogger library and added several new columns to our log file. These new data points add additional dimensions for analyzing our data. With our new capability of capturing high-resolution time we are set up perfectly to begin gathering runtime metrics next chapter.

Visualizing the New Data

Now let's have some fun with our new data! There are some great data points that we can look at: What is our average load time user agent? On average, what part of the HTTP transaction process takes the most time? And what is our general load time distribution? So let's get started.

A sample of our data looks like this:

```
IP, TestID, StartTime, StopTime, RunTime, URL, UserAgent, PerceivedLoadTime, PageRenderTime,
RoundTripTime, TCPConnectionTime, DNSLookupTime, CacheTime, RedirectTime
75.149.106.130,page_render,1341243219599,1341243220218,619,http://www.tom-barker.com/
blog/?p=x,Mozilla/5.0 (Macintosh; Intel Mac OS X 10.5; rv:13.0) Gecko/20100101 Firef
ox/13.0.1790,261,-2,36,0,-4,0
75.149.106.130,page_render,633.36499998695,973.8049999869,340.43999999994,http://www.tom-barker.
com/blog/?p=x,Mozilla/5.0 (Macintosh; Intel Mac OS X 10_5_8) AppleWebKit/536.11 (KHTML like
Gecko) Chrome/20.0.1132.43 Safari/536.11633,156,-1341243238576,30,0,0,0
75.149.106.130,page_render,1498.2289999898,2287.9749999847,789.74599999492,http://www.tom-
barker.com/blog/?p=x,Mozilla/5.0 (Macintosh; Intel Mac OS X 10_5_8) AppleWebKit/536.11 (KHTML
like Gecko) Chrome/20.0.1132.43 Safari/536.111497,979,788,0,0,0,0
```

First let's look at the frequency distribution of perceived load times. at a large enough scale, this will give us a pretty good idea of what the general experience is like for most users. We already have performance data being read into the perflogs variable back from the R script that we've been assembling since Chapter 3, so let's just draw a histogram using that variable:

```
hist(perflogs$PerceivedLoadTime, main="Distribution of Perceived Load Time", xlab="Perceived Load
Time in Milliseconds", col=c("#CCCCCC"))
```

This creates the graph that we see in Figure 5-14.

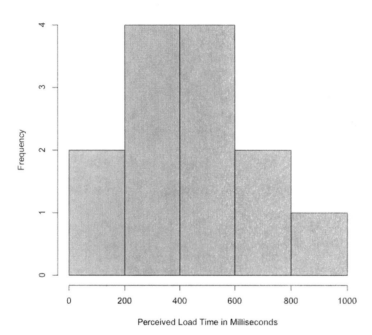

Figure 5-14. Histogram of perceived load time, frequency representing number of visits

Pretty simple so far. You just need to wrap it in a call to the pdf() function to save this as a file we can reference later:

```
loadTimeDistrchart <- paste(chartDirectory, "loadtime_distribution.pdf", sep="")
pdf(loadTimeDistrchart, width=10, height=10)
    hist(perflogs$PerceivedLoadTime, main="Distribution of Perceived Load Time", xlab="Perceived
Load Time in Milliseconds", col=c("#CCCCCC"))
dev.off()
```

Now let's take a look at all of the data that we have collected from our full HTTP request and break down the average time spent on each part of the request. This will give us a full picture of how long each step takes.

First create a new variable to hold the path to our next chart, and a new function to hold this in, called avgTimeBreakdownInRequest:

```
requestBreakdown <- paste(chartDirectory, "avgtime_inrequest.pdf", sep="")
avgTimeBreakdownInRequest <- function(){
}
```

Within the function you'll do some things to clean up the data. If the numbers are large enough, R may store them in exponential notation. This is great for referencing large numbers, but to visualize these numbers for general consumption we should unfurl the exponential notation for ease of reading. To do this, pass the scipen parameter to the options() function. The options() function allows us to set global options in R, and scipen takes a numeric value; the higher the value passed in, the greater the chance that R will display numbers in fixed position, not in exponential notation:

```
options(scipen=100)
```

Next address some of those negative numbers that we see in the data. Negative numbers don't make sense in this context. They appear because sometimes the window.performance object returns 0 for values, and we are doing subtraction between values to derive our saved performance data.

You have some choices here; you could remove the rows where negative numbers occur, or just zero out the negatives. You could wipe out the whole row if you thought one bad column indicated that the rest of the row was unreliable, but that's not the case here. To avoid losing the values in the other columns that may be good, just zero out the negatives.

To zero out the negatives, we simply check for any values that are less than 0 in each column, and set those columns to 0. Do this for each column to graph:

```
perflogs$PageRenderTime[perflogs$PageRenderTime < 0] <- 0
perflogs$RoundTripTime[perflogs$RoundTripTime < 0] <- 0
perflogs$TCPConnectionTime[perflogs$TCPConnectionTime < 0] <- 0
perflogs$DNSLookupTime[perflogs$DNSLookupTime < 0] <- 0
```

Next you will create a data frame that contains the average value for each column. To do this, use the data.frame() function and pass in a call to mean() for each column that should be averaged. Then set the column names for this new data frame:

```
avgTimes <- data.frame(mean(perflogs$PageRenderTime), mean(perflogs$RoundTripTime), mean(perflogs$T
CPConnectionTime), mean(perflogs$DNSLookupTime))

colnames(avgTimes) <- c("PageRenderTime", "RoundTripTime", "TCPConnectionTime", "DNSLookupTime")
```

Finally, create the chart. It will be a horizontal bar chart, much like we've made in previous chapters, and save this as a PDF.

```
pdf(requestBreakdown, width=10, height=10)
opar <- par(no.readonly=TRUE)
    par(las=1, mar=c(10,10,10,10))
    barplot(as.matrix(avgTimes), horiz=TRUE, main="Average Time Spent\nDuring HTTP Request",
xlab="Milliseconds")
par(opar)
dev.off()
```

Your completed function should look as follows, and the chart it generates can be seen in Figure 5-15.

```
avgTimeBreakdownInRequest <- function(){
#expand exponential notation
options(scipen=100)

#set any negative values to 0
```

```
perflogs$PageRenderTime[perflogs$PageRenderTime < 0] <- 0
perflogs$RoundTripTime[perflogs$RoundTripTime < 0] <- 0
perflogs$TCPConnectionTime[perflogs$TCPConnectionTime < 0] <- 0
perflogs$DNSLookupTime[perflogs$DNSLookupTime < 0] <- 0

#capture avg times
avgTimes <- data.frame(mean(perflogs$PageRenderTime), mean(perflogs$RoundTripTime), mean(perflogs$T
CPConnectionTime), mean(perflogs$DNSLookupTime))
colnames(avgTimes) <- c("PageRenderTime", "RoundTripTime", "TCPConnectionTime", "DNSLookupTime")

pdf(requestBreakdown, width=10, height=10)
opar <- par(no.readonly=TRUE)
    par(las=1, mar=c(10,10,10,10))
    barplot(as.matrix(avgTimes), horiz=TRUE, main="Average Time Spent\nDuring HTTP Request",
xlab="Milliseconds")
par(opar)
dev.off()
}
```

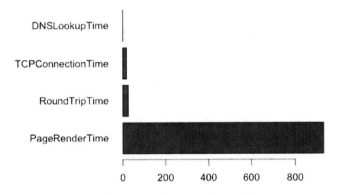

Figure 5-15. *Avg Time for each step in HTTP Request*

This is an interesting result. You may have figured already that the rendering of the page would take the longest, since it would have the most overhead and the most to do; it's making sense of the message, not just transmitting it. But you may not have thought that the TCP connection time and round trip time were the same or that they would be so significantly higher than the DNS lookup time.

The final chart that we'll look at for this chapter is a breakdown of perceived load time by browser. Notice that the sample data above stores the full user agent string, which gives not just the browser name, but the version, the sub-version, the operating system, and even the render engine. This is great, but if you want to roll up to a high level of browser information, irrespective of versioning or OS, we can search the user agent string for the specific high level browser name.

You can search for strings in data frame columns using grep(). The grep() function accepts the string to search for as its first parameter and the vector or object to search through as the second parameter. For our purposes we'll use the grep() function as a filtering option that we pass into a data frame:

```
data frame[grep([string to search for], [data frame column to search])]
```

Create a function called getDFByBrowser() that will allow you to generalize the search by passing in a data frame to search and a string to search for:

```
getDFByBrowser<-function(data, browsername){
    return(data[grep(browsername, data$UserAgent),])
}
```

Next create a variable to hold the path to our new chart, loadtime_bybrowser:

```
loadtime_bybrowser <- paste(chartDirectory, "loadtime_bybrowser.pdf", sep="")
```

Next create a function to hold the main functionality for this chart; call it printLoadTimebyBrowser():

```
printLoadTimebyBrowser <- function(){
}
```

This function first creates data frames for each browser that we want to include in our graph:

```
chrome <- getDFByBrowser(perflogs, "Chrome")
firefox <- getDFByBrowser(perflogs, "Firefox")
ie <- getDFByBrowser(perflogs, "MSIE")
```

Next create a data frame to hold the average perceived load time for each browser, much as you did in the previous example for steps in the HTTP request. Also give the data frame descriptive column names:

```
meanTimes <- data.frame(mean(chrome$PerceivedLoadTime), mean(firefox$PerceivedLoadTime),
mean(ie$PerceivedLoadTime))
colnames(meanTimes) <- c("Chrome", "Firefox", "Internet Explorer")
```

And finally, create the graph as a bar chart and save it as a pdf:

```
pdf(loadtime_bybrowser, width=10, height=10)
    barplot(as.matrix(meanTimes), main="Average Perceived Load Time\nBy Browser", ylim=c(0,
600), ylab="milliseconds")
dev.off()
```

Your completed functionality should look like the following, and the finished chart should look like Figure 5-16.

```
getDFByBrowser<-function(data, browsername){
    return(data[grep(browsername, data$UserAgent),])
}

printLoadTimebyBrowser <- function(){
    chrome <- getDFByBrowser(perflogs, "Chrome")
    firefox <- getDFByBrowser(perflogs, "Firefox")
    ie <- getDFByBrowser(perflogs, "MSIE")

    meanTimes <- data.frame(mean(chrome$PerceivedLoadTime), mean(firefox$PerceivedLoadTime),
mean(ie$PerceivedLoadTime))
    colnames(meanTimes) <- c("Chrome", "Firefox", "Internet Explorer")
```

```
        pdf(loadtime_bybrowser, width=10, height=10)
            barplot(as.matrix(meanTimes), main="Average Perceived Load Time\nBy Browser",
ylim=c(0, 600), ylab="milliseconds")
        dev.off()
}
```

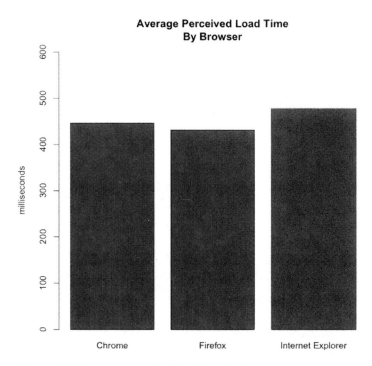

Figure 5-16 *Average perceived load time by browser*

Interestingly enough, the results of our tests show that Firefox has the best perceived load time, followed by Chrome, and finally Internet Explorer. This is just the smallest taste of a comparison; we could expand this by looking at versions and sub-versions if we wanted to.

The full updated R file should now look like this:

```
dataDirectory <- "/Applications/MAMP/htdocs/lab/log/"
chartDirectory <- "/Applications/MAMP/htdocs/lab/charts/"
testname = "page_render"

perflogs <- read.table(paste(dataDirectory, "runtimeperf_results.csv", sep=""), header=TRUE,
sep=",")
perfchart <- paste(chartDirectory, "runtime_",testname, ".pdf", sep="")

loadTimeDistrchart <- paste(chartDirectory, "loadtime_distribution.pdf", sep="")
requestBreakdown <- paste(chartDirectory, "avgtime_inrequest.pdf", sep="")
loadtime_bybrowser <- paste(chartDirectory, "loadtime_bybrowser.pdf", sep="")
```

```
pagerender <- perflogs[perflogs$TestID == "page_render",]
df <- data.frame(pagerender$UserAgent, pagerender$RunTime)
df <- by(df$pagerender.RunTime, df$pagerender.UserAgent, mean)
df <- df[order(df)]

pdf(perfchart, width=10, height=10)
opar <- par(no.readonly=TRUE)
    par(las=1, mar=c(10,10,10,10))
    barplot(df, horiz=TRUE)
par(opar)
dev.off()


getDFByBrowser<-function(data, browsername){
    return(data[grep(browsername, data$UserAgent),])
}


printLoadTimebyBrowser <- function(){
    chrome <- getDFByBrowser(perflogs, "Chrome")
    firefox <- getDFByBrowser(perflogs, "Firefox")
    ie <- getDFByBrowser(perflogs, "MSIE")

    meanTimes <- data.frame(mean(chrome$PerceivedLoadTime), mean(firefox$PerceivedLoadTime),
mean(ie$PerceivedLoadTime))
    colnames(meanTimes) <- c("Chrome", "Firefox", "Internet Explorer")
    pdf(loadtime_bybrowser, width=10, height=10)
        barplot(as.matrix(meanTimes), main="Average Perceived Load Time\nBy Browser",
ylim=c(0, 600), ylab="milliseconds")
    dev.off()
}


pdf(loadTimeDistrchart, width=10, height=10)
    hist(perflogs$PerceivedLoadTime, main="Distribution of Perceived Load Time", xlab="Perceived
Load Time in Milliseconds", col=c("#CCCCCC"))
dev.off()

avgTimeBreakdownInRequest <- function(){

#expand exponential notation
options(scipen=100, digits=3)

#set any negative values to 0
perflogs$PageRenderTime[perflogs$PageRenderTime < 0] <- 0
perflogs$RoundTripTime[perflogs$RoundTripTime < 0] <- 0
perflogs$TCPConnectionTime[perflogs$TCPConnectionTime < 0] <- 0
perflogs$DNSLookupTime[perflogs$DNSLookupTime < 0] <- 0

#capture avg times
```

107

```
avgTimes <- data.frame(mean(perflogs$PageRenderTime), mean(perflogs$RoundTripTime), mean(perflogs$T
CPConnectionTime), mean(perflogs$DNSLookupTime))
colnames(avgTimes) <- c("PageRenderTime", "RoundTripTime", "TCPConnectionTime", "DNSLookupTime")
pdf(requestBreakdown, width=10, height=10)
opar <- par(no.readonly=TRUE)
    par(las=1, mar=c(10,10,10,10))
    barplot(as.matrix(avgTimes), horiz=TRUE, main="Average Time Spent\nDuring HTTP Request",
xlab="Milliseconds")
par(opar)
dev.off()

}


#invoke our new functions
printLoadTimebyBrowser()
avgTimeBreakdownInRequest()
```

Summary

This chapter explored the window.performance object, a new standardized way from the W3C to gather performance metrics from the browser. We incorporated the Performance object into our existing perfLogger project, including the performance metrics in each test that we run, as well as building in support for window.performance's high-resolution time, if the browser supports it.

We used this new data to look at the overall web performance of our sites.

We touched upon the emerging possibilities of looking at client machine memory usage from a browser, specifically Chrome's implementation, and a brief look at how to get Firefox to expose similar data.

The next chapter will take a look at optimizing web performance; you will run multivariate tests with the tools that we've developed to look at the results of our optimizations.

CHAPTER 6

■ ■ ■

Web Performance Optimizations

The last chapter explored the results of the W3C's first steps at standardizing performance in a browser, the Performance object. Chapter 5 looked at each of the APIs in the Performance object; you saw how to gather and derive performance metrics from the Performance Timing object, how to use the Performance Navigation object to determine how users are coming to your sites, and how the Performance object exposes high-resolution time to allow us to track timing data below the millisecond limit.

Based on all of that, you updated perfLogger library to incorporate all of the great metrics that the Performance object provides. You built shims into perfLogger in order to use high-resolution time with browsers that support it, and fall back gracefully for those that don't.

You then took all of this new data and expanded the R scripts to chart out what this data says about our users, their connections, and their browsers.

And now this chapter you will use all of the tools that we have created thus far, and all of the tools that we looked at in Chapter 2, to quantify the benefits possible from some web performance optimization tips— specifically, how JavaScript can block page rendering and how you can use JavaScript to postpone the loading of heavier pieces of content. Remember that web performance is the time that your content takes to be delivered to your end user, including network latency and browser render time.

Optimizing Page Render Bottlenecks

The first place we will look to optimize is the rendering of content in the browser. This issue is outside of any network latency concerns; it simply means how fast the browser will process and render content to present to the end user. Let's first take a look at how drawing our content to the screen works in modern browsers.

As discussed in Chapter 1, modern browsers are made up of several interacting components. There is a UI layer that draws the client-facing interface for the browser, including the location bar, the back and forward buttons, and any other chrome that the browser may have. The end user interacts with the UI layer and from the UI layer drives the rest of the application.

We have a network layer that handles network connections, establishing TCP connections, and performing the HTTP roundtrips. The network layer also provides content to the rendering engine.

The rendering engine handles painting the content to the screen. When it encounters JavaScript, it hands it off to the JavaScript interpreter. See Figure 6-1 for an annotated look at the high-level architecture of modern browsers.

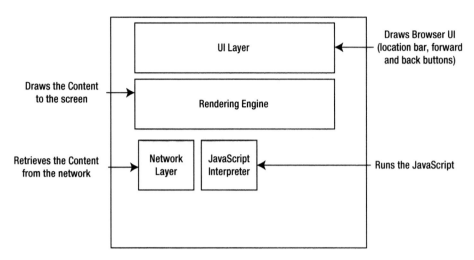

Figure 6-1. *Annotated browser architecture*

So as I said, the rendering engine— be it Gecko, or WebKit, or what have you—retrieves content from the network layer. It has a finite bus size, so it pulls in the data in chunks and passes the chunks into its own workflow.

The workflow is a process with several steps. First the content is parsed, meaning that the markup is read as characters and undergoes *lexical analysis,* in which the characters are compared to a rule set and converted to tokens based on the rule set. The rule set is the DTD that we define in our HTML document; it specifies the tags that make up the version of the language that we will use. The tokens are just the characters broken into meaningful segments.

For example, the network layer may return the following string:

```
<!DOCTYPE html><html><head><meta charset="UTF-8"/>
```

This string would get tokenized into meaningful chunks:

```
<!DOCTYPE html>
<html>
<head>
<meta charset="UTF-8"/>
```

The rendering engine then takes the tokens and converts them to DOM elements. The DOM elements are laid out in a render tree that the rendering engine then iterates over. In the first iteration the rendering engine lays out the positioning of the DOM elements, and in the next it paints them to the screen. See Figure 6-2 for this workflow.

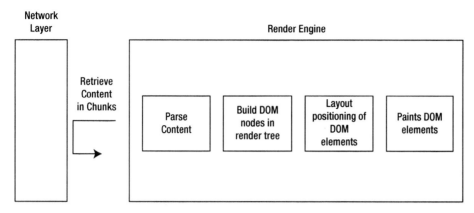

Figure 6-2. *Rendering engine workflow*

Normally during this process, if the rendering engine identifies an external script during tokenization, it pauses parsing the content and begins downloading the script. The rendering engine only resumes parsing after the script has been downloaded and executed. This causes a potential bottleneck in the time it takes for content to be displayed to the end user. See Figure 6-3 for a flowchart of this potential bottleneck.

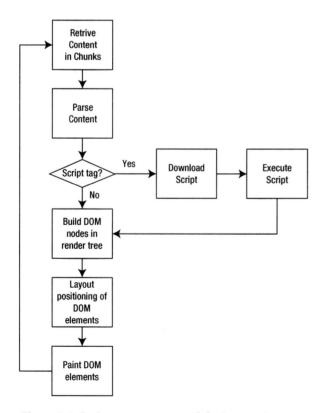

Figure 6-3. *Script tags encountered during parsing*

To get around this potential issue it has generally been good practice[1] to place all script tags at the bottom of your HTML, so that any pause in rendering to process the JavaScript is done after the page is fully rendered.

Script Loading

Another option is to load remote JavaScript files programmatically. This is called *script loading* and allows us to trick the rendering engine, let's look at how.

Remember that the workflow we've just explored for how the rendering engine pauses applies to external scripts. The browser looks for the src attribute of the script tag, which tells it that it must download a remote resource. If it encounters a script tag without a src attribute, the rendering engine simply passes the code to the JavaScript Interpreter for execution.

So what we can do is create inline JavaScript to append script tags to the document dynamically, like so:

```
<script>
var script = window.document.createElement('SCRIPT');
script.src = src;
window.document.getElementsByTagName('HEAD')[0].appendChild(script);
</script>
```

This code snippet uses the document.createElement() function to create a new script tag and store it in a variable named script. It sets the src attribute of the new script tag to point to a remote JavaScript file, and appends the new script tag to the Head section of the document.

That's fairly simple, so let's flesh that out into a real example that we can use.

First create a namespace, which you can call remoteLoader:

```
var remoteLoader = function remoteLoader(){

return{

}
}();
```

Within remoteLoader, create a private function to construct the script tags, using much the same logic outlined in the previous snippet. Call the function constructScriptTag() and pass in a URL to use as the source of the script tag:

```
function constructScriptTag(src){
    var script = window.document.createElement('SCRIPT');
    script.src = src;
return script;
}
```

Within the returned object, create a single public function called loadJS(), with a parameter named script_url:

```
loadJS: function(script_url){

}
```

---

1   At least since Steve Souders wrote about it in his book *High Performance Web Sites: Essential Knowledge for Front-End Engineers* (O'Reilly 2007).

Within loadJS you'll put in some branching logic to test whether the passed-in value is an array or a string. That will provide some flexibility to use our API to load either a single JavaScript file or a list of JavaScript files.

To test this, look at the typeof the variable. Arrays return a type of "object", and strings return "string". To be able to tell an array from other types of objects, you need to use the instanceof operator on the variable. The instanceof operator tests whether the object on the left has an instance of the constructor on the right in its prototype chain— In other words, is it an instance of that constructor?

```
if(typeof script_url === "object"){
if(script_url instanceof Array){
}
}else if(typeof script_url === "string"){

}
```

Flesh out the string branch first, since it will be the simplest. Just make a call to the constructScriptTag() function and pass in script_url. Then append the element that gets returned to the head of the document.

```
else if(typeof script_url === "string"){
window.document.getElementsByTagName('HEAD')[0].appendChild(constructScriptTag(script_url));
}
```

The array branch will iterate through the array of URLs, create a new script tag for each one, and use a document fragment to store all of the new elements. It will then append them all at once to the head. I'll talk at length about document fragments in the next chapter.

```
if(script_url instanceof Array){
var frag = document.createDocumentFragment();
    for(var ind = 0; ind < script_url.length; ind++){
        frag.appendChild(constructScriptTag(script_url[ind]));
    }
window.document.getElementsByTagName('HEAD')[0].appendChild(frag.cloneNode(true) );
}
```

Your completed code should look like this:

```
var remoteLoader = function remoteLoader(){
    function constructScriptTag(src){
        var script = window.document.createElement('SCRIPT');
        script.src = src;
        return script;
    }

    return{
        loadJS: function(script_url){
            if(typeof script_url === "object"){
                if(script_url instanceof Array){
                    var frag = document.createDocumentFragment();
                    for(var ind = 0; ind < script_url.length; ind++){
                        frag.appendChild(constructScriptTag(script_url[ind]));
                    }
                    window.document.getElementsByTagName('HEAD')[0].appendChild(frag.
cloneNode(true) );
                }
```

113

```
                    }else if(typeof script_url === "string"){
                        window.document.getElementsByTagName('HEAD')[0].appendChild(constructScriptTag(
script_url));
                    }
                }
            }
}();
```

To use it you can pass in either a string or an array, as shown in the following code snippets:

```
<script>
    remoteLoader.loadJS("/lab/perfLogger.js"); // passing in a string
</script>
```

```
<script>
    remoteLoader.loadJS(["/lab/perfLogger.js", "jquery.js"]); // passing in an array
</script>
```

async

Another option to prevent blocking the rendering engine is to use the async attribute for script tags. Introduced in HTML 5, the async option is a native attribute that will tell the browser to load the script asynchronously. It is supported in all modern browsers, and even Internet Explorer starting with version 10. (Prior to version 10 Internet Explorer used a proprietary attribute called defer.) The async attribute optionally accepts a Boolean value; just including it in a script tag with no value defaults to true.

```
<script src="[URL]" async=true></script>
<script src="[URL]" async></script>
```

When using async you don't know when the file will be downloaded, so you can attach an onload event handler to the script tag. This will allow you to invoke or instantiate any code that will need to be run when the file is downloaded:

```
<script src="[URL"] async onload="init();]"></script>
```

Compare Results

If you've read this far you know what will come next—let's run a multivariate test and compare the results of each method that we have just covered!

For this test you will create a baseline, a page with no optimizations for external scripts at all. Load perfLogger.js in the head of this baseline file.

```
<head>
… [snip head content]
<script src="/lib/perfLogger.js"></script>
<script>
perfLogger.startTimeLogging("page_render", "timing page render", true, true);
</script>
</head>
```

Now create a file that uses remoteLoader to load in perfLogger.js via code. You'll load remoteLoader.js in the head, and then invoke loadJS in the body section:

```
<head>
…[snip head content]
<script src="/lib/remoteLoader.js"></script>
</head>
<body>
<script>
remoteLoader.loadJS("/lab/perfLogger.js");
</script>
… [snip body content]
<script>
perfLogger.showPerformanceMetrics();
</script>
</body>
```

And finally, create a page that uses the async attribute in the script tag:

```
<head>
…[snip head content]
<script async src="/lab/perfLogger.js"></script>
</head>
<body>
… [snip body content]
<script>
perfLogger.showPerformanceMetrics();
</script>
</body>
```

Now take each of these pages and run them through WebPagetest.

Use the same content for each of these pages—a snapshot of the main page of my web site tom-barker.com. The URLs are as follows:

URL to Test	Test Result URL
tom-barker.com/lab/baseline.html	http://www.webpagetest.org/result/120712_D2_16a7c450629a5765171f4a4c2d9e016e/
tom-barker.com/lab/scriptloaded.html	http://www.webpagetest.org/result/120712_9W_408ca6d9d9e428f28e7f3e1adff126d7/
tom-barker.com/lab/asyncloaded.html	http://www.webpagetest.org/result/120712_90_1f667f8a71811c39ee0cc9066f78645d/

Figures 6-4 to 6-6 show our high-level summary times for each test.

Figure 6-4. WebPagetest results summary for baseline

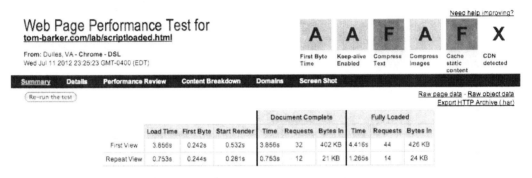

Figure 6-5. WebPagetest results summary for script dynamically loaded

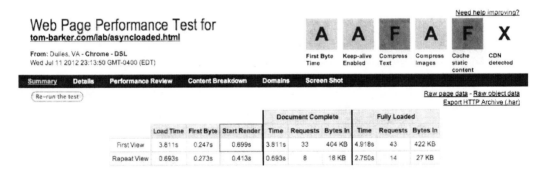

Figure 6-6. WebPagetest results summary for script async

From these results you can see that the difference in overall load times is negligible, but the consistent difference here is the first byte time and start render. The remoteLoader.js page gives the best start render time, over 350 milliseconds faster than the baseline and 160 milliseconds faster than the async page.

There are tradeoffs; the total load time is longer, but the page is rendered faster so it looks like it loads faster to our end users.

To see why the start render is faster, let's look at the waterfall charts. Figures 6-7 to 6-9 show the waterfall charts for our tests.

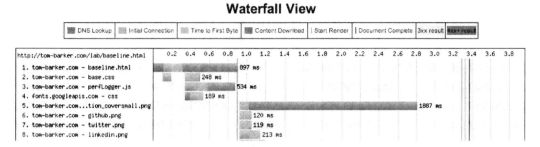

Figure 6-7. Waterfall chart for our baseline file

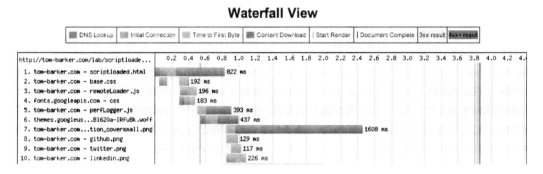

Figure 6-8. Waterfall chart for our scriptloader file

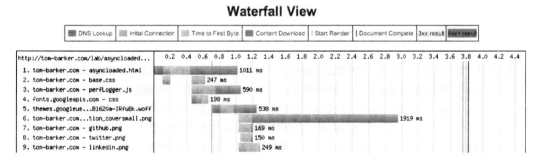

Figure 6-9. *Waterfall chart for our async file*

In these waterfall charts we can see how perfLogger.js impacts the items below it in the sequence.

For the baseline (Figure 6-7) we can see that while the browser is connecting to perfLogger.js it is also connecting to and downloading our web font, but once the browser begins downloading perfLogger.js, all other progress is halted until that download is finished. This is evidenced on lines 5 to 8 of Figure 6-7, where each PNG on those lines waits until around the 897 millisecond mark before it begins, which is when perfLogger.js finishes downloading.

For our script-loaded test (Figure 6-8) you can see that the browser is not blocked by downloading perfLogger.js. On line 6 you see our web font file downloading in parallel with perfLoader.js.

The same goes for our `async` test (Figure 6-9), where we can see that the browser downloads an external CSS file and a web font file both in parallel with our `perfLoader.js` file. We can see these on lines 3 to 5.

And finally, let's take a look at the results of our `perfLogger` metrics for each page.

Test	Results (in Milliseconds)
baseline	Perceived Time: 342 Redirect Time: 0 Cache Time: 0 DNS Lookup Time: 0 TCP Connection Time: 0 roundTripTime: 162 pageRenderTime: 263
scriptloaded	Perceived Time: 277 Redirect Time: 0 Cache Time: 0 DNS Lookup Time: 0 TCP Connection Time: 0 roundTripTime: 196 pageRenderTime: 207
async	Perceived Time: 343 Redirect Time: 0 Cache Time: 0 DNS Lookup Time: 0 TCP Connection Time: 0 roundTripTime: 158 pageRenderTime: 212

We can see that there are improvements in the perceived time and page render time at an individual test level, but if we run these tests at a large scale, will these improvements be averaged out or do they reflect a larger performance improvement?

Luckily we built `perfLogger` to save all of our results, so let's take a look at our log file and parse the results in R.

First write a new R function to create data frames by URL:

```
getDFByURL<-function(data,url){
    return(data[grep(,url, data$URL)])
}
```

Next create a new function called `comparePerfMetricsbyURL`:

```
comparePerfMetricsbyURL<-function(){
}
```

Within this function create variables for each test, using the `getDFByURL()` function that you just created:

```
baseline <- getDFByURL(perflogs, "http://tom-barker.com/lab/baseline.html")
scripted <- getDFByURL(perflogs, "http://tom-barker.com/lab/scriptloaded.html")
async <- getDFByURL(perflogs, "http://tom-barker.com/lab/asyncloaded.html")
```

Then create a data frame to hold the mean page render times for each test URL, and a data frame to hold the mean load time for each test URL. You'll also update the column names for each data frame to make sure you get neat descriptive x-axis values for the chart:

```
meanRenderTimes <- data.frame(mean(baseline$PageRenderTime), mean(scripted$PageRenderTime),
mean(async$PageRenderTime))

colnames(meanRenderTimes) <- c("Baseline", "Script Loaded", "Async")

meanLoadTimes <- data.frame(mean(baseline$PerceivedLoadTime), mean(scripted$PerceivedLoadTime),
mean(async$PerceivedLoadTime))

colnames(meanLoadTimes) <- c("Baseline", "Script Loaded", "Async")
```

And finally create bar charts with these data frames:

```
barplot(as.matrix(meanRenderTimes), main="Average Render Time\nBy Test Type", ylim=c(0, 400),
ylab="milliseconds")

barplot(as.matrix(meanLoadTimes), main="Average Load Time\nBy Test Type", ylim=c(0, 700),
ylab="milliseconds")
```

Our completed function should look like this:

```
comparePerfMetricsbyURL<-function(){
    baseline <- getDFByURL(perflogs, "http://tom-barker.com/lab/baseline.html")
    scripted <- getDFByURL(perflogs, "http://tom-barker.com/lab/scriptloaded.html")
    async <- getDFByURL(perflogs, "http://tom-barker.com/lab/asyncloaded.html")

    meanRenderTimes <- data.frame(mean(baseline$PageRenderTime), mean(scripted$PageRenderTime),
mean(async$PageRenderTime))
    colnames(meanRenderTimes) <- c("Baseline", "Script Loaded", "Async")
    meanLoadTimes <- data.frame(mean(baseline$PerceivedLoadTime), mean(scripted$PerceivedLoadTi
me), mean(async$PerceivedLoadTime))
    colnames(meanLoadTimes) <- c("Baseline", "Script Loaded", "Async")

    barplot(as.matrix(meanRenderTimes), main="Average Render Time\nBy Test Type", ylim=c(0,
400), ylab="milliseconds")
    barplot(as.matrix(meanLoadTimes), main="Average Load Time\nBy Test Type", ylim=c(0, 700),
ylab="milliseconds")
}
```

The charts that this code generates can be seen in Figures 6-10 and 6-11.

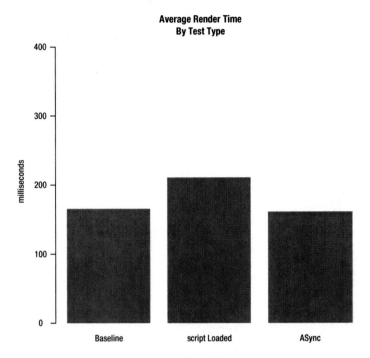

Figure 6-10. Average render time for each test

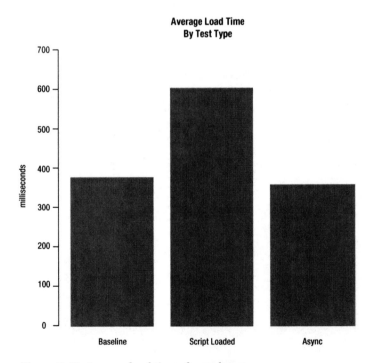

Figure 6-11. *Average load timer for each test*

So we can see that these benefits are somewhat intangible. The page is visible sooner to the end user, so it appears to load faster, but according to our technical measurements it doesn't really load faster. In fact, it looks like it takes slightly longer to load in the case of the script loader because there are extra assets to load. Remember, performance is a moving target and highly nuanced.

The thing to keep in mind is that the way we are measuring our performance with these charts, it looks like it's taking about as long, or a little longer because we are counting done at the onload event of the page. If we don't need our external scripts available before the onload event we can use a design pattern called *lazy loading* to load our scripts after the onload.

Lazy Loading

We will now look at lazy loading, a way to programmatically delay the loading of assets. We will look at what lazy loading is, as a design pattern, and how we can use it tactically to improve the web performance of our pages.

The Art of Lazy Loading

At a very high level, lazy loading is a design pattern in which we postpone the creation or initialization of something until it is absolutely necessary (See Figure 6-12).

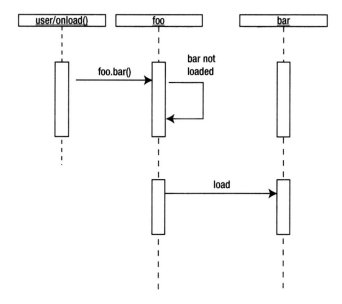

Figure 6-12. Lazy loading sequence diagram

There are several implementations of this pattern:

- The virtual proxy pattern
- The lazy initialization pattern
- Value holder pattern

In the virtual proxy pattern, shown in Figure 6-13, we instantiate a stub and load in the actual implementation when it is needed and expose it (usually via composition). This pattern is generally used when applications have modules or components that are not always needed, or needed immediately—much like JavaScript files that may not be needed before the page loads.

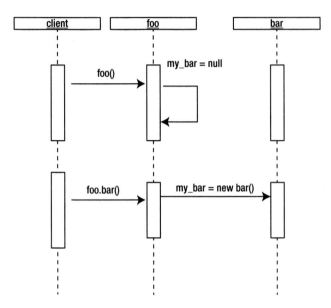

Figure 6-13. *The Virtual Proxy pattern*

In the lazy initialization pattern we check whether the object exists (is it null?), and if it doesn't yet exist, we instantiate it. This is probably the pattern that most people have used and never even realized it was lazy initialization. This pattern is most often used when declaring objects or namespaces in JavaScript. If our namespace exists, use it; if not, create it.

```
if (obj == null){
     obj = new obj();
}
return obj;
```

Finally the value holder pattern is where we call a public function of an object to get an instance of the object. The object is instantiated only on the first call of the function. The value holder pattern is most commonly used as part of the implementation of a singleton pattern.

___

■ **Note**   Design patterns are core algorithmic patterns that have been identified and named to create a vocabulary that describes in a simple vernacular the steps needed to solve common problems. The seminal work on design patterns is the original book *Design Patterns: Elements of Reusable Object-Oriented Software*, by Erich Gamma, et.al. (Addison-Wesley 1994).

The idea of anti-patterns has since been identified as well. Anti-patterns are the inverse of design patterns, common, systemic repeatable mistakes that once identified can be avoided. It is hugely useful to learn at least some of both.

All of human history and science is built on the idea of recording previous learning and building on top of it. We avoid re-inventing the wheel. This is the idea of design patterns and anti-patterns: we've identified issues and the most effective way to solve them; let's instead focus on new challenges and solve those, and preserve our new findings for future posterity.

It is also much simpler and takes fewer words to refer to something as a factory rather than refer to that same something as an object that generates other objects.

Lazy Loading Scripts

When we don't need our JavaScript code to be available as soon as the page loads, we can script-load our external JavaScript after the `window.onload` event. This is lazy loading our scripts. Let's take a look at how we can lazy-load our scripts and see what kind of benefit to performance we can get from that. Then we'll evaluate the results.

Set Up Lazy Loading

To start with, create a new test URL to experiment with. You'll take the script-loaded page from the previous examples and rename it `lazyloadscript.html`. You'll also be updating our `remoteLoader` object.

In the new `lazyloadscript.html` page, you'll add a script tag and some JavaScript. This will check whether the `window.attachEvent` function is available in the current browser. The `attachEvent` function accepts two parameters: the event to attach to, and the function to invoke when the event occurs. If the current browser supports `window.attachEvent`, you'll pass in the onload event and the call to `remoteLoader.loadJS` to load the remote scripts.

If `attachEvent` is not supported, instead use `window.addEventListener()` to the same effect. Here's the code:

```
<script>
if (window.attachEvent)
    window.attachEvent('onload', remoteLoader.loadJS("/lab/perfLogger.js"));
else
    window.addEventListener('load', remoteLoader.loadJS("/lab/perfLogger.js"), false);
</script>
```

Technically, you've just lazy-loaded the remote script loading—but there's an issue. Right now we don't know when the remote script has finished loading. If you try to make the call to `perfLogger.showPerformanceMetrics()` and the script hasn't just loaded but also executed, then you will get an error.

So you need to make some modifications. You need to be able to know when the script has loaded and run the performance test after it is loaded. So you need to make the `remoteLoader.loadJS` function accept a callback.

■ **Note**   callback can then execute the callback function. This is one of the very beautiful things about functional programming, that we can pass functions around between functions or objects. it opens up other ways of changing functionality without inheritance.

So let's go into remoteLoader and update the constructScriptTag() and loadJS() functions. Add a second parameter to their signature, this will be the callback function.

```
loadJS: function(script_url, f){
}

function constructScriptTag(src, func){
}
```

Within constructScriptTag(), you'll check to see if a callback has been passed in; and if it has, add an onload attribute to the script object and assign the callback function to that onload attribute. This will make the browser execute this callback function when the script has completed loading the file. In truth, it will act different ways, depending on the browser. It may call the callback function every time the state changes on the connection, just like an AJAX transaction. So you'll code defensively around this in the callback function:

```
if(func){
script.onload  = func;
}
```

Your updated remoteLoader file should now look like this:

```
var remoteLoader = function remoteLoader(){
    function constructScriptTag(src, func){
        var script = window.document.createElement('SCRIPT');
        script.src = src;
        if(func){
            script.onload  = func;
            }
        return script;
    }

    return{
        loadJS: function(script_url, f){
            if(typeof script_url === "object"){
                if(script_url instanceof Array){
                    var frag = document.createDocumentFragment();
                    for(var ind = 0; ind < script_url.length; ind++){
                        frag.appendChild(constructScriptTag(script_url[ind]), f);
                    }
                    window.document.getElementsByTagName('HEAD')[0].appendChild(frag.
cloneNode(true));
                }
            }else if(typeof script_url === "string"){
                window.document.getElementsByTagName('HEAD')[0].appendChild(constructScriptTag(sc
ript_url, f))
            }
        }
    }
}();
```

Now update your code snippet in the page to pass in a callback function. Stub out the function and just call it init:

```
<script>
if (window.attachEvent)
    window.attachEvent('onload', remoteLoader.loadJS("/lab/perfLogger.js"), init);
else
    window.addEventListener('load', remoteLoader.loadJS("/lab/perfLogger.js", init), false);
</script>
```

Next let's flesh out our init function. We know we want to call perfLogger.showPerformanceMetrics() here, but since it's possible for the browser to call this function when the script is loaded (but not yet executed) and then again when the interpreter has executed the script, you'll need to check if perfLogger has been initialized yet.

```
<script>
function init(){
    if(perfLogger){
        perfLogger.showPerformanceMetrics()
    }
}
</script>
```

Your complete code example should look like this:

```
<script src="/lab/remoteLoader.js"></script>
<script>
function init(){
    if(perfLogger){
        perfLogger.showPerformanceMetrics()
    }
}

if (window.attachEvent)
    window.attachEvent('onload', remoteLoader.loadJS("/lab/perfLogger.js"), init);
else
    window.addEventListener('load', remoteLoader.loadJS("/lab/perfLogger.js", init), false);
</script>
```

Analyze and Chart Your Results

If you put this up in a production environment and gather data from end users you'll then be able to visualize the metrics for this page and compare it to our other methods.

To do that, let's update our R script to compare our lazy loaded example against our previous examples.

In the comparePerfMetricsbyURL() function, add a new data frame for the new URL:

```
lazy <- getDFByURL(perflogs, "http://tom-barker.com/lab/lazyloadscript.html")
```

And include the new variable in the meanRenderTimes and meanLeadTimes data frames:

```
meanRenderTimes <- data.frame(mean(baseline$PageRenderTime), mean(scripted$PageRenderTime),
mean(async$PageRenderTime), mean(lazy$PageRenderTime))

colnames(meanRenderTimes) <- c("Baseline", "Script Loaded", "Async", "Lazy Loaded")
```

```
meanLoadTimes <- data.frame(mean(baseline$PerceivedLoadTime), mean(scripted$PerceivedLoadTime),
mean(async$PerceivedLoadTime),mean(lazy$PerceivedLoadTime))

colnames(meanLoadTimes) <- c("Baseline", "Script Loaded", "Async", "Lazy Loaded")
```

Your updated comparePerfMetricsbyURL() function should now look like this:

```
comparePerfMetricsbyURL<-function(){
    baseline <- getDFByURL(perflogs, "http://tom-barker.com/lab/baseline.html")
    scripted <- getDFByURL(perflogs, "http://tom-barker.com/lab/scriptloaded.html")
    async <- getDFByURL(perflogs, "http://tom-barker.com/lab/asyncloaded.html")
    lazy <- getDFByURL(perflogs, "http://tom-barker.com/lab/lazyloadscript.html")


    meanRenderTimes <- data.frame(mean(baseline$PageRenderTime), mean(scripted$PageRenderTime),
mean(async$PageRenderTime), mean(lazy$PageRenderTime))
    colnames(meanRenderTimes) <- c("Baseline", "Script Loaded", "Async", "Lazy Loaded")
    meanLoadTimes <- data.frame(mean(baseline$PerceivedLoadTime), mean(scripted$PerceivedLoadTi
me), mean(async$PerceivedLoadTime),mean(lazy$PerceivedLoadTime))
    colnames(meanLoadTimes) <- c("Baseline", "Script Loaded", "Async", "Lazy Loaded")

    barplot(as.matrix(meanRenderTimes), main="Average Render Time\nBy Test Type", ylim=c(0,
400), ylab="milliseconds")
    barplot(as.matrix(meanLoadTimes), main="Average Load Time\nBy Test Type", ylim=c(0, 700),
ylab="milliseconds")
}
```

Let's look at the charts that this code generates, shown in Figures 6-14 and 6-15.

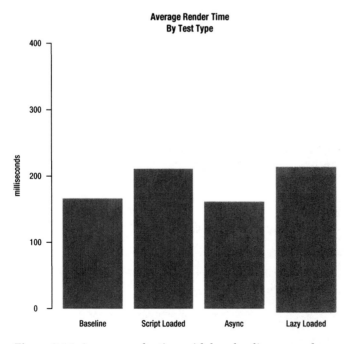

Figure 6-14. Average render time with lazy loading example

Figure 6-14 is the average render time. Remember from Chapter 5 that we calculate render time as being `Date.now()` minus `performance.timing.domLoading`, where `domLoading` is when the document begins to load. That means that this metric is actually rendered meaningless when we lazy-load, because we don't start lazy loading until after the document is finished loading, so `Date.now()` is delayed to whenever the asynchronous loading of the script file is complete.

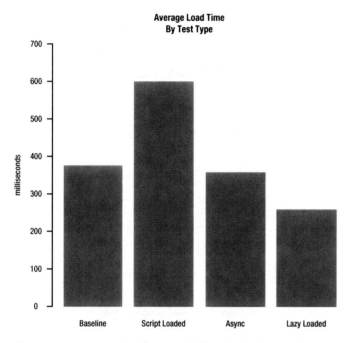

Figure 6-15. *Average load time with lazy loaded example*

Now Figure 6-15 begins to tell the real story. It charts the times spent from the beginning of the navigation request to when the page is loaded, the lazy-loaded script is loaded, and the init function is called. This is a genuine representation of the full load time, and from here you can see that we get significant gains by lazy loading. The results are 100 milliseconds faster on average than our baseline and `async` tests, and 350 milliseconds faster on average than our script-loaded test.

▓ **Note**   We didn't just mechanically look at our charts and declare a winner. We considered the context of what the charts were telling us; we thought about the full picture of the data in the charts and made sense of them.

Let's see how this test fares in WebPagetest. Our test URL and our test results URL are as follows:

URL to Test	Test Result URL
tom-barker.com/lab/lazyloadscript.html	http://www.webpagetest.org/result/120718_7X_d30b018b195bed1954d93baf25570f92/

For Figure 6-16 when we compare the raw numbers to our previous tests we see benefits. Our repeat view load time and repeat view document complete are the fastest out of every test. But the real victory here is the repeat view document Fully Loaded time, 2 seconds faster than our async time, 500 milliseconds faster than our script loaded test, and 100 milliseconds faster than our baseline.

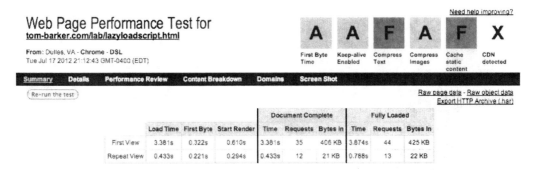

Figure 6-16. *WebPagetest summary results for lazy-loaded test (note the first view and repeat view rows)*

You can see in Figure 6-17 that just as in our script-loaded example, we don't have the overhead of the initial time to connect, but with our lazy load test we have a much smaller download time, and the total time is only 113 milliseconds, compared to 534 milliseconds in our baseline test and 393 milliseconds for our script-loaded example.

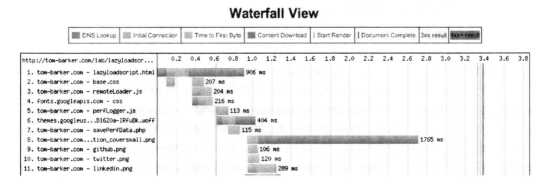

Figure 6-17. *WebPagetest waterfall view for our lazy load test*

Clearly lazy loading our scripts is the way to go for optimal load times; we just need to be sure to fire off our subsequent code that uses these scripts in a callback function. And we need to be sure that we don't need these scripts before the page load.

Lazy Loading CSS

We're on a roll and seeing great results with lazy loading, so let's keep going! Let's build on the success we saw with lazy loading our external JavaScript and lazy load our CSS as well. Then we'll look at our results.

Set Up CSS Lazy Loading

First take our lazy loaded page and save it as a new file, lazyloadcss.html. We'll keep our JavaScript files being lazy loaded and we'll augment the file, as well as our remoteLoader.js file to handle lazy loading our CSS files.

In lazyloadcss.html create a function called fetch(). This function will hold the call to remoteLoader. loadJS. Also stub out calls to a function that we will define soon called loadCSS(). Your complete fetch function should look like the following:

```
<script>
function fetch(){
    remoteLoader.loadJS("/lab/perfLogger.js", init)
    remoteLoader.loadCSS(["/style/base.css", "http://fonts.googleapis.com/css?family=Metrophobi
c&amp;v2"])
}
</script>
```

Next update the code that attaches the lazy-loading functionality to the window load event. Replace the call to remoteLoader with a call to the fetch function. We'll use fetch() to lazy load all of our JavaScript and all of our CSS, including our web fonts.

```
<script>
if (window.attachEvent)
    window.attachEvent('onload', fetch);
else
    window.addEventListener('load', fetch, false);
</script>
```

The updated JavaScript in lazyloadcss.html should now look like the following:

```
<script>
function init(){
    if(perfLogger){
        perfLogger.showPerformanceMetrics()
    }
}

function fetch(){
    remoteLoader.loadJS("/lab/perfLogger.js", init)
    remoteLoader.loadCSS(["/style/base.css", "http://fonts.googleapis.com/css?family=Metrophobi
c&amp;v2"])
}

if (window.attachEvent)
    window.attachEvent('onload', fetch);
else
    window.addEventListener('load', fetch, false);
</script>
```

Next let's update our remoteLoader file. Start by renaming the constructScriptTag function to constructTag to make it more general, and pass in a third parameter to specify the type of tag that you'll be constructing:

```
function constructTag(src, func, type){
}
```

Within constructTag you will first create a variable to hold whatever tag you create, and then branch the logic based on the value of type, which identifies whether it's for JavaScript or for CSS. And after the if else if statement, return el.

```
function constructTag(src, func, type){
    var el;
    if(type === "JS"){

    }}else if(type==="CSS"){

}
return el;
}
```

In the JavaScript branch, put the logic held over from constructScripTag, but retrofitted to use the new el variable. Remember, that means building a script tag, setting the src attribute, and assigning the callback:

```
if(type === "JS"){
el = window.document.createElement('SCRIPT');
    el.src = src;
    if(func){
        el.onload  = func;
    }
}
```

In your CSS branch, build a link element, set the type attribute, set the rel, and finally set the href to point to the passed-in CSS file:

```
else if(type==="CSS"){
el = document.createElement('link');
    el.type = 'text/css';
    el.rel = 'stylesheet';
    el.href = src
}
```

Now you need to pull all of the functionality out of loadJS and move it to its own function, which you can call processURLs. Pass in the same parameters, and add in a parameter for type that you will pass in to constructTag:

```
function processURLs(script_url, f, type){
    if(typeof script_url === "object"){
        if(script_url instanceof Array){
            var frag = document.createDocumentFragment();
            for(var ind = 0; ind < script_url.length; ind++){
                frag.appendChild(constructTag(script_url[ind]), f, type);
            }
window.document.getElementsByTagName('HEAD')[0].appendChild(frag.cloneNode(true));
        }
    }else if(typeof script_url === "string")}
window.document.getElementsByTagName('HEAD')[0].appendChild(constructTag(script_url, f, type))
```

```
    }
}
```

And finally, you'll add the load statements:

```
loadCSS:function(script_url){
processURLs(script_url, null, "CSS")
},

loadJS: function(script_url, f){
processURLs(script_url, f, "JS")
}
```

Your updated remoteLoader file should now look like the following:

```
var remoteLoader = function remoteLoader(){
    function constructTag(src, func, type){
        var el;
        if(type === "JS"){
            el = window.document.createElement('SCRIPT');
            el.src = src;
            if(func){
                el.onload  = func;
                }
        }else if(type==="CSS"){
            el = document.createElement('link');
            el.type = 'text/css';
            el.rel = 'stylesheet';
            el.href = src
        }
        return el;
    }

    function processURLs(script_url, f, type){
        if(typeof script_url === "object"){
            if(script_url instanceof Array){
                var frag = document.createDocumentFragment();
                for(var ind = 0; ind < script_url.length; ind++){
                    frag.appendChild(constructTag(script_url[ind]), f, type);
                }
                window.document.getElementsByTagName('HEAD')[0].appendChild(frag.
cloneNode(true));
            }
        }else if(typeof script_url === "string"){
            window.document.getElementsByTagName('HEAD')[0].appendChild(constructTag(script_url,
f, type))
        }
    }

    return{
        loadCSS:function(script_url){
            processURLs(script_url, null, "CSS")
```

```
        },

        loadJS: function(script_url, f){
            processURLs(script_url, f, "JS")
        }
    }
}();
```

Analysis and Visualization

Great! Now let's take a look at our new test page in WebPagetest (see Figure 6-18). Our URLs are as follows:

URL to Tests	Test Result URL
http://tom-barker.com/lab/lazyloadcss.html	http://www.webpagetest.org/result/120719_CP_94a98c 18918b49d36912378ffc5d435f/

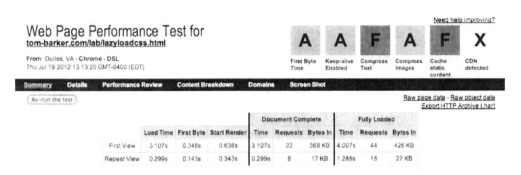

Figure 6-18. WebPagetest summary results for lazy loading

Look at these results! Our load times and start-render times are around 200 milliseconds better for our first view and repeat view. Our document complete times have similar benefits. The waterfall chart in Figure 6-19 helps us see why this is.

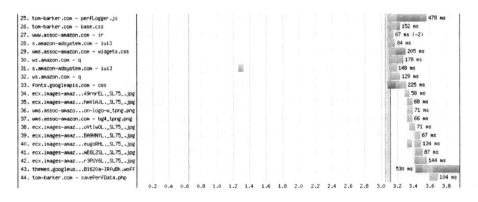

Figure 6-19. WebPagetest waterfall view for our lazy loading test

From the waterfall chart we can see that `perfLogger.js`, `base.css`, and our web fonts were all pushed down to after the page had loaded, lines 25, 26, 33 and 43 respectively.

This means that the actual content of the page was loaded first, the page was usable, and it was available to our audience before the heaviest of the presentation layer content was loaded. That's definitely a win.

Let's look to see if our Navigation Performance bears that out as well (see Figures 6-20 and 6-21).

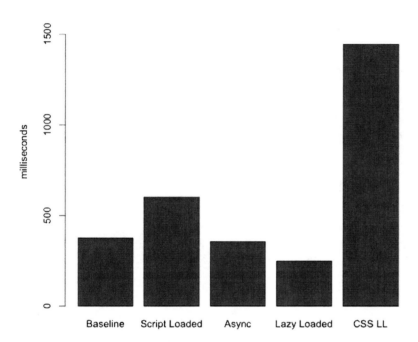

Figure 6-20. Comparing average load time for each test type

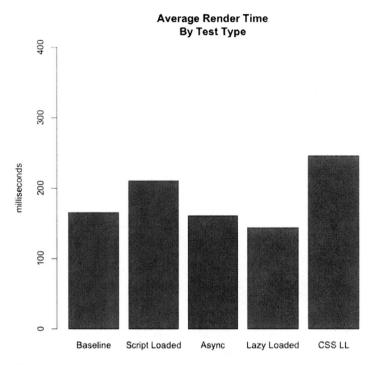

Figure 6-21. *Comparing average page render time for each test type*

What is this? Clearly lazy loading alters our timing data because of how the sequence of events is altered. But here we see that even our render time is thrown off by lazy loading our CSS and the JavaScript that we use to gather the metrics.

We can adjust this by not lazy loading perfLogger.js. If we put perfLogger back inline we see the data in Figures 6-22 and 6-23 instead:

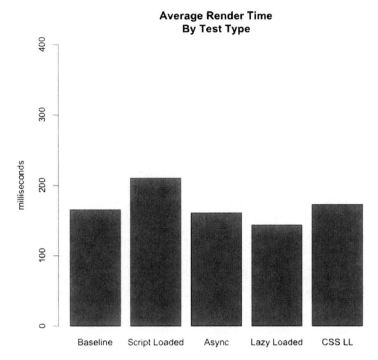

Figure 6-22. *Adjusted Results of Average Page Render Time, with perfLogger not lazy loaded*

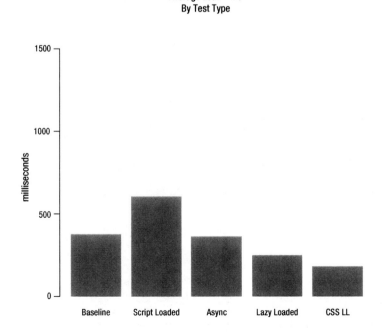

Figure 6-23. *Adjusted results of average page load time, with perfLogger not lazy loaded.*

That's better. By inlining perfLogger, we no longer block the loading and executing of it, so that our methodology doesn't interfere with the recording of our data.

This is a valuable lesson— always be careful that your metrics are not being altered by the way you are capturing them. The only way to do this is to give your data a thorough analysis; never take your results at face value.

Why Not to Lazy Load Images

After what we've explored so far this chapter, it might be tempting to go and try to lazy load as much as possible. But lazy loading is not a silver bullet. You need to be sure that the content isn't needed on page load. You also need to understand how your page will function with JavaScript turned off.

The way we would lazy load images would be to alter the HTML of the page to remove the contents of the src attribute of each image. We could just move the contents of the src attribute to an attribute in the image tag of our own design, maybe the rel attribute. This would prevent the images from being downloaded:

```
<img src="#" rel="[path to image]" />
```

Then, on loading we could use JavaScript to iterate through all of the image tags on the page and set each one's src attribute to the content of the new attribute:

```
<script>
function lazyloadImages(){
    var img = document.getElementsByTagName("img");
    for(var x = 0; x<img.length; x++){
        img[x].src = img[x].rel;
    }
}
</script>
```

But there are several reasons or scenarios where that's not a good idea, mostly because of issues that prevent our JavaScript from loading the images at all. If a user comes to our site with JavaScript turned off, they won't get any images loaded at all. If we use third-party ads on our site, it's possible for the third party JavaScript code to have an error and prevent any of our images from loading. When search engine spiders come to index our pages there is a chance that they won't see our images, so they will cache our page with no images and display our page preview with no images. The most significant reason, though, is that using the rel attribute to hold the image path is not a semantically correct way to use the markup.

Note that being semantically correct in the context of HTML means that we are retaining the meaning of the tag name in our usage of the tag; we use HTML tags because of what the tags say about the data that they contain, instead of what visual decoration the browser may assign to the tag. If we use tags meaningfully—for example using <p> tags for paragraphs not for visual spacing—then external applications accessing our pages, like search engines or screen readers should be able to parse the information in the pages meaningfully. It also allows us to separate content from presentation.

Summary

This chapter explored in greater detail how we can use JavaScript to improve aspects of web performance, specifically how the browsers parse and render our content, and the potential bottlenecks in this process. We looked at ways to prevent the blocking of other content by downloading of external JavaScript file, including using the new async attribute, and creating the script tags programmatically.

We explored the lazy-loading design pattern and used it to download our external JavaScript after all of our other content was loaded on the page. We expanded that concept to lazy load our CSS files, and considered how we could lazy load our images as well, but some reasons why we may not want to.

In each example we used the tools that we developed and existing tools to analyze and visualize our results.

Chapter 7 will look at ways to improve our runtime performance.

CHAPTER 7

■ ■ ■

Runtime Performance

The last chapter explored ways to optimize web performance with JavaScript. You learned several ways to avoid having external JavaScript block the parsing of the rest of the page. We looked at the `async` attribute, which is new to HTML 5, and at drawing script tags with JavaScript.

You learned about the lazy load pattern, and applied it to our example's script tags, adding them to the page only after the page has loaded. We expanded that idea to apply to our CSS; lazy loading our CSS files only after the document has loaded.

You ran tests for each of these scenarios; you captured data about each one and visualized comparisons of the results.

In this chapter we will now look at runtime performance optimizations in the browser. We will look at caching references across the scope chain to save time on look-ups. You will learn about using frameworks such as JQuery and compare the runtime performance of operations in JQuery and pure JavaScript. You'll even try to quantify a long-held belief that using `eval()` hurts performance. And finally the chapter looks at how to streamline DOM interaction, and quantify the incremental cost of nesting loops.

Keep in mind that because each browser uses a different JavaScript engine, runtime performance numbers can be different for each browser. So for the examples we will look at in this chapter you will first write the code to test, using our perfLogger library, and then look at the perfLogger results in a single browser, and then presumably put the code in a public place where you can crowd-source traffic to it or run it through our own browser lab - where you hit the page many times from a number of different browsers. I'll talk more about how to implement these changes in production next chapter. And finally we chart the difference in aggregate for each test grouped by browser.

■ **Note**   Some of these tests have results in the sub-millisecond range, so for best results we'll use browsers that support high-resolution time. Also remember that your results may vary based on the browsers that you test on or that your clients use. As you'll see in this chapter's tests, each browser has varying degrees of efficiency in different areas of execution. The point of this chapter is to learn how to make your own tests and analyze those results, as browsers and client configurations change, to continually evaluate your own best practices based on your end users.

Cache Variables and Properties across Scope

The first optimization to consider is caching variables and object properties.

Let's look at what this means. Normally when you reference variables in other scopes— at the global level, in other namespaces, and so on—the interpreter needs to traverse the stack to get to the variable.

Let's use `document.location` as an example. If you reference `document.location` from within an object, the interpreter will need to go from the function that references the variable, up out of the namespace to the global window scope, down to the document scope, and get the location value. See Figure 7-1.

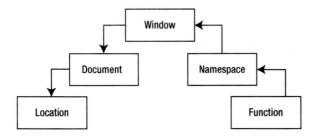

Figure 7-1. *Tracing through the stack to get to document.location*

This is based on the efficiency of the interpreter and the inheritance hierarchy that you create— if there are namespaces 4 or 5 or 10 objects deep, it will take just that much longer to get to the global scope and then back down to the scope of your intended variable.

To get around this, you can create a locally scoped variable to hold that value, and reference that variable instead. This allows you to create a shortcut to the variable reference and reap a runtime performance boost. See Figure 7-2.

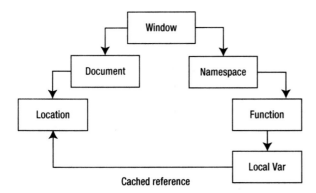

Figure 7-2. *Creating a local variable to cache the reference to document.location*

Let's quantify this performance boost with a practical example.

Creating a New File

First create a new file, called `cache_locationcomparison.html`, and create an HTML skeletal structure of just the doctype, html, head, title, character set, and body tags. This structure will be the base structure that you start each test with for the remainder of this chapter.

```
<!DOCTYPE html>
<html>
<head>
<meta charset="UTF-8" />
<title>Cache Location Comparison</title>
</head>
<body>
</body>
</html>
```

In the head, add our perfLogger and a function you can call populateArray that creates and returns an array of whatever size is passed into the function:

```
<script src="/lab/perfLogger.js"></script>
<script>
function populateArray(len){
        var retArray = new Array(len)
        for(var i = 0; i < len; i++){
            retArray[i] = i;
        }
        return retArray
}
</script>
```

In the body, you'll create a new script tag and instantiate a new array of size 400 that you will use for the remainder of these tests:

```
<script>
tempArray = populateArray(400);

</script>
```

Creating Tests

Now that we are done with setup, let's create our first test. In this test you'll capture ad hoc timing data for referencing the document.location. Start by calling perfLogger.startTimeLogging, pass in an ID of "uncached_location", give a description of the test, and set the test to be displayed on the screen as well as saved in our log file. Refer to Chapter 4 for the perfLogger API.

```
// Capture ad hoc timing data for referencing uncached document.location
perfLogger.startTimeLogging("uncached_location", "Capture ad hoc timing data for referencing
document.location", true, true, true)
```

Immediately after the call to startTimeLogging, you will run the code for the test. Create a for loop, and have it iterate through tempArray using tempArray's length property, and each step in the array, set a variable loc to document.location:

```
for(var i = 0; i < tempArray.length; i++){
    var loc = document.location;
}
```

Finally, after the loop call perfLogger.stopTimeLogging and pass in the "uncached_location" ID to stop the test, display it to the screen, and log it to the server:

```
perfLogger.stopTimeLogging("uncached_location");
```

Your completed test should look like the following:

```
// Capture ad hoc timing data for referencing uncached document.location
perfLogger.startTimeLogging("uncached_location", "Capture ad hoc timing data for referencing
document.location", true,true, true)
for(var i = 0; i < tempArray.length; i++){
    var loc = document.location;
}
perfLogger.stopTimeLogging("uncached_location");
```

If you view it in the browser, you'll see the test output:

```
Capture ad hoc timing data for referencing document.location
run time: 0.2339999999749125ms
path: http://tom-barker.com/lab/cache_locationcomparison.html
useragent: Mozilla/5.0 (Macintosh; Intel Mac OS X 10_5_8) AppleWebKit/536.11 (KHTML, like Gecko)
Chrome/20.0.1132.47 Safari/536.11
Perceived Time: 40370
Redirect Time: 0
Cache Time: 0
DNS Lookup Time: 0
tcp Connection Time: 0
roundTripTime: 12636
pageRenderTime: 107
```

Let's make another test, this time benchmarking the for loop just shown. First wrap the loop in a function called uncachedLoc():

```
//benchmark timing data for uncached document.location
function uncachedLoc(){
    for(var i = 0; i < tempArray.length; i++) {
     var loc = document.location;
    }
}
```

Then call perfLogger.logBenchmark, pass in an ID of "LocationUnCached_benchmark", tell it to run the function 10 times, pass in the function to benchmark, and have it display to the page and log to the server:

```
perfLogger.logBenchmark("LocationUnCached_benchmark", 10, uncachedLoc, true, true);
```

Your completed test should look like this:

```
//benchmark timing data for uncached document.location
function uncachedLoc(){
    for(var i = 0; i < tempArray.length; i++) {
     var loc = document.location;
    }
}
perfLogger.logBenchmark("LocationUnCached_benchmark", 10, uncachedLoc, true, true);
```

OK. These tests are your baseline, they are direct references to document.location. What you will do now is create two more tests, optimized to cache the reference to document.location.

First create a variable called l; this will hold the reference to document.location:

```
var l = document.location;
```

Then recreate the logic from the baseline ad hoc test, but instead of setting loc to document.location within the loop, set it to l.

Your complete test should look like the following:

```
// Capture ad hoc timing data for referencing cached document.location
var l = document.location;
perfLogger.startTimeLogging("cached_location", "Capture ad hoc timing data for referencing
document.location", true,true, true)
for(var i = 0; i < tempArray.length; i++){
    var loc = l;
}
perfLogger.stopTimeLogging("cached_location");
```

Finally, you'll benchmark the cached test. Just you did before, create a function called cacheLoc where you create a variable l to reference document.location and reference, that variable in the loop. The completed test looks like this:

```
//benchmark timing data for cached document.location

function cachedLoc(){
    var l = document.location;
    for(var i = 0; i < tempArray.length; i++){
        var loc = l;
    }
}

perfLogger.logBenchmark("LocationCached_benchmark", 10, cachedLoc, true, true);
```

Now your completed cache_locationcomparison.html page should look like the following:

```
<!DOCTYPE html>
<html>
<head>
<meta charset="UTF-8" />
<title>Cache Location Comparison</title>
<script src="/lab/perfLogger.js"></script>
<script>
function populateArray(len){
        var retArray = new Array(len)
        for(var i = 0; i < len; i++){
            retArray[i] = i;
        }
        return retArray
}
</script>
</head>
<body>
<script>
tempArray = populateArray(400);

// Capture ad hoc timing data for referencing uncached document.location
```

```
perfLogger.startTimeLogging("uncached_location", "Capture ad hoc timing data for referencing
document.location", true,true, true)
for(var i = 0; i < tempArray.length; i++){
    var loc = document.location;
}
perfLogger.stopTimeLogging("uncached_location");

//benchmark timing data for uncached document.location

function uncachedLoc(){
    for(var i = 0; i < tempArray.length; i++) {
     var loc = document.location;
     }
}

perfLogger.logBenchmark("LocationUnCached_benchmark", 10, uncachedLoc, true, true);


// Capture ad hoc timing data for referencing cached document.location
var l = document.location;
perfLogger.startTimeLogging("cached_location", "Capture ad hoc timing data for referencing
document.location", true,true, true)
for(var i = 0; i < tempArray.length; i++){
    var loc = l;
}
perfLogger.stopTimeLogging("cached_location");


//benchmark timing data for cached document.location

function cachedLoc(){
    var l = document.location;
    for(var i = 0; i < tempArray.length; i++){
        var loc = l;
    }
}

perfLogger.logBenchmark("LocationCached_benchmark", 10, cachedLoc, true, true);


</script>
</body>
</html>
```

When you view the page in a browser, you should see the following output (with the Performance Navigation data trimmed out for clarity):

```
Capture ad hoc timing data for referencing document.location
run time: 0.23800000781193376ms
path: http://localhost:8888/lab/chapter7/cache_locationcomparison.html
```

```
useragent: Mozilla/5.0 (Macintosh; Intel Mac OS X 10_5_8) AppleWebKit/536.11 (KHTML, like Gecko)
Chrome/20.0.1132.47 Safari/536.11

Benchmarking function uncachedLoc(){ for(var i = 0; i < tempArray.length; i++) { var loc =
document.location; }        }
average run time: 0.08210000523831695ms
path: http://localhost:8888/lab/chapter7/cache_locationcomparison.html
useragent: Mozilla/5.0 (Macintosh; Intel Mac OS X 10_5_8) AppleWebKit/536.11 (KHTML, like Gecko)
Chrome/20.0.1132.47 Safari/536.11

Capture ad hoc timing data for referencing document.location
run time: 0.027000001864507794ms
path: http://localhost:8888/lab/chapter7/cache_locationcomparison.html
useragent: Mozilla/5.0 (Macintosh; Intel Mac OS X 10_5_8) AppleWebKit/536.11 (KHTML, like Gecko)
Chrome/20.0.1132.47 Safari/536.11

Benchmarking function cachedLoc(){        var l = document.location; for(var i = 0; i < tempArray.
length; i++){ var loc = l; }        }
average run time: 0.012399995466694236ms
path: http://localhost:8888/lab/chapter7/cache_locationcomparison.html
useragent: Mozilla/5.0 (Macintosh; Intel Mac OS X 10_5_8) AppleWebKit/536.11 (KHTML, like Gecko)
Chrome/20.0.1132.47 Safari/536.11
```

Excellent! You can see from both the ad hoc tests and the benchmarking tests that we gain a significant performance improvement by caching the scope chain reference.

Visualizing Our Results

Now let's chart our results in R. Open up runtimePerformance.R from the perfLogger project. Remember that in this file you have already read the runtimeperf_results flat file into a variable named perflogs.

So start by creating a function that accepts the ID of a test and returns a subset of perflogs that has a TestID that matches the passed in value. Name this function ParseResultsbyTestID(). You'll use this in a little bit to create variables that will hold data frames for each test that you run:

```
ParseResultsbyTestID <- function(testname){
    return(perflogs[perflogs$TestID == testname,])
}
```

You already have the function getDFByBrowser() in runtimePerformance.R; you'll be using it as well. Remember, this function returns the subset of the data frame passed in that has a UserAgent column that contains the browser name, which is also passed in.

```
getDFByBrowser<-function(data, browsername){
    return(data[grep(browsername, data$UserAgent),])
}
```

Next create a variable that you'll call avg_loc_uncache_chrome, which will hold the average runtime for the uncached location test in Chrome browsers. To get this value, you will call ParseResultsbyTestID and pass in the test ID of "LocationUnCached_benchmark". Pass the results of that function call into getDFByBrowser, along with the string "Chrome":

```
avg_loc_uncache_chrome <- mean(getDFByBrowser(ParseResultsbyTestID("LocationUnCached_
benchmark"), "Chrome")$RunTime)
```

If you print the value in the console, you'll see something like this.

```
> avg_loc_unucache_chrome
[1] 1.75
```

Great! Next do the same for Firefox, and then again the same for the "LocationCached_benchmark" test for both Chrome and Firefox (and any other browser you want to track).

```
avg_loc_cache_chrome <- mean(getDFByBrowser(ParseResultsbyTestID("LocationCached_benchmark"),
"Chrome")$RunTime)

avg_loc_uncache_firefox <- mean(getDFByBrowser(ParseResultsbyTestID("LocationUnCached_
benchmark"), "Firefox")$RunTime)

avg_loc_cache_firefox <- mean(getDFByBrowser(ParseResultsbyTestID("LocationCached_benchmark"),
"Firefox")$RunTime)
```

Excellent. You now have the mathematical mean for each test in each browser. Now create a data frame to hold all of these and assign meaningful names to the columns of the data frame:

```
location_comparison <- data.frame(avg_loc_uncache_chrome, avg_loc_cache_chrome, avg_loc_uncache_
firefox, avg_loc_cache_firefox)

colnames(location_comparison) <- c("Chrome\nUncached", "Chrome\nCached", "Firefox\nUncached",
"Firefox\nCached")
```

And finally, create a bar chart from this data frame:

```
barplot(as.matrix(location_comparison), main="Comparison of average benchmark time in
milliseconds")
```

The complete R code that you would need for this example looks like this:

```
ParseResultsbyTestID <- function(testname){
    return(perflogs[perflogs$TestID == testname,])
}

getDFByBrowser<-function(data, browsername){
    return(data[grep(browsername, data$UserAgent),])
}

avg_loc_uncache_chrome <- mean(getDFByBrowser(ParseResultsbyTestID("LocationUnCached_
benchmark"), "Chrome")$RunTime)

avg_loc_cache_chrome <- mean(getDFByBrowser(ParseResultsbyTestID("LocationCached_benchmark"),
"Chrome")$RunTime)

avg_loc_uncache_firefox <- mean(getDFByBrowser(ParseResultsbyTestID("LocationUnCached_
benchmark"), "Firefox")$RunTime)

avg_loc_cache_firefox <- mean(getDFByBrowser(ParseResultsbyTestID("LocationCached_benchmark"),
"Firefox")$RunTime)

location_comparison <- data.frame(avg_loc_uncache_chrome, avg_loc_cache_chrome, avg_loc_uncache_
firefox, avg_loc_cache_firefox)
```

```
colnames(location_comparison) <- c("Chrome\nUncached", "Chrome\nCached", "Firefox\nUncached",
"Firefox\nCached")

barplot(as.matrix(location_comparison), main="Comparison of average benchmark time in
milliseconds")
```

And from this R code you generate the bar chart shown in Figure 7-3.

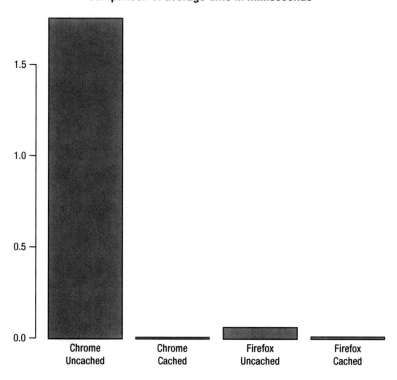

Figure 7-3. *Comparison of benchmarking results for cached and uncached scope chain references, by browser*

So from this example and our own sample data, we can see that for the client browsers used, both Chrome and Firefox saw performance improvements. Chrome saw the most significant improvement, averaging almost a 2 millisecond improvement. By itself this is insignificant, but at a larger scale we can begin to see value.

Property Reference Example

You've just looked at caching variables in different stacks, now let's look at caching property references. The way you can test this technique is to loop through an array, using the length of the array as the loop terminator. This will be your baseline. You can then loop through another array, store the array length in a local variable, and use this local variable as the loop terminator. If you compare the results for the two techniques, you should be able to quantify the performance benefit of caching the property reference.

```
<!DOCTYPE html>
<html>
<head>
<meta charset="UTF-8" />
<title>Loop Comparison</title>
<script src="/lab/perfLogger.js"></script>
<script>
function populateArray(len){
        var retArray = new Array(len)
        for(var i = 0; i < len; i++){
            retArray[i] = i;
        }
        return retArray
}
</script>
</head>
<body>
<script>
tempArray = populateArray(400);

// Capture ad hoc timing data for JavaScript for loop with uncached length variable

perfLogger.startTimeLogging("js_forloop_uncached", "Capture ad hoc timing data for JavaScript
for loop with uncached length variable", true,true, true)
for(var i = 0; i < tempArray.length; i++) {

}
perfLogger.stopTimeLogging("js_forloop_uncached");



// Capture ad hoc timing data for JavaScript for loop with cached length variable

perfLogger.startTimeLogging("js_forloop_cached", "Capture ad hoc timing data for JavaScript for
loop with cached length variable", true,true, true)
var l = tempArray.length
for(var i = 0; i < l; i++) {

}
perfLogger.stopTimeLogging("js_forloop_cached");

//benchmark timing data for uncached length variable

function uncachedLen(){
    for(var i = 0; i < tempArray.length; i++) {

    }
}
```

```
perfLogger.logBenchmark("JSForLoopUnCached_benchmark", 10, uncachedLen, true, true);


//benchmark timing data for cached length variable

function cachedLen(){
    for(var i = 0; i < l; i++) {

    }
}

perfLogger.logBenchmark("JSForLoopCached_benchmark", 10, cachedLen, true, true);


</script>
</body>
</html>
```

This produces the following results:

```
Capture ad hoc timing data for JavaScript for loop with uncached length variable
run time: 41.936000023270026ms
path: http://localhost:8888/lab/chapter7/loopcomparison.html
useragent: Mozilla/5.0 (Macintosh; Intel Mac OS X 10_5_8) AppleWebKit/536.11 (KHTML, like Gecko)
Chrome/20.0.1132.47 Safari/536.11

Capture ad hoc timing data for JavaScript for loop with cached length variable
run time: 14.304999989690259ms
path: http://localhost:8888/lab/chapter7/loopcomparison.html
useragent: Mozilla/5.0 (Macintosh; Intel Mac OS X 10_5_8) AppleWebKit/536.11 (KHTML, like Gecko)
Chrome/20.0.1132.47 Safari/536.11

benchmarking function uncachedLen(){ for(var i = 0; i < tempArray.length; i++) { }       }
average run time: 29.685899993637577ms
path: http://localhost:8888/lab/chapter7/loopcomparison.html
useragent: Mozilla/5.0 (Macintosh; Intel Mac OS X 10_5_8) AppleWebKit/536.11 (KHTML, like Gecko)
Chrome/20.0.1132.47 Safari/536.11

benchmarking function cachedLen(){       for(var i = 0; i < l; i++) { }      }
average run time: 19.58730000187643ms
path: http://localhost:8888/lab/chapter7/loopcomparison.html
useragent: Mozilla/5.0 (Macintosh; Intel Mac OS X 10_5_8) AppleWebKit/536.11 (KHTML, like Gecko)
Chrome/20.0.1132.47 Safari/536.11
```

Once again this individual test shows significant performance improvements gained from caching the property reference. Now try it from multiple browsers and chart the results in R.

Create a variable for each test/browser combination. In each variable, store the averaged results of a call to your function getDFByBrowser:

```
avg_loop_uncache_chrome <- mean(getDFByBrowser(ParseResultsbyTestID("JSForLoopUnCached_
benchmark"), "Chrome")$RunTime)
```

```
avg_loop_uncache_firefox <- mean(getDFByBrowser(ParseResultsbyTestID("JSForLoopUnCached_
benchmark"), "Firefox")$RunTime)

avg_loop_cache_chrome <- mean(getDFByBrowser(ParseResultsbyTestID("JSForLoopCached_benchmark"),
"Chrome")$RunTime)

avg_loop_cache_firefox <- mean(getDFByBrowser(ParseResultsbyTestID("JSForLoopCached_benchmark"),
"Firefox")$RunTime)
```

Next create a data frame to aggregate the variables that you just created and generate a bar plot from this data frame:

```
loop_comparison <- data.frame(avg_loop_uncache_chrome, avg_loop_cache_chrome, avg_loop_uncache_
firefox, avg_loop_cache_firefox)

colnames(loop_comparison) <- c("Chrome\nUncached", "Chrome\nCached", "Firefox\nUncached",
"Firefox\nCached")

barplot(as.matrix(loop_comparison), main="Comparison of average benchmark time \nfor cache and
uncached properties \nin milliseconds")
```

This produces the chart shown in Figure 7-4.

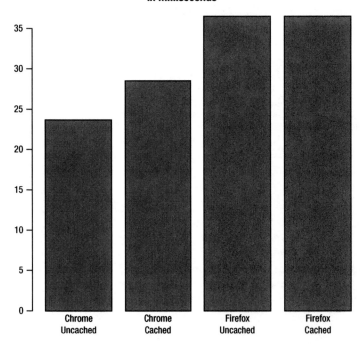

Figure 7-4. *Comparison of benchmark results for cached and uncached property reference by browser*

This is interesting—while you may see performance benefits at an individual test level for Firefox, when you scale the benchmark to many tests, you see that the benefit in Firefox is averaged out, but the benefit in Chrome is over five milliseconds for this test. We can generalize this to an observed 16.6% performance improvement in Chrome:

```
> (1 - (avg_loop_uncache_chrome / avg_loop_cache_chrome)) * 100
[1] 16.6
```

Comparison of Core JavaScript versus Frameworks

Something that I've noticed over the years both in the classroom with new students coming in, and in interviewees coming for open positions, is that both groups tend to know how to use a framework, usually JQuery, instead of knowing core JavaScript.

This is problematic because not everything should be done using frameworks. Frameworks are an author-time efficiency, meaning that they make coding tasks much simpler by abstracting the real work that goes into doing those tasks. The upside of this is that in addition to wrapping lots of functionality in a little API, they also usually wrap lots of error checking and cross-browser support. But all of this wrapped functionality is available in the core language, and sometimes it runs faster in the core language because we can do only what we need to do, not what is needed to support every user of the framework. If we only know the framework, we lose the ability to write our functionality, to fork existing projects and update them for our own purposes, and in general to create something new. We become consumers and aggregators of functionality instead of creators.

That raises a question: Is core JavaScript more performant— in terms of run time performance—than using a framework? Logically it would seem so, but let's run through some examples to benchmark most common uses of frameworks, using JQuery as a point of comparison.

▓ **Note**   JQuery is a JavaScript framework, created in 2006 by John Resig. Maintenance of JQuery was taken over by the JQuery Project in 2009. As of this writing JQuery is the most widely used JavaScript framework.

JQuery vs JavaScript: Looping

Let's start by comparing the timing of loops, for loops in JavaScript versus .each in JQuery. Create a new page called jquerycomparison.html. In jquerycomparison.html you'll start with an empty skeletal HTML document and include jQuery and perfLogger. Also include our populateArray function:

```
<!DOCTYPE html>
<html>
<head>
<meta charset="UTF-8" />
<title>Framework Comparison</title>
<script src="jquery.js"></script>
<script src="/lab/perfLogger.js"></script>
<script>
function populateArray(len){
        var retArray = new Array(len)
        for(var i = 0; i < len; i++){
            retArray[i] = i;
```

```
        }
            return retArray
    }
    </script>

    </head>
    <body>
    </body>
    </html>
```

Next create a function called JQueryEach that loops through tempArray using JQuery.each. Then pass that function to perfLogger.logBenchmark to benchmark it.

```
function JQueryEach(){
    jQuery.each(tempArray, function(i, val) {
    });
}
perfLogger.logBenchmark("JQueryEach_benchmark", 10, JQueryEach, true, true);
```

Finally, create a function called JSForLoop to loop through a for loop using the prior optimization of caching the length property of the iteration, and pass that function into perfLogger.logBenchmark:

```
function JSForLoop(){
    var l = tempArray.length
    for(var i = 0; i < l; i++) {
    }
}
perfLogger.logBenchmark("JSForLoop_benchmark", 10, JSForLoop, true, true);
```

Your complete page should now look like this:

```
<!DOCTYPE html>
<html>
<head>
<meta charset="UTF-8" />
<title>Framework Comparison</title>
<script src="jquery.js"></script>
<script src="/lab/perfLogger.js"></script>
<script>
function populateArray(len){
        var retArray = new Array(len)
        for(var i = 0; i < len; i++){
            retArray[i] = i;
        }
        return retArray
}
</script>
</head>
<body>
<script>
tempArray = populateArray(400);

//benchmark timing data for JQuery .each loop
```

```
function JQueryEach(){
    jQuery.each(tempArray, function(i, val) {
    });
}
perfLogger.logBenchmark("JQueryEach_benchmark", 10, JQueryEach, true, true);


//benchmark timing data for JS for loop

function JSForLoop(){
    var l = tempArray.length
    for(var i = 0; i < l; i++) {
    }
}
perfLogger.logBenchmark("JSForLoop_benchmark", 10, JSForLoop, true, true);

</script>

</body>
</html>
```

When you look at the test page in a browser, you should see something like the following:

```
benchmarking function JQueryEach(){ jQuery.each(tempArray, function(i, val) { });      }
average run time: 0.10279999987687916ms
path: http://tom-barker.com/lab/jquerycomparison.html
useragent: Mozilla/5.0 (Macintosh; Intel Mac OS X 10_5_8) AppleWebKit/536.11 (KHTML, like Gecko)
Chrome/20.0.1132.47 Safari/536.11
benchmarking function JSForLoop(){ var l = tempArray.length for(var i = 0; i < l; i++) { } }
average run time: 0.0035999983083456755ms
path: http://tom-barker.com/lab/jquerycomparison.html
useragent: Mozilla/5.0 (Macintosh; Intel Mac OS X 10_5_8) AppleWebKit/536.11 (KHTML, like Gecko)
Chrome/20.0.1132.47 Safari/536.11
```

Wow! That's orders of magnitude difference. Let's chart this in R.

Just as in the previous tests, create variables to hold the average values for each test for each browser:

```
avg_jquery_loop_chrome <- mean(getDFByBrowser(ParseResultsbyTestID("JQueryEach_benchmark"),
"Chrome")$RunTime)

avg_for_loop_chrome <- mean(getDFByBrowser(ParseResultsbyTestID("JSForLoop_benchmark"),
"Chrome")$RunTime)

avg_jquery_loop_firefox <- mean(getDFByBrowser(ParseResultsbyTestID("JQueryEach_benchmark"),
"Firefox")$RunTime)

avg_for_loop_firefox <- mean(getDFByBrowser(ParseResultsbyTestID("JSForLoop_benchmark"),
"Firefox")$RunTime)
```

Once again, create a data frame to hold the average values, and assign column names to the data frame:

```
jquery_comparison <- data.frame(avg_jquery_loop_chrome, avg_for_loop_chrome, avg_jquery_loop_
firefox, avg_for_loop_firefox)
```

```
colnames(jquery_comparison) <- c("Chrome\nJQuery", "Chrome\nJavascript", "Firefox\nJQuery",
"Firefox\nJavaScript")
```

And finally, chart out the data frame:

```
barplot(as.matrix(jquery_comparison), main="Comparison of average benchmark time \nfor looping
in JQuery vs core JavaScript \nin milliseconds")
```

The finished R code should look like this:

```
avg_jquery_loop_chrome <- mean(getDFByBrowser(ParseResultsbyTestID("JQueryEach_benchmark"),
"Chrome")$RunTime)
```

```
avg_for_loop_chrome <- mean(getDFByBrowser(ParseResultsbyTestID("JSForLoop_benchmark"),
"Chrome")$RunTime)
```

```
avg_jquery_loop_firefox <- mean(getDFByBrowser(ParseResultsbyTestID("JQueryEach_benchmark"),
"Firefox")$RunTime)
```

```
avg_for_loop_firefox <- mean(getDFByBrowser(ParseResultsbyTestID("JSForLoop_benchmark"),
"Firefox")$RunTime)
```

```
jquery_comparison <- data.frame(avg_jquery_loop_chrome, avg_for_loop_chrome, avg_jquery_loop_
firefox, avg_for_loop_firefox)
```

```
colnames(jquery_comparison) <- c("Chrome\nJQuery", "Chrome\nJavascript", "Firefox\nJQuery",
"Firefox\nJavaScript")
```

```
barplot(as.matrix(jquery_comparison), main="Comparison of average benchmark time \nfor looping
in JQuery vs core JavaScript \nin milliseconds")
```

This creates the chart that we see in Figure 7-5.

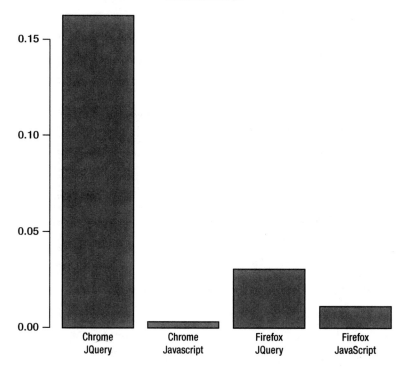

**Comparison of average benchmark time
for looping and JQuery vs core JavaScript
in milliseconds**

Figure 7-5. *Comparison of benchmark results for looping with JQuery versus looping with core JavaScript, by browser*

There is a 63.4% performance improvement for Firefox:

```
> (1 - (avg_for_loop_firefox / avg_jquery_loop_firefox)) * 100
[1] 63.4
```

But a 98.2% improvement in Chrome:

```
> (1 - (avg_for_loop_chrome / avg_jquery_loop_chrome)) * 100
[1] 98.2
```

RESPECTING THE DRY PRINCIPLE

Let's go down a tangent for a moment. I don't know about you. but I'm tired of writing the same R code over and over again with only slight variations just to get and chart our benchmarking test results. In software engineering there is the concept known as the DRY principle: Don't Repeat Yourself. It's a primal, inherent thing, the concept that anything we need to do more than once we should automate. It was named and popularized in *The Pragmatic Programmer*, by Andy Hunt and Dave Thomas (Addison-Wesley 1999).

So let's respect the DRY principle and automate this bit of R code that we've been writing and rewriting to fit our needs for each test.

Make a function called `PlotResultsofTestsByBrowser` and pass in three values to this function: `testList`, a vector of test names, `browserList`, a vector of browser names, and `descr`, a string that will be the chart header :

```
PlotResultsofTestsByBrowser <- function(testList, browserList, descr){


}
```

Within the function, declare an empty data frame, which you will use to hold the averages, and an empty list, which you will use to construct the column names of the data frame:

```
df <- data.frame()
```

```
colnameList <- c()
```

Next, the function steps through each browser name in `browserList`, and within that loop iterates through each test name in `testList`. Within the inner loop the code constructs the column name for the particular Test/Browser combination that we are on and pushes that value into `colnameList`. To make sure that the test name fits in our chart, truncate the name to hold only ten characters.

Call `ParseResultsbyTestID` and pass in the current test name; then pass that value to `getDFByBrowser` along with the current browser name value, and get the mean of that returned value and store it in a temporary variable you can call `tmp`. And finally add `tmp` to our data frame `df`:

```
for(browser in browserList){

for(test in testList){

        colnameList <- c(colnameList, paste(browser, "\n", substr(test, 1,10)

))

        tmp <- mean(getDFByBrowser(ParseResultsbyTestID(test), browser)$RunTime)

        df <- rbind(df , tmp)

    }

}
```

This functionality will step through each test and browser combination until it constructs a data frame that looks something like the following:

```
> df

 X0.0050476189047619

1               0.00505

2               0.02979

3               0.00125

4               0.00716
```

That's great; that's what we want. From there all you need to do is transpose the data frame.

```
df <- t(df)
```

Transposing the data puts it on its side so that it looks like this.

```
> df
```

	1	2	3	4

```
X0.0050476189047619 0.00505 0.0298 0.00125 0.00716
```

Then just set the column names of the data frame to be the list of column names that you've been building and create the chart:

```
colnames(df) <- colnameList
```

```
barplot(as.matrix(df), main=descr)
```

The completed function looks like the following. You will use this from now on to generate charts to demonstrate test results.

```
PlotResultsofTestsByBrowser <- function(testList, browserList, descr){
        df <- data.frame()
        colnameList <- c()


        for(browser in browserList){
        for(test in testList){
                colnameList <- c(colnameList, paste(browser, "\n", test))
                tmp <- mean(getDFByBrowser(ParseResultsbyTestID(test), browser)$RunTime)
                df <- rbind(df , tmp)
            }
        }
        df <- t(df)
        colnames(df) <- colnameList
        barplot(as.matrix(df), main=descr)
}
```

JQuery vs JavaScript: DOM Access

Next let's compare the cost of DOM interaction, with JQuery and with pure JavaScript. You'll create a test that compares the time it takes to loop through an array and write the value from the array to a div on the page both using JQuery and using JavaScript.

First create the skeletal structure of the page, with JQuery, perfLogger, and our populateArray function included in the head:

```
<!DOCTYPE html>
<html>
<head>
<meta charset="UTF-8" />
```

```
<title>Framework Comparison</title>
<script src="jquery.js"></script>
<script src="/lab/perfLogger.js"></script>
<script>
function populateArray(len){
        var retArray = new Array(len)
        for(var i = 0; i < len; i++){
            retArray[i] = i;
        }
        return retArray
}
</script>
</head>
<body>
</body>
</html>
```

Next you'll include two divs on the page, one with an id of DOMtest, where the JavaScript test will write to the JavaScript case, and the other with an id of JQueryDomtest, where the JQuery test will writeo.

```
<div id="DOMtest"><p>Dom Test</p></div>
<div id="JQueryDomtest"><p>JQuery Dom Test</p></div>
```

Then add in a script tag, and within the script tag create a tempArray of size 400. Also add a function called JQueryDOM that will loop through the array and append the index number to the JQueryDomtest div. Finally, benchmark this function using perfLogger.logBenchmark.

```
<script>
tempArray = populateArray(400);

function JQueryDOM(){
    var l = tempArray.length
    for(var i = 0; i < l; i++) {
        $("#JQueryDomtest").append(i);
    }
}
perfLogger.logBenchmark("JQueryDOM_benchmark", 10, JQueryDOM, true, true);
```

Next create a function called JSDOM, which iterates through tempArray, using document.getElementById to access the div and innerHTML to append the content to the div. And finally, use perfLogger.logBenchmark to benchmark this function:

```
function JSDOM(){
    var l = tempArray.length
    for(var i = 0; i < l; i++) {
        document.getElementById("DOMtest").innerHTML += i;
    }
}
perfLogger.logBenchmark("JSDOM_benchmark", 10, JSDOM, true, true);

</script>
```

The complete page looks like this:

```html
<!DOCTYPE html>
<html>
<head>
<meta charset="UTF-8" />
<title>Framework Comparison</title>
<script src="jquery.js"></script>
<script src="/lab/perfLogger.js"></script>
<script>
function populateArray(len){
        var retArray = new Array(len)
        for(var i = 0; i < len; i++){
            retArray[i] = i;
        }
        return retArray
}
</script>
</head>
<body>
<div id="DOMtest"><p>Dom Test</p></div>
<div id="JQueryDomtest"><p>JQuery Dom Test</p></div>
<script>
tempArray = populateArray(400);

//benchmark timing data for JQuery DOM access

function JQueryDOM(){
    var l = tempArray.length
    for(var i = 0; i < l; i++) {
        $("#JQueryDomtest").append(i);
    }
}
perfLogger.logBenchmark("JQueryDOM_benchmark", 10, JQueryDOM, true, true);


//benchmark timing data for JS DOM access

function JSDOM(){
    var l = tempArray.length
    for(var i = 0; i < l; i++) {
        document.getElementById("DOMtest").innerHTML += i;
    }
}
perfLogger.logBenchmark("JSDOM_benchmark", 10, JSDOM, true, true);

</script>
</body>
</html>
```

When you view this in a browser, you see the following.

```
benchmarking function JQueryDOM(){ var l = tempArray.length for(var i = 0; i < l; i++) {
$("#JQueryDomtest").append(i); } }
average run time: 0.4493000014917925ms
path: http://tom-barker.com/lab/jquery_dom_compare.html
useragent: Mozilla/5.0 (Macintosh; Intel Mac OS X 10_5_8) AppleWebKit/536.11 (KHTML, like Gecko)
Chrome/20.0.1132.47 Safari/536.11
```

```
benchmarking function JSDOM(){ var l = tempArray.length for(var i = 0; i < l; i++) { document.
getElementById("DOMtest").innerHTML += i; } }
average run time: 0.19499999471008778ms
path: http://tom-barker.com/lab/jquery_dom_compare.html
useragent: Mozilla/5.0 (Macintosh; Intel Mac OS X 10_5_8) AppleWebKit/536.11 (KHTML, like Gecko)
Chrome/20.0.1132.47 Safari/536.11
```

Note that as for every test result, your individual results may vary, depending on the browser and system used.

Let's plot this in R. With our new function, it takes only one line to do this, by passing in a list of the names of the tests we want, JQueryDOM_benchmark and JSDOM_benchmark.

```
PlotResultsofTestsByBrowser(c("JQueryDOM_benchmark", "JSDOM_benchmark"), c("Chrome","Firefox"),
"Comparison of average benchmark time \nfor using JQuery to access the DOM versus pure
JavaScript \nin milliseconds")
```

This creates the bar chart shown in Figure 7-6.

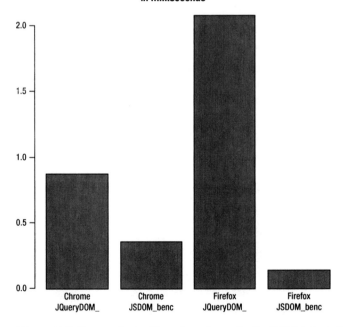

Figure 7-6. *Comparison of benchmark results for DOM interaction with JQuery and with JavaScript, by browser*

That's a 60% improvement for Chrome and a 93% improvement for Firefox, just by using core JavaScript instead of JQuery.

The True Cost of Eval

If you aren't familiar with it, eval is a JavaScript native function that accepts a string and executes the string as JavaScript. It basically fires up the interpreter and allows the passed-in string to be parsed and interpreted at the time of invocation.

We've all heard that eval is evil and should be avoided at all cost[1]. The rationale is that it is potentially dangerous because it is essentially injecting code directly to the interpreter, and that because the interpreter is being accessed it causes a hit on performance. It's become good practice over the years to avoid the use of eval. Even in the cases where it was accepted and commonplace, like to de-serialize JSON, we now have standard solutions that don't use eval.

I would contend that code injection is a perfectly legitimate solution *sometimes*, with a history that dates back to inlining assembler in C code for performance boosts and low-level control. Having a console available in our browser that lets us execute ad hoc code client-side also negates this aspect of the argument against eval.

But let's quantify the impact on performance of this long held belief for ourselves. Let's run a test that compares the run time performance of passing a string that contains a function to eval versus invoking the function directly.

Just as in our previous tests, start with our basic HTML skeletal structure, with perfLogger:

```
<!DOCTYPE html>
<html>
<head>
<meta charset="UTF-8" />
<title>Cache Location Comparison</title>
<script src="/lab/perfLogger.js"></script>
</head>
<body>
</body>
</html>
```

Next create a `script` tag in the body and a function called getAvg. The getAvg function iterates from 0 to 200, adds each consecutive number, and then averages it.

```
<script>
function getAvg(){
    var avg = 0;
    for(var x = 0; x < 200; x++){
        avg += x;
    }
    return(avg/200);
}
```

Create two functions, one that will convert the getAvg function to a string and pass it to eval and store the return value in a variable, and the other function that will simply invoke the getAvg function and store the result:

---

1 http://blogs.msdn.com/b/ericlippert/archive/2003/11/01/53329.aspx

```
function evalAverage(){
    var average = eval(getAvg.toString());
}

function invokeAverage(){
    var average = getAvg()
}
```

And finally call perfLogger.logBenchmark for each test, having it run each test 1000 times:

```
perfLogger.logBenchmark("EvalTime", 1000, evalAverage, true, true);
```

```
perfLogger.logBenchmark("InvokeTime", 1000, invokeAverage, true, true);
```

The completed page follows:

```
<!DOCTYPE html>
<html>
<head>
<meta charset="UTF-8" />
<title>Cache Location Comparison</title>
<script src="/lab/perfLogger.js"></script>
</head>
<body>
<script>
function getAvg(){
    var avg = 0;
    for(var x = 0; x < 200; x++){
        avg += x;
    }
    return(avg/200);
}

function evalAverage(){
    var average = eval(getAvg.toString());
}

function invokeAverage(){
    var average = getAvg()
}

perfLogger.logBenchmark("EvalTime", 1000, evalAverage, true, true);

perfLogger.logBenchmark("InvokeTime", 1000, invokeAverage, true, true);
</script>
</body>
</html>
```

In the browser you see the following results:

```
benchmarking function evalAverage(){ var average = eval(getAvg.toString()); }
average run time: 0.03299599998717895ms
path: http://tom-barker.com/lab/eval_comparison.html
```

useragent: Mozilla/5.0 (Macintosh; Intel Mac OS X 10_5_8) AppleWebKit/536.11 (KHTML, like Gecko) Chrome/20.0.1132.47 Safari/536.11

benchmarking function invokeAverage(){ var average = getAvg() }
average run time: 0.004606999973475467ms
path: http://tom-barker.com/lab/eval_comparison.html
useragent: Mozilla/5.0 (Macintosh; Intel Mac OS X 10_5_8) AppleWebKit/536.11 (KHTML, like Gecko) Chrome/20.0.1132.47 Safari/536.11

Great! Let's point some users at the page or run it through our test lab and chart the data in R (see Figure 7-7):

```
PlotResultsofTestsByBrowser(c("EvalTime", "InvokeTime"), c("Chrome","Firefox"), "Comparison of
average benchmark time \nfor using Eval compared to Function invocation \nin milliseconds")
```

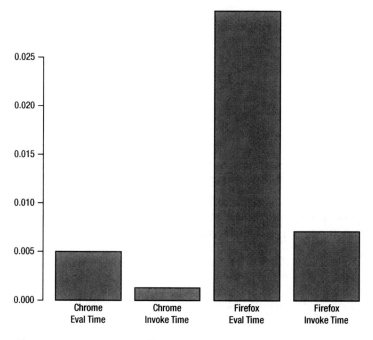

Figure 7-7. Comparison of benchmark results for using eval versus direct function invocation, by browser

DOM Access

The browser makers are constantly working to make DOM access more efficient[2], but the fact remains that DOM access involves interfacing with an aspect of the browser outside the JavaScript interpreter, the render engine, which makes it inherently the slowest part of JavaScript development.

But there are ways to optimize interaction with the DOM. Let's look at some.

Queue Changes to DOM Elements

When we are making multiple changes to the content of a DOM element, we can queue those changes and then append them to the element at once. Let's take a look at an example of this.

Start with a skeletal HTML structure, our perfLogger library, and our populateArray function as in the previous tests. In the body of the page, add a div with an id of DOMtest and a script tag. In the script tag, create tempArray.

```
<div id="DOMtest"><p>Dom Test</p></div>
<script>
tempArray = populateArray(400);
</script>
```

So with all of the setup out of the way, you'll create a function called sequentialWrites().This function will loop through tempArray and update the innerHTML of DOMtest each step in the iteration. You'll then benchmark this function:

```
function sequentialWrites(){
    var l = tempArray.length
    for(var i = 0; i < l; i++) {
        document.getElementById("DOMtest").innerHTML += i;
    }
}
perfLogger.logBenchmark("SequentialWrites", 10, sequentialWrites, true, true);
```

Next create a function, called queueWrites, that will loop through tempArray, but at each step through the iteration will instead concatenate the changes to a string variable. After the loop is complete, the function will insert the updated string variable into the div. Finally, benchmark the queueWrites function:

```
function queueWrites(){
    var l = tempArray.length,
        writeVal = "";
    for(var i = 0; i < l; i++) {
        writeVal += i
    }
    document.getElementById("DOMtest").innerHTML += writeVal;
}
perfLogger.logBenchmark("QueueWrites", 10, queueWrites, true, true);
```

Your complete test script should look like the following.

```
<div id="DOMtest"><p>Dom Test</p></div>
<script>
tempArray = populateArray(400);
```

---

2 http://updates.html5rocks.com/2012/04/Big-boost-to-DOM-performance---WebKit-s-innerHTML-is-240-faster

```
//benchmark timing data for JS DOM access
function sequentialWrites(){
    var l = tempArray.length
    for(var i = 0; i < l; i++) {
        document.getElementById("DOMtest").innerHTML += i;
    }
}
perfLogger.logBenchmark("SequentialWrites", 10, sequentialWrites, true, true);

//benchmark timing data for JS DOM access
function queueWrites(){
    var l = tempArray.length,
        writeVal = "";
    for(var i = 0; i < l; i++) {
        writeVal += i
    }
    document.getElementById("DOMtest").innerHTML += writeVal;
}
perfLogger.logBenchmark("QueueWrites", 10, queueWrites, true, true);

</script>
```

In the browser you should see something like the following results:

```
benchmarking function sequentialWrites(){ var l = tempArray.length for(var i = 0; i < l; i++) {
document.getElementById("DOMtest").innerHTML += i; } }
average run time: 146.904400002677ms
path: http://tom-barker.com/lab/dom_interactions.html
useragent: Mozilla/5.0 (Macintosh; Intel Mac OS X 10_5_8) AppleWebKit/536.11 (KHTML, like Gecko)
Chrome/20.0.1132.47 Safari/536.11


benchmarking function queueWrites(){ var l = tempArray.length, writeVal = ""; for(var i = 0; i <
l; i++) { writeVal += i } document.getElementById("DOMtest").innerHTML += writeVal; }
average run time: 2.8286000015214086ms
path: http://tom-barker.com/lab/dom_interactions.html
useragent: Mozilla/5.0 (Macintosh; Intel Mac OS X 10_5_8) AppleWebKit/536.11 (KHTML, like Gecko)
Chrome/20.0.1132.47 Safari/536.11
```

That's a significant difference between the sequential and queued write—146 milliseconds versus 2.8 milliseconds. But that's for an individual test. Let's chart these results at scale in R.

If you plug the following into our R console, you'll get the chart shown in Figure 7-8. The difference in scale between the two tests is so significant that we lose almost all granular details of the smaller number when compared to the larger.

```
PlotResultsofTestsByBrowser(c("SequentialWrites", "QueueWrites"), c("Chrome","Firefox"),
"Comparison of average benchmark time \n Sequential DOM element updates versus Queued DOM
element updates \nin milliseconds")
```

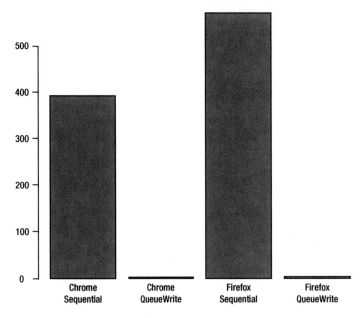

**Comparison of average benchmark time
sequential DOM element updated versus queued DOM element update
in milliseconds**

Figure 7-8. *Results of individual writes to the DOM compared to a single queued write*

Queue Adding New Node

Let's apply the same principle when adding new nodes to the DOM. When we need to add multiple DOM elements to a page we can queue the creation of these elements, add them to a DocumentFragment and then append the DocumentFragment to the page. As described in the W3C page at http://www.w3.org/TR/DOM-Level-2-Core/core.html#ID-B63ED1A3, a DocumentFragment is a lightweight Document object. Its intended use is to be a staging environment for Document changes, and once all changes are staged in a DocumentFragment, we simply copy the nodes in the DocumentFragment to the Document. Let's explore a test of this concept.

We'll use the same page as our queued versus sequential DOM write test and just add some new tests to benchmark.

First create a function called useAppendChild. This function will loop through tempArray, at each step through creating a new script element and append it to the head of the document. Then benchmark the function:

```
function useAppendChild(){
    var l = tempArray.length,
        writeVal = "";
    for(var i = 0; i < l; i++) {
        window.document.getElementsByTagName('HEAD')[0].appendChild(window.document.
createElement('SCRIPT'));
    }
}
perfLogger.logBenchmark("AppendChildWrites", 10, useAppendChild, true, true);
```

Finally, create a function useDocFragments to do the same thing, except that instead of appending to the Document it should append to a DocumentFragment. Once the loop is complete, merge the changes from DocumentFragment to the Document:

```
<script>

//documentfragment vs append child for multiple updates
function useDocFragments(){
    var l = tempArray.length,
        writeVal = "",
        frag = document.createDocumentFragment();
    for(var i = 0; i < l; i++) {
            frag.appendChild(window.document.createElement('SCRIPT'));
        }
    window.document.getElementsByTagName('HEAD')[0].appendChild(frag.cloneNode(true));
}
perfLogger.logBenchmark("DocFragmentWrites", 10, useDocFragments, true, true);
```

The complete code from these tests is as follows:

```
<script>
function useAppendChild(){
    var l = tempArray.length,
        writeVal = "";
    for(var i = 0; i < l; i++) {
        window.document.getElementsByTagName('HEAD')[0].appendChild(window.document.
createElement('SCRIPT'));
    }
}
perfLogger.logBenchmark("AppendChildWrites", 10, useAppendChild, true, true);

</script>
```

When you view these tests in a browser, you should see something like the following:

```
benchmarking function useDocFragments(){ var l = tempArray.length, writeVal = "", frag =
document.createDocumentFragment(); for(var i = 0; i < l; i++) { frag.appendChild(window.
document.createElement('SCRIPT')); } window.document.getElementsByTagName('HEAD')[0].
appendChild(frag.cloneNode(true));        }
average run time: 2.3462999932235107ms
path: http://localhost:8888/lab/chapter7/dom_interactions.html
useragent: Mozilla/5.0 (Macintosh; Intel Mac OS X 10_5_8) AppleWebKit/536.11 (KHTML, like Gecko)
Chrome/20.0.1132.47 Safari/536.11

benchmarking function useAppendChild(){ var l = tempArray.length, writeVal = ""; for(var i = 0;
i < l; i++) { window.document.getElementsByTagName('HEAD')[0].appendChild(window.document.
createElement('SCRIPT')); }        }
average run time: 2.593400003388524ms
path: http://localhost:8888/lab/chapter7/dom_interactions.html
useragent: Mozilla/5.0 (Macintosh; Intel Mac OS X 10_5_8) AppleWebKit/536.11 (KHTML, like Gecko)
Chrome/20.0.1132.47 Safari/536.11
```

To chart this test run at scale, use the following call to PlotResultsofTestsByBrowser to generate the chart shown in Figure 7-9. You can see that using DocumentFragment gives a 9.6% performance increase in Chrome and a 10% increase in Firefox.

```
PlotResultsofTestsByBrowser(c("AppendChildWrites","DocFragmentWrites"), c("Chrome","Firefox"),
"Comparison of average benchmark time \n Individual append child calls vs document fragment \nin
milliseconds")
```

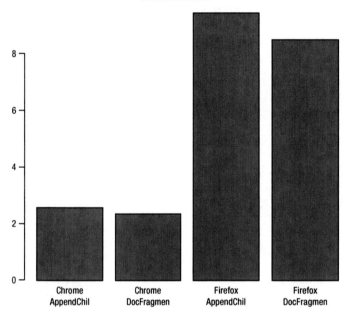

Figure 7-9. Comparison of benchmark results for multiple additions to DOM versus single DOM interaction via DocumentFragment, by browser

The Cost of Nested Loops

We know that loops in general cost more in performance than unfurling the code and executing it sequentially. This is because each loop is synchronous and blocks execution of the rest of the application until it is complete. As you saw in Chapter 2, that was one of Google's Closure Compiler's optimizations, and Chapter 8 explores that concept. But even more expensive than loops are nested loops.

There are ways to avoid nested loops, such as loop unwinding, as Closure Compiler does, or loop fusion, where we merge the execution of the sub-loops into a single loop. But to see why we would do that let's explore the cost of nested loops.

Make a new page, starting out with the basic HTML skeletal structure, with the perfLogger library and populateArray function. In the body of the page, create a script tag and our tempArray variable.

Within the script tag you will create functions, each with increasing depth of nested loops. The twoLoopsDeep function has a nested loop, threeLoopsDeep has a loop with two nested loops, and so on until we get to fiveLoopsDeep.

Finally, you'll benchmark each function. To be able to test these in a browser, you'll need to keep the number of times we run the functions low; otherwise you'll get slow script warnings or even crash the browser.

```
<script>
tempArray = populateArray(20);

function twoLoopsDeep(){
    var l = tempArray.length;
    for(var a = 0; a < l; a++){
        for(var b = 0; b < l; b++){

        }
    }
}

function threeLoopsDeep(){
    var l = tempArray.length;
    for(var a = 0; a < l; a++){
        for(var b = 0; b < l; b++){
            for(var c = 0; c < l; c++){

            }
        }
    }
}

function fourLoopsDeep(){
    var l = tempArray.length;
    for(var a = 0; a < l; a++){
        for(var b = 0; b < l; b++){
            for(var c = 0; c < l; c++){
                for(var d = 0; d < l; d++){

                }
            }
        }
    }
}

function fiveLoopsDeep(){
    var l = tempArray.length;
    for(var a = 0; a < l; a++){
        for(var b = 0; b < l; b++){
            for(var c = 0; c < l; c++){
                for(var d = 0; d < l; d++){
                    for(var e = 0; e < l; e++){

                    }
                }
            }
```

```
            }
        }
    }

perfLogger.logBenchmark("TwoLoops", 10, twoLoopsDeep, true, true);
perfLogger.logBenchmark("ThreeLoops", 10, threeLoopsDeep, true, true);
perfLogger.logBenchmark("FourLoops", 10, fourLoopsDeep, true, true);
perfLogger.logBenchmark("FiveLoops", 10, fiveLoopsDeep, true, true);
</script>
```

When you view the page in a browser you should see the following:

```
benchmarking function oneLoop(){ var l = tempArray.length; for(var a = 0; a < l; a++){ } }
average run time: 0.008299996261484921ms
path: http://tom-barker.com/lab/cyclomaticcomplexity.html
useragent: Mozilla/5.0 (Macintosh; Intel Mac OS X 10_5_8) AppleWebKit/536.11 (KHTML, like Gecko)
Chrome/20.0.1132.47 Safari/536.11


benchmarking function twoLoopsDeep(){ var l = tempArray.length; for(var a = 0; a < l; a++){
for(var b = 0; b < l; b++){ } } }
average run time: 0.012399998377077281ms
path: http://tom-barker.com/lab/cyclomaticcomplexity.html
useragent: Mozilla/5.0 (Macintosh; Intel Mac OS X 10_5_8) AppleWebKit/536.11 (KHTML, like Gecko)
Chrome/20.0.1132.47 Safari/536.11


benchmarking function threeLoopsDeep(){ var l = tempArray.length; for(var a = 0; a < l; a++){
for(var b = 0; b < l; b++){ for(var c = 0; c < l; c++){ } } } }
average run time: 0.06290000164881349ms
path: http://tom-barker.com/lab/cyclomaticcomplexity.html
useragent: Mozilla/5.0 (Macintosh; Intel Mac OS X 10_5_8) AppleWebKit/536.11 (KHTML, like Gecko)
Chrome/20.0.1132.47 Safari/536.11


benchmarking function fourLoopsDeep(){ var l = tempArray.length; for(var a = 0; a < l; a++){
for(var b = 0; b < l; b++){ for(var c = 0; c < l; c++){ for(var d = 0; d < l; d++){ } } } } }
average run time: 1.022299993201159ms
path: http://tom-barker.com/lab/cyclomaticcomplexity.html
useragent: Mozilla/5.0 (Macintosh; Intel Mac OS X 10_5_8) AppleWebKit/536.11 (KHTML, like Gecko)
Chrome/20.0.1132.47 Safari/536.11


benchmarking function fiveLoopsDeep(){ var l = tempArray.length; for(var a = 0; a < l; a++){
for(var b = 0; b < l; b++){ for(var c = 0; c < l; c++){ for(var d = 0; d < l; d++){ for(var e =
0; e < l; e++){ } } } } } }
average run time: 6.273999999393709ms
path: http://tom-barker.com/lab/cyclomaticcomplexity.html
useragent: Mozilla/5.0 (Macintosh; Intel Mac OS X 10_5_8) AppleWebKit/536.11 (KHTML, like Gecko)
Chrome/20.0.1132.47 Safari/536.11
```

Now let's chart the data in R! If we plot out two to five loops in a single chart, we lose the perspective between each incremental increase, so at first we'll chart out two to three then four to five. Then finally we'll look at the full scope of two to five loops in a single browser.

First look at the increase in latency between two and three loops:

```
PlotResultsofTestsByBrowser(c("TwoLoops","ThreeLoops"), c("Chrome","Firefox"), "Comparison of
average benchmark time \n For Increasing Depth of Nested Loops \nin milliseconds")
```

This creates the chart we see in Figure 7-10.

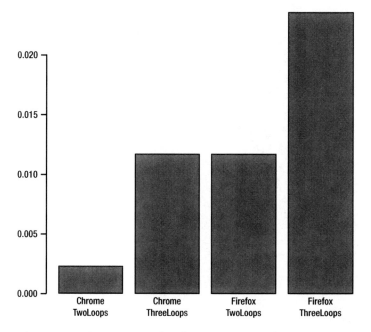

Figure 7-10. *Comparison of performance impact for increasing nesting of loops from two to three, by browser*

That's a 420% increase in latency for Chrome and a 103% increase for Firefox.
Next plot the increase in latency between four and five nested loops:

```
PlotResultsofTestsByBrowser(c("FourLoops","FiveLoops"), c("Chrome","Firefox"), "Comparison of
average benchmark time \n For Increasing Depth of Nested Loops \nin milliseconds")
```

This creates the chart that we see in Figure 7-11.

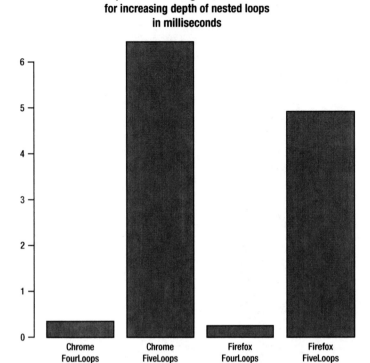

Figure 7-11. Comparison of performance impact for increasing nesting of loops from four to five, by browser

That's a 1774% increase for Chrome and an 1868% increase for Firefox!

And finally, you can look at the larger picture, from two to five loops to appreciate the full scale of the impact on performance:

```
PlotResultsofTestsByBrowser(c("TwoLoops", "ThreeLoops", "FourLoops","FiveLoops"), c("Chrome"),
"Comparison of average benchmark time \n For Increasing Depth of Nested Loops \nin
milliseconds")
```

This creates the chart shown in Figure 7-12.

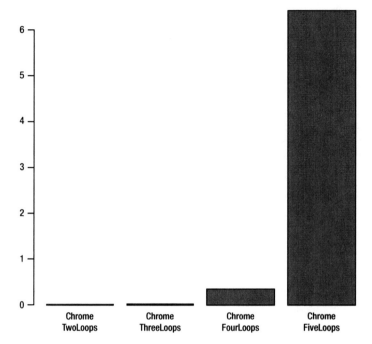

Figure 7-12. Comparison of benchmark results for nested for loops in Chrome

This is a 285677% increase in latency!

So we can see the true cost of incrementally increasing the number of loops deep that we nest. From our findings we see that as soon as we make the leap from two loops deep to three, the performance impact is dramatic and just increases exponentially as we nest deeper.

Summary

This chapter took a deep dive into runtime performance, exploring concepts like taking variables and properties in other scope chains and storing them locally to avoid the performance hit of retrieving across the scope stack.

You learned about the benefit of using pure JavaScript instead of frameworks for everything, and compared benchmark results from looping and DOM access using JQuery and JavaScript to prove the performance gain from doing so.

One example quantified the cost of using eval compared to directly invoking a function. This speaks to the performance benefit we gather from using functions as parameters instead of passing strings and passing them to eval. You also saw that eval might not be as evil as has been the long-standing belief.

You saw the performance benefits from queueing writes to the DOM, both updates to DOM elements and using DocumentFragment objects to queue adding new DOM elements.

And finally we quantified the increase in latency we get from increasing the depth of nested loops.

Chapter 8 talks about balancing performance with readability and modularity.

■ ■ ■

Balancing Performance with Software Engineering Best Practices and Running in Production

Chapter 7 explored ways to improve runtime performance. You quantified these improvements using the example perfLogger library and charted the results with R. That has been a theme throughout this book— measure and prove a point with data. If I had to choose a single sentence to serve as a thesis statement for this book, it would have to be something that I said in the first chapter that deserves repeating: Any journeyman can create something to spec, but a master crafts with excellence and proves that excellence with empirical data.

We've strived to do that so far throughout this book, creating our own tools to instrument our code and monitor the web performance of our web sites. We crafted data visualizations to prepare our data for easier consumption.

But this chapter is a little different. We will still look at raw data and performance optimizations, but the focus will be on balancing the need to optimize with other needs, like adhering to coding standards and best practices, readability, and making our code modular for use across a larger team.

We'll also take a closer look at how to generate test data at scale, either making our own test lab using virtual machines, or putting our code on a production web site to crowd-source the data.

Balancing Performance with Readability, Modularity, and Good Design

At the time of this writing the size of the group that I lead is roughly 20 to 25 engineers, managers, and engineering leads. That's a lot of hands to have making changes in just two to three code repositories. I track our performance like a hawk would track a field mouse. I chart out our web performance from WebPagetest for tens of URLs. I meet with the team regularly to discuss the output of these reports, going over our first view and repeat view data to make sure we are making efficient use of cache. We look at all of the aspects of performance and try to eke out as many optimizations as we can.

But there are other things that I track as well; among them are things like: What is our defect density? What is our incident rate for each product in production? Those things can be harmful to a product brand, arguably more than performance, depending on the severity of the issue.

In looking at things like defects and production incidents, one of the leading root causes, in my experience, is communication. Are the engineers talking to the QA staff updating them on features? Are the engineers talking with the production operations staff about how to support the features? And are the engineers talking with each other? But communication issues don't stop there. With literally millions of lines of code, does everyone know what all of the code does? Are libraries written to modularize functionality? Does everyone know about these libraries? If I were to read through a piece of code, would I know what it does and how to use it? How readable is the code?

When code is breaking in production, it is more important to me that all twenty of my engineers know how to use all of the code and functionality available to them than to wring out an extra millisecond or two of performance.

That's why we strive for modularity, reusability, and readability.

We try to practice modular code design, in that we try to write code in small self-contained and interchangeable modules. Writing code in modules minimizes the potential harm that can come from changes—because the modules communicate with each other via their interfaces, we can easily unit-test the interface and create integration tests around how they interact.

By striving for reusability we reduce the chances of creating new bugs. Ideally, the code that we are reusing has been tested and proven already.

Making our code readable means we try to make it obvious what our code does. This includes

- Abstracting complex logic into clearly and meaningfully named functions or self-contained objects or modules (it's all circular).

- Using consistent formatting that we have all agreed upon as our standard.

- Using good and clear naming patterns for our variable names.

While all of those are good practices, they generally also work counter to having the leanest, most performant code humanly possible. Long, meaningful variable names take up characters that add to file size, which increases the payload of a page. The same principle applies to the extra lines of code needed to write functions and constructors, not to mention the extra overhead for the interpreter of creating these objects in the heap, managing their garbage collection, and traversing their scope chain.

But having our code in objects and functions abstracts our logic to meaningfully named, atomic pieces that can be updated and maintained without having too much of an impact on the rest of the system.

It's all about perspective and finding balance. That's part of what we will talk about this chapter.

Scorched-Earth Performance

In earlier chapters I've mentioned the term *scorched-earth performance*. That's a term I've coined that indicates that we have sacrificed all else in the ultimate pursuit of performance. In this section we look at some scorched-earth practices, and we quantify the benefit, but also discuss the cost involved to give the full picture.

Inlining Functions

Let's first look at the run-time performance benefit that we get from inlining functions. In past chapters we've looked at the overhead cost of having and traversing memory structures. Last chapter we talked about this in the context of differing memory scopes, but the same concept applies to object hierarchies we create.

Ostensibly there is a runtime performance boost that we can gain by coalescing all of our functionality into a single function, instead of abstracting out functionality into separate functions or even objects. Let's look at this.

In the next example you'll create a single page where you will benchmark the results of coalescing functionality into a single function, breaking the code into different functions, and creating objects to contain functionality. Let's get started!

Creating the Example

First create a new page with the basic skeletal HTML structure and include the perfLogger.js library:

```
<!DOCTYPE html>
<html>
<head>
<meta charset="UTF-8" />
<title>Methodology Comparison</title>
<script src="/lab/perfLogger.js"></script>
</head>
<body>
</body>
</html>
```

Next you'll create a script tag in the body of the page and create a function that will combine everything that we want to do. Call the function unwoundfunction():

```
<script>
function unwoundfunction(){

}
</script>
```

Within unwoundfunction() you'll create a variable named sum, iterate through a for loop 300 times and sum up the incremental value of each step in the loop:

```
var sum = 0;
for(var x = 0; x < 300; x++){
    sum += x;
}
```

Then you will create a variable named average, iterate 300 times, sum up the incrementor, and divide the sum by 300. This gives you two operations to calculate—summing up series of numbers and finding an average.

```
var average = 0;
for(var x = 0; x < 300; x++){
    average += x;
}
average = average/300;
```

The completed function should look like the following. It is this function that you will benchmark to get the time for coalescing functionality:

```
function unwoundfunction(){
    var sum = 0;
    for(var x = 0; x < 300; x++){
        sum += x;
    }

    var avgerage = 0;
    for(var x = 0; x < 300; x++){
        avgerage += x;
    }
    avgerage = avgerage/300;
}
```

Next create two new functions, one to handle summing the numbers and the other to handle the averaging of the result:

```
function getAvg(p){
    var avg = 0;
    for(var x = 0; x < p; x++){
        avg += x;
    }
    return(avg/p);
}

function getSum(a){
    var sum = 0;
    for(var x = 0; x < a; x++){
        sum += x;
    }
    return(sum);

}
```

Next create a third function that will invoke getSum() and getAvg(). You'll benchmark this function as an example of using functions:

```
function usingfunctions(){
    var average = getAvg(300);
    var sum = getSum(300)
}
```

Now create an object constructor to handle this functionality. You can call this object simpleMath and give it two public methods, sum() and avg():

```
function simpleMath(){
    this.sum = function(a){
        var sum = 0;
        for(var x = 0; x < a; x++){
            sum += x;
        }
        return(sum);
    }
```

```
    this.avg = function(p){
        var avg = 0;
        for(var x = 0; x < p; x++){
            avg += x;
        }
        return(avg/p);
    }
}
```

Then create a function called usingobjects that will instantiate a new simpleMath object and call the sum and avg methods. You will benchmark this function to get the metrics for using objects.

```
function usingobjects(){
    var m = new simpleMath();
    var average = m.avg(300);
    var sum = m.sum(300);
}
```

And finally you'll benchmark these functions, having perfLogger execute each function 100 times:

```
perfLogger.logBenchmark("UsingObjects", 100, usingobjects, true, true);
perfLogger.logBenchmark("UsingFunctions", 100, usingfunctions, true, true);
perfLogger.logBenchmark("unwoundfunction", 100, unwoundfunction, true, true);
```

The complete test page should look like this:

```
<!DOCTYPE html>
<html>
<head>
<meta charset="UTF-8" />
<title>Methodology Comparison</title>
<script src="/lab/perfLogger.js"></script>
<script>
function getAvg(p){
    var avg = 0;
    for(var x = 0; x < p; x++){
        avg += x;
    }
    return(avg/p);
}

function getSum(a){
    var sum = 0;
    for(var x = 0; x < a; x++){
        sum += x;
    }
    return(sum);

}


function simpleMath(){
    this.sum = function(a){
```

```
            var sum = 0;
            for(var x = 0; x < a; x++){
                 sum += x;
            }
            return(sum);
        }

        this.avg = function(p){
            var avg = 0;
            for(var x = 0; x < p; x++){
                 avg += x;
            }
            return(avg/p);
        }
    }
    </script>
    </head>
    <body>
    <script>

    function usingfunctions(){
        var average = getAvg(300);
        var sum = getSum(300)
    }

    function usingobjects(){
        var m = new simpleMath();
        var average = m.avg(300);
        var sum = m.sum(300);
    }

    function unwoundfunction(){
        var sum = 0;
        for(var x = 0; x < 300; x++){
             sum += x;
        }

        var average = 0;
        for(var x = 0; x < 300; x++){
             average += x;
        }
        average = average/300;
    }


    perfLogger.logBenchmark("UsingObjects", 100, usingobjects, true, true);
    perfLogger.logBenchmark("UsingFunctions", 100, usingfunctions, true, true);
    perfLogger.logBenchmark("unwoundfunction", 100, unwoundfunction, true, true);

    </script>
    </body>
```

```
</html>
```

Viewing this page in a browser you should see something like the following results:

```
benchmarking function usingobjects() { var m = new simpleMath; var average = m.avg(300); var sum
= m.sum(300); }
average run time: 0.025260580000000914ms
path: http://tom-barker.com/lab/useFunctions.html
useragent: Mozilla/5.0 (Macintosh; Intel Mac OS X 10.5; rv:16.0) Gecko/16.0 Firefox/16.0

benchmarking function usingfunctions() { var average = getAvg(300); var sum = getSum(300); }
average run time: 0.020855050000000687ms
path: http://tom-barker.com/lab/useFunctions.html
useragent: Mozilla/5.0 (Macintosh; Intel Mac OS X 10.5; rv:16.0) Gecko/16.0 Firefox/16.0

benchmarking function unwoundfunction() { var sum = 0; for (var x = 0; x < 300; x++) { sum += x;
} var avgerage = 0; for (var x = 0; x < 300; x++) { avgerage += x; } avgerage = avgerage / 300;
}
average run time: 0.01648929999999666ms
path: http://tom-barker.com/lab/useFunctions.html
useragent: Mozilla/5.0 (Macintosh; Intel Mac OS X 10.5; rv:16.0) Gecko/16.0 Firefox/16.0
```

Once again you'll put this either in production or in a test lab to get traffic pointed at the code to give a nice breadth of results in the log file.

Let's grab these results and chart them in R!

Analyzing Results

For charting you can reuse the PlotResultsofTestsByBrowser() function from the last chapter, and pass in the ID of each test. This will create the chart shown in Figure 8-1.

```
PlotResultsofTestsByBrowser(c("unwoundfunction", "UsingFunctions", "UsingObjects"),
c("Firefox"), "Comparison of average benchmark time \nfor coding methodology \nin milliseconds")
```

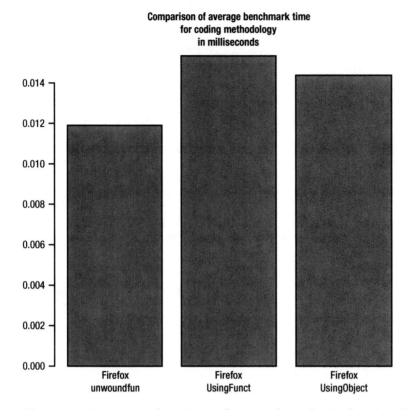

Figure 8-1. *Comparison of runtime performance for coalescing functionality, using functions, and using objects*

So you can see that there is a performance increase by stripping out all overhead and writing the code as line-by-line imperative statements. In this simple example the differences are less than a millisecond in scope, but the percentages are significant. From the smallest to the largest there is a 23% improvement in performance for coalescing functionality compared to using functions, and an 18% improvement in performance for coalescing functionality over using objects. In situations where performance is everything, as in financial transactions, this is a significant difference.

But splitting our functionality into functions makes our code much more readable. It's fairly obvious what code like average = getAvg or sum = getSum does.

Creating objects takes that improvement even further. You can reuse objects between projects, pass the objects between applications, extend the objects into new ones, or decorate the prototype chain, to reuse functionality.

In most cases the extra overhead is worth the reusability and readability gains.

Closure Compiler

Another case of scorched-earth performance is what Google's Closure Compiler does to JavaScript when using Advanced mode. I touched a little on Closure Compiler back in Chapter 2, but let's now look at a fleshed-out example.

Closure Compiler can be run in either of two modes:

- In Simple mode it mostly performs like most other minifiers, removing whitespace, line breaks, and comments

- In Advanced mode it rewrites the JavaScript by renaming variables and functions from longer descriptive names to single letters to save file size, and it inlines functions, coalescing them into single functions wherever it determines that it can.

It is Advanced mode that I would consider scorched-earth. Let's take a look at an example.

Creating an Example

First create a baseline file called benchmarkobjects.html. On this page you will create two objects, a user object and a video object. The user will be able to add video to their favorites list. You'll exercise this ability in a function and benchmark that function.

Start with the familiar basic skeletal HTML structure and include the perfLogger library:

```
<!DOCTYPE html>
<html>
<head>
<meta charset="UTF-8" />
<title>Loop Comparison</title>
<script src="/lab/perfLogger.js"></script>
</head>
<body>
</body>
</html>
```

In the body, create a script tag and start making object constructors. First create the constructor for the video object; it will accept a parameter that becomes the video title, and it has a public method called printInfo() that simply returns the video title.

```
<script>
function video(title){
        this.title = title;
        this.printInfo = function(){
            return this.title;
        }


    }
</script>
```

Next create the constructor for the user object. The user object accepts a parameter that is set as the user name, and it has two public methods: addToFavorite(), which pushes the passed-in object into the user's favoriteList, and showFavorites(), which loops through the favoriteList. The user object then console-logs the return value from calling printInfo on each video in the favoriteList:

```
function user(uname){
    this.username = uname;
    this.favoriteList = [];
    this.addToFavorite = function(a){
        this.favoriteList[this.favoriteList.length] = a;
    }
```

```
    this.showFavorites = function(){
        for(var f = 0; f < this.favoriteList.length; f++){
            var t = this.favoriteList[f].printInfo();
            console.log(t);
        }
    }
}
```

Finally, create a function that will exercise the functionality you just created and benchmark that function. It will create a new user object and iterate 20 times, creating a new video object each step and adding that new video to the user's favoriteList:

```
function testUserObject(){
    var u1 = new user("tom");
    for(var i = 0; i < 20; i++){
        u1.addToFavorite(new video("video "+ i));
    }
    u1.showFavorites();
}
```

```
perfLogger.logBenchmark("benchmarkObject", 10, testUserObject, true, true);
```

Your completed page should look like this:

```
<!DOCTYPE html>
<html>
<head>
<meta charset="UTF-8" />
<title>Loop Comparison</title>
<script src="/lab/perfLogger.js"></script>
</head>
<body>
    <script>
    function user(uname){
        this.username = uname;
        this.favoriteList = [];
        this.addToFavorite = function(a){
            this.favoriteList[this.favoriteList.length] = a;
        }

        this.showFavorites = function(){
            for(var f = 0; f < this.favoriteList.length; f++){
                var t = this.favoriteList[f].printInfo();
                console.log(t);
            }
        }
    }

    function video(title){
        this.title = title;
        this.printInfo = function(){
            return this.title;
```

```
        }

    }

    function testUserObject(){
        var u1 = new user("tom");
        for(var i = 0; i < 20; i++){
            u1.addToFavorite(new video("video "+ i));
        }
        u1.showFavorites();
    }

    perfLogger.logBenchmark("benchmarkObject", 10, testUserObject, true, true);
    </script>
</body>
</html>
```

And when you look at the page in a browser, you should see something like the following:

```
benchmarking function testUserObject(){ var u1 = new user("tom"); for(var i = 0; i < 20; i++){
u1.addToFavorite(new video("video "+ i)); } u1.showFavorites();          }
average run time: 0.6119000026956201ms
path: http://tom-barker.com/lab/benchmarkobjects.html
useragent: Mozilla/5.0 (Macintosh; Intel Mac OS X 10_5_8) AppleWebKit/536.11 (KHTML, like Gecko)
Chrome/20.0.1132.47 Safari/536.11
```

Run Through Closure Compiler

Now you are ready to run the code through Closure Compiler. The easiest way to do that is to use the Closure Compiler UI, accessible here: http://closure-compiler.appspot.com/home.

Closure Compiler UI is a web application (see Figure 8-2). On the left you enter the JavaScript and choose from a number of options, and on the right is the output of Closure Compiler.

Figure 8-2. *The Closure Compiler UI*

The options on the top left are:

- A text box where you can enter the URL of a remote JavaScript file to be included in the compilation. To use this, simply type in the URL and click the Add button. You'll see the URL reflected in the large text area in the bottom, like so:

```
// @code_url http://tom-barker.com/lib/perfLogger.js
```

- A series of radio buttons that indicate the mode that Closure Compiler should run in, either Whitespace Only, Simple, or Advanced. Whitespace Only does just what it sounds like; it removes comments, line breaks, and unneeded whitespace. Simple compilation removes whitespace, line breaks, and comments but it also renames local variables to use smaller names. As you've already seen, Advanced compilation completely rewrites the JavaScript.

- Your choice of formatting. Pretty Print includes line breaks and indents for easier reading, and Print Input Delimiter allows you to pass in a string that will function as boundaries between blocks of passed-in code—if we pass in multiple remote files, the input delimiter will print (in comments) between the code from each file so that we can tell which code block came from which file.

- A Compile button, and finally a large text area where you can enter your options and any additional code you want to compile.

On the right side is a large text area where the compiled code is output. There are also tabs to see any warnings or errors that were generated during compilation.

For this test if you include perfLogger.js as a file include and compile it, you get a JavaScript error when trying to use the results because Closure Compiler has renamed the shim for performance.now(); see Figure 8-3.

Figure 8-3. JavaScript error thrown when running perfLogger through Closure Compiler Advanced Compilation

So to make the test work you can just copy and paste the contents of perfLogger into the text area on the right side, and change the performance.now references to Date.now().Then copy the contents of the script tag from benchmarkobjects.html into the text area below the contents of perfLogger. See Figure 8-4.

Figure 8-4. Running perfLogger through Closure Compiler UI

Then create a new page with just the basic HTML skeletal structure, put a script tag in the body, and copy and paste the compiled JavaScript into the script tag. The test file should look like the following:

```
<!DOCTYPE html>
<html>
<head>
<meta charset="UTF-8" />
<title>Closure Compiler Benchmark</title>
</head>
<body>
<script>
var c, e;
function f() {
}
function g(a) {
```

```
 var d = f.prototype, b;
 for(b in d) {
   a[b] = d[b]
 }
 return a
}
function j(a) {
 var d = document.getElementById("debug"), b = "<p><strong>" + k[a].description + "</
strong><br/>", b = k[a].c ? b + ("average run time: " + k[a].c + "ms<br/>") : b + ("run time: "
+ k[a].j + "ms<br/>"), b = b + ("path: " + k[a].url + "<br/>"), b = b + ("useragent: " + k[a].v
+ "<br/>"), b = b + ("Perceived Time: " + k[a].g + "<br/>"), b = b + ("Redirect Time: " + k[a].h
+ "<br/>"), b = b + ("Cache Time: " + k[a].d + "<br/>"), b = b + ("DNS Lookup Time: " + k[a].e +
"<br/>"), b = b + ("tcp Connection Time: " +
 k[a].m + "<br/>"), b = b + ("roundTripTime: " + k[a].i + "<br/>"), b = b + ("pageRenderTime: "
+ k[a].f + "<br/>"), a = b + "</p>";
 d ? d.innerHTML += a : (d = document.createElement("div"), d.id = "debug", d.innerHTML = a,
document.body.appendChild(d))
}
function l(a) {
 a = "data=" + JSON.stringify(g(k[a]));
 console.log(a);
 var d = new XMLHttpRequest;
 d.open("POST", m, !0);
 d.setRequestHeader("Content-type", "application/x-www-form-urlencoded");
 d.setRequestHeader("Content-length", a.length);
 d.setRequestHeader("Connection", "close");
 d.onreadystatechange = function() {
 };
 d.send(a)
}
var m = "savePerfData.php", k = [];
if(window.D) {
 var n = Date.now() - performance.a.C || 0, o = performance.a.G - performance.a.H || 0, p =
performance.a.p - performance.a.B || 0, q = performance.a.A - performance.a.p || 0, r =
performance.a.w - performance.a.o || 0, t = performance.a.I - performance.a.o || 0, u = Date.
now() - performance.a.z || 0
}
c = f.prototype;
c.g = n;
c.h = o;
c.d = p;
c.e = q;
c.m = r;
c.i = t;
c.f = u;
e = {k:function(a, d, b, h) {
 k[a] = new f;
 k[a].id = a;
 k[a].startTime = Date.now();
 k[a].description = d;
 k[a].q = b;
```

```
 k[a].s = h
}, l:function(a) {
 k[a].u = Date.now();
 k[a].j = k[a].u - k[a].startTime;
 k[a].url = window.location.href;
 k[a].v = navigator.userAgent;
 k[a].q && j(a);
 k[a].s && l(a)
}, r:function(a, d, b, h, v) {
 for(var i = 0, s = 0;s < d;s++) {
   e.k(a, "benchmarking " + b, !1, !1), b(), e.l(a), i += k[a].j
 }
 k[a].c = i / d;
 h && j(a);
 v && l(a)
}, g:function() {
 return n
}, h:function() {
 o
}, d:function() {
 return p
}, e:function() {
 return q
}, m:function() {
 return r
}, i:function() {
 return t
}, f:function() {
 return u
}, J:function() {
 this.k("no_id", "draw perf data to page", !0, !0);
 this.l("no_id")
}};
function w() {
 this.K = "tom";
 this.b = [];
 this.n = function(a) {
   this.b[this.b.length] = a
 };
 this.t = function() {
   for(var a = 0;a < this.b.length;a++) {
     console.log(this.b[a].title)
   }
 }
}
function x(a) {
 this.title = a;
 this.F = function() {
   return this.title
 }
}
```

```
e.r("benchmarkClosureCompiler", 10, function() {
 for(var a = new w, d = 0;20 > d;d++) {
   a.n(new x("video " + d))
 }
 a.t()
}, !0, !0);
</script>
</body>
</html>
```

If you view this in a browser you should see the following.

```
benchmarking function () { for(var a = new w, d = 0;20 > d;d++) { a.n(new x("video " + d)) }
a.t() }
average run time: 0.9ms
path: http://tom-barker.com/lab/benchmarkclosurecompiler.html
useragent: Mozilla/5.0 (Macintosh; Intel Mac OS X 10_5_8) AppleWebKit/536.11 (KHTML, like Gecko)
Chrome/20.0.1132.47 Safari/536.11
```

When checking the log file, you can see that the Closure Compiler–rewritten code doesn't quite save all of the fields to the log file. This is because Closure Compiler renamed most of the variables, including runtime. If you console.log the serialized data, you can see that the data being posted looks like this:

```
data={"id":"benchmarkClosureCompiler","startTime":1344114475936,"description":"benchmarking
function () {\n    for (var a = new w, d = 0; 20 > d; d++) {\n        a.n(new x(\"video \" +
d));\n    }\n    a.t();\n}","q":false,"s":false,"u":1344114475943,"j":7,"url":"http://tom-
barker.com/lab/benchmarkclosurecompiler.html","v":"Mozilla/5.0 (Macintosh; Intel Mac OS X 10.5;
rv:16.0) Gecko/16.0 Firefox/16.0","c":18.6}
```

The runtime variable is that little "c" value at the end. Good luck trying to parse that out of the stew that the compiled source code is now. To be fair, there are ways to preserve property names, like using quoted string property names—for example by using testResult["runtime"] instead of obj.runTime. For more information about this, see Google's documentation here: https://developers.google.com/closure/compiler/docs/api-tutorial3.

When you pass the data back to savePerfData.php, that code is expecting a variable runTime or avgRunTime, not c, so runtime data is never retrieved.

But that's OK; the benefit we are interested in here is in web performance, so we'll compare the two pages in WebPagetest.

Compare and Analyze

Let's go to webpagetest.com and run tests for both of our URLs. The following table has the URLs tested and the test result URLs for the tests that I ran.

URL to Test	Test Result URL
tom-barker.com/lab/benchmarkobjects.html	http://www.webpagetest.org/result/120803_WS_ad105844519fccc308dd9f678bc0caae/
tom-barker.com/lab/benchmarkclosurecompiler.html	http://www.webpagetest.org/result/120803_BO_20df854313c5101e6339e24bb0d958ec/

The summary results are shown in Figures 8-5 and 8-6.

Figure 8-5. Summary Web Performance Results for benchmarkobject.html

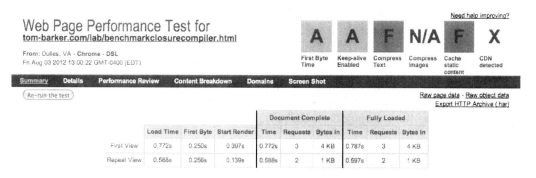

Figure 8-6. Summary Web Performance Results for benchmarkclosurecompiler.html

From the result screens just shown, you can see that the Closure Compiler–generated test has a load time that is 200 milliseconds faster, a first byte time that is 100 milliseconds faster, a start render time that is almost 600 milliseconds faster, a document complete time that is 145 milliseconds faster, and a fully loaded time that is 291 milliseconds faster. Clearly there are significant gains to be had by using Closure Compiler's Advanced mode.

But at this point you should also be able to see the downside. It was necessary to alter the original code just for the compiled code to work in the browser without generating errors. Once it was working in a browser, you saw that some of the hooks into the back-end stopped working.

And all of this is just a small test example, very self-contained. Imagine if we had third-party ad code embedded in the page. Imagine if we interacted with plug-ins with our JavaScript.

Now imagine adding new features to our original code and doing this all over again. Every week. With 20 people having their hands in the code base.

We've had to alter our workflow and introduce at least one extra debugging step, testing that everything actually works after compilation. We've added a level of complexity, a new breakpoint for our code to stop working. And debugging at this level, after everything has been obfuscated, is degrees of magnitude harder than debugging our own native code that we have already written.

Are the gains in performance that we see worth the extra effort and additional level of complexity that would be entailed in maintaining and updating compiled code?

Next Steps: From Practice to Practical Application

Throughout the book so far we have been creating tests and talking about and looking at data that is being generated from these tests at scale. We now look at the tactics of doing this on the job.

Monitoring Web Performance

This is fairly straightforward. You'll just need to choose a number of URLs that you want to monitor, plug them into WPTRunner, and begin tracking those URLs over time.

As you gather data you should review that data with your team. Identify areas for improvement—are your images not optimized, is your content not gzipped, how can you minimize HTTP requests? Set performance goals and begin working toward those goals with your team.

Instrumenting Your Site

The next thing you want to do, if you aren't doing so already, is to instrument your site—to put benchmarking code live in production to gather real live performance data for your pages that are already out in the wild.

To do this, you just need to choose what pages you want to monitor, choose a set of metrics that you want to gather—maybe the perceived load time of the page, maybe the runtime of the more complex pieces of functionality—and integrate perfLogger into those pages to capture that data. Note that you probably don't want to use the benchmark feature of perfLogger, since that will impact the performance of the pages, but rather use the startTimeLogging and stopTimeLogging functions to capture timing information.

I do this on my own site. In Figure 8-7 you can see a screenshot of my home page with perfLogger debug information on the far right side of the page.

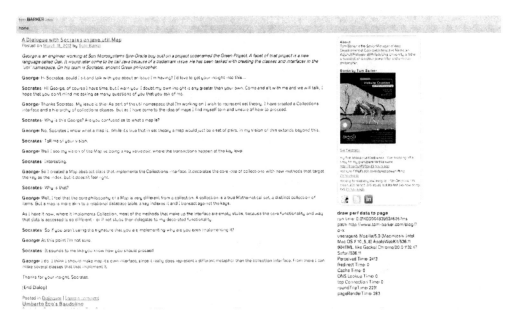

Figure 8-7. *The tom-barker.com site with performance data drawn to the screen*

The benefit of putting instrumentation on our live sites is that we get real live data from our actual users. We track this data over time and look for issues as conditions change—new browsers and browser versions get introduced, new features get promoted to production, and so on. Issues can appear as spikes in performance numbers to indicate that something is suddenly running much slower, or even unexpected drops in performance numbers, which could indicate that your site might be unavailable to your users.

Instrumenting your site is something that is done as regular maintenance of your site.

Benchmark in Your Test Lab

So we instrument our code in production and we monitor our web performance regularly, but how do we make sure our code is performant before we release it? We benchmark in a test lab.

A test lab can be a physical lab full of workstations, or it can be one or two machines with virtual machines running on them.

If you have the scale, budget, and staff for a physical test lab, then that's awesome! That's how it's done for real world-class web applications. But for 7 out of the last 12 companies that I've worked at, that was a pipe dream. My developers and I would have to test and certify our own code on our own machines. And in some cases that may be all that you need.

In either case your first order of business is to establish a browser support matrix—how else can you know what browsers and clients to assemble if you don't have a clear list of what you will support. At the bare minimum a browser support matrix is a list of browsers and browser versions and what level of support you will provide for those browsers. In my own experience there are generally three levels of support—will we provide support to an end user using this browser (Support in Production), should our QA team test with this browser in their regular testing (Test in QA), and should our engineers be conducting developer testing with these browsers, at least making sure that features function in these browsers (Developer Testing)? See Figure 8-8 for an example of this sort of browser matrix.

Browser	Support in Production	Test in QA	Developer Testing
IE 10	N	Y	Y
IE 9	Y	Y	Y
IE 8	Y	Y	N
IE 7	Y	Y	N
Chrome 21b	N	Y	Y
Chrome 20	Y	Y	Y
Chrome 19	Y	Y	N
Firefox Aurora	N	N	Y
Firefox Beta	N	Y	Y
Firefox 14	Y	Y	Y
Firefox 13	Y	Y	N
Safari 5.5	Y	Y	Y
Safari 5.0x	N	Y	N

Figure 8-8. A bare-minimum browser support matrix

Ideally and eventually, though, your browser support matrix should include things like plug-ins, as well as a breakdown of features, because not every feature may work in every browser. See Figure 8-9 for a more robust browser support matrix.

Browser	Support in Production	Test in QA	Developer Testing	Expandable Left Nav	Content Reflow	Ad Break Out	On Load Fade
iOS 5.0	Y	Y	Y	Y	Y	Y	Y
iOS 4.3	Y	Y	N	Y	Y	Y	Y
Android 4.0	Y	Y	Y	Y	Y	Y	Y
Android 3.1	Y	Y	N	Y	Y	Y	Y
IE 10	N	Y	Y	Y	Y	Y	Y
IE 9	Y	Y	Y	Y	Y	Y	Y
IE 8	Y	Y	N	Y	N	Y	N
IE 7	Y	Y	N	N	N	Y	N
Chrome 21b	N	N	Y	Y	Y	Y	Y
Chrome 20	Y	Y	Y	Y	Y	Y	Y
Chrome 19	Y	Y	N	Y	Y	Y	Y
Firefox Aurora	N	N	Y	Y	Y	Y	Y
Firefox Beta	N	N	Y	Y	Y	Y	Y
Firefox 14	Y	Y	Y	Y	Y	Y	Y
Firefox 13	Y	Y	N	Y	Y	Y	Y
Safari 5.5	Y	Y	Y	Y	Y	Y	Y
Flash 11	Y	Y	Y	N/A	N/A	N/A	N/A
Flash 10	Y	Y	N	N/A	N/A	N/A	N/A
Silverlight 5	Y	Y	Y	N/A	N/A	N/A	N/A
Silverlight 4	Y	Y	N	N/A	N/A	N/A	N/A

Figure 8-9. A more detailed browser support matrix

The way you start to choose your browser matrix is by looking at your logs—what browsers are most used by your clients? Make sure you take into account at least the most active browsers, which won't always be the most attractive browsers. (How many years did you need to support IE 6 just because your user base was locked into it because of corporate upgrade policy?) But don't assume that because a certain set of browsers are being used to visit your site, you only need to focus on those browsers. It may just be that your site only works best on those browsers. Also make sure you include beta and earlier browsers in your matrix as well, so that you can code for the future.

Once you have your browser support matrix, you can begin gathering workstations or virtual machines to test on those. Even if you have a QA staff that handles testing, as web developers the onus is on us to make sure that what we create is functional and in a good state before handing off to QA. That includes benchmarking our code against our browser matrix.

If you are going to use virtual machines (VMs), my favorite option is to use Virtual Box from Oracle, available at https://www.virtualbox.org/. It's a completely free, open source, lightweight, professional-level solution for running VMs. See Figure 8-10 for the Virtual Box homepage.

Figure 8-10. The homepage for Virtual Box

You simply go to the download section and choose the correct binary for your native operating system. See Figure 8-11 for the Virtual Box download page.

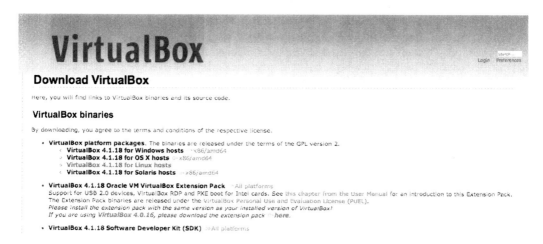

Figure 8-11. The Virtual Box download page

Once you've downloaded and installed Virtual Box, you can simply add new virtual machines by following the instructions in the application. Note that you'll need the install disk or the disk images for each operating system that you want to run. Once you have all of your VMs set up, your Virtual Box installation should look something like Figure 8-12.

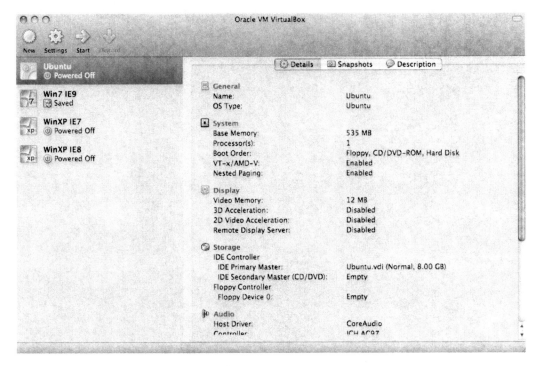

Figure 8-12. Virtual Box with multiple VMs

In this post-PC era don't forget to include mobile browsers in your matrix. Your best bet is, of course, to have devices on hand to test on, but barring that you can run an emulator/simulator on your laptop or use a third party like Keynote Device Anywhere that can make available a complete test center full of devices, available for manual or scripted testing remotely. More information about Keynote Device Anywhere can be found at their website, http://www.keynotedeviceanywhere.com/.

The iOS simulator comes bundled in with XCode, but getting and installing the Android emulator it is a bit more involved. You must first download the Android SDK from http://developer.android.com/sdk/index.html. Figure 8-13 shows the download page.

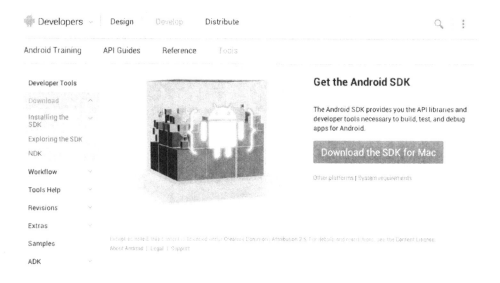

Figure 8-13. *Android SDK download page*

Once it's downloaded you'll need to expand the compressed file and navigate to the tools directory to get to the SDK Manager. On a Windows machine you can simply double-click the SDK Manager executable in the tools directory. On a Mac or Linux box you need to go into Terminal, cd to the directory, and launch android sdk:

```
>cd /android-sdk-macosx/tools
> ./android sdk
```

This opens the SDK Manager, shown in Figure 8-14. From the SDK Manager you can download and install an Android Platform and a set of platform tools. The platform you download will be the device image that you load up.

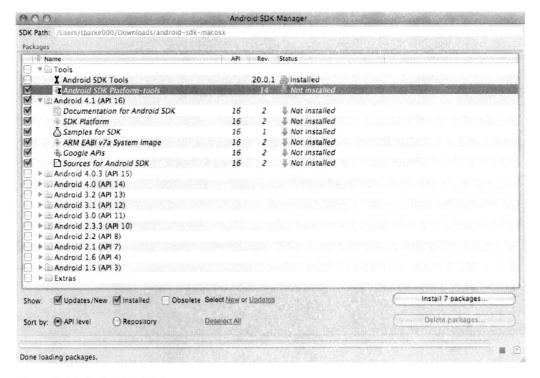

Figure 8-14. Android SDK Manager

Once you have downloaded a platform and the platform tools, you next need to launch the Android Virtual Device Manager, by running android avd in the tools directory:

`./android avd`

The Android Device Manager, much like Virtual Box, will allow you to create and run virtual machines. See Figure 8-15 for the Android Virtual Device Manager.

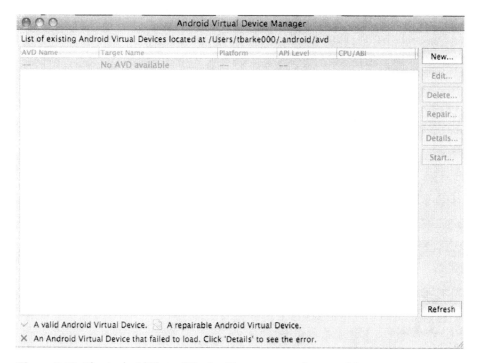

Figure 8-15. *The Android Virtual Device Manager, running on a Mac*

In the Android Virtual Device Manager you can create a new virtual device from the platform that you just downloaded. To do so, just click the New button to bring up the screen shown in Figure 8-16. Here you configure your new virtual device.

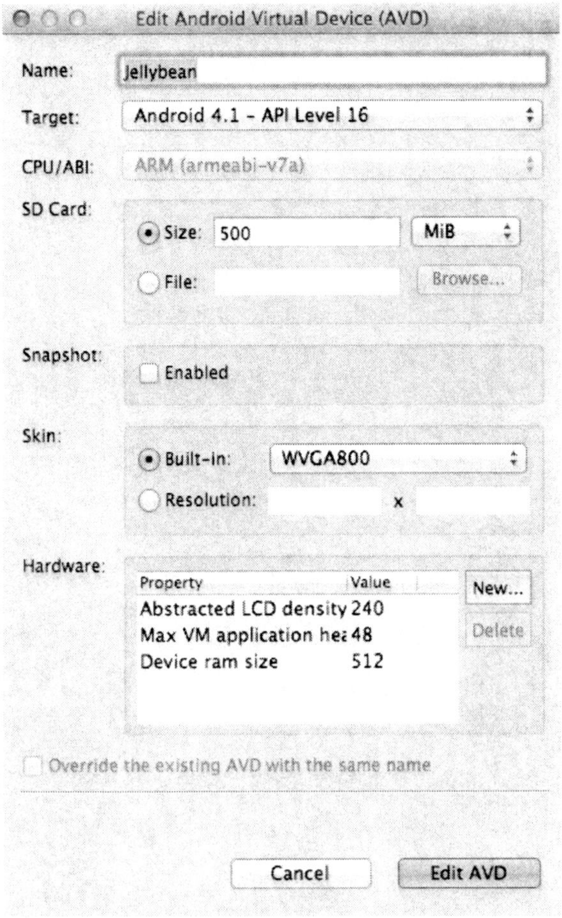

Figure 8-16. Adding an Android Virtual Device

When you are done you can launch the device and load up the browser. See Figure 8-17 for the emulator in action.

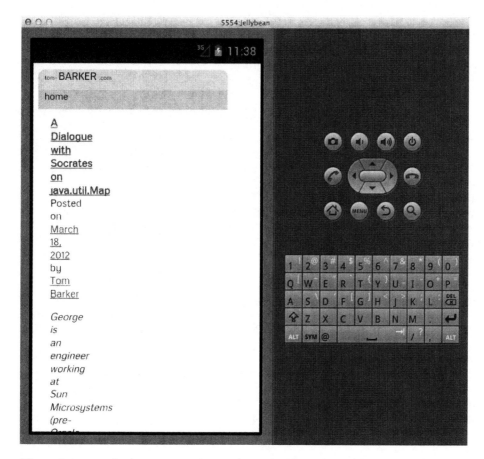

Figure 8-17. tom-barker.com running on the Android emulator

OK. You're instrumenting your production code, monitoring the web performance of your pages in production, and benchmarking the code in a test lab against your browser matrix. What now?

Share Your Findings

Benchmarking, instrumenting, and monitoring are great, but if you don't tell anyone, what is the point? Share your findings with your team. But first analyze your data—I mean really understand your data so that you can speak to each data point and have an idea about the cause or implication of each finding.

Use the data visualization skills that you have been refining throughout the course of the book to generate charts, assemble the charts into a report, and share your analysis. Play with different types of charts to see which ones better communicate your point.

Have an open mind, and consider the context. Are you missing something that can explain a larger picture? Get second opinions and double-check your tests. Maybe the test you are benchmarking is flawed in some way, like an improperly scoped variable throwing off your results.

Once you have your findings double-checked your analysis complete, and your charts created, you should assemble your results into a report, maybe an email, maybe a PDF, maybe a wiki entry; it just needs to be something in which you can include not just your graphs but your analysis and context as well, and that can be distributed.

Review your report with your team, go over root causes, and come up with a plan of attack to address the areas for improvement. Above all else always strive to improve.

Summary

In this chapter we explored some closing thoughts about performance.

We talked about balancing performance with keeping the best practices of readability, reuse, and modularity. We looked at scorched-earth performance practices. We looked at the practice of inlining functions, coalescing them into a single function to reduce overhead that the JavaScript interpreter must go through to construct and execute function and object hierarchy. We created a test to compare the runtime performance of inlining functions versus using functions versus using objects.

While we saw performance gains with this scorched-earth performance practice, we also lost the gains of modularity, readability, and reusability that good software design gives us.

We also looked at running our code through Google's Closure Compiler. We saw significant web performance benefits. But we also saw that compiling our JavaScript down to the barest minimum also made our code much harder to debug, and would add a much more difficult layer of abstraction to maintain and update.

The point of these two examples was not just the raw numbers, it was that in all things we do we must strive to find balance. Performance is immensely important, but there are other aspects of quality just as important, if not more so.

We also talked about how to implement the things that we have learned. We discussed monitoring the web performance of our production sites using WPTRunner. We talked about using perfLogger to instrument our code live in the wild. We talked about assembling a browser support matrix and creating a test lab to benchmark our code in our test lab.

And finally we talked about the importance of sharing our data; using our findings as a feedback loop to identify areas of improvement in our continual quest to be excellent.

Index

Runtime performance, eval true cost (*cont.*)
- evalAverage () function, 162
- getAvg function, 161
- HTML skeletal structure, 161
- interpreter, 161
- perfLogger.logBenchmark, 162
- JQuery *vs.* Javascript (*see* JQuery *vs.* Javascript)
- nested loop
  - benchmarking function results, 170
  - code execution, 168
  - increasing depth chart, 171–173
  - script tag and tempArray variable creation, 168
  - slow script warnings, 169–170
- numbers, 139

■ S

Scorched-earth performance
- Closure Compiler
  - Advanced mode, 183, 191
  - basic skeletal HTML structure, 183
  - benchmarkobjects.html, 183
  - completed page, 184–185
  - debugging, 191
  - favoriteList, 184
  - JavaScript error, 187
  - printInfo(), 183
  - running perfLogger, 187
  - Simple mode, 183
  - test file, 187–190
  - testUserObject function, 184
  - UI, 185, 186
  - URLs test, 190
  - user object, 183
  - video function, 183
  - web performance results, 191
- inlining functions
  - basic skeletal HTML structure, 177
  - coalescing functionality, 182
  - getAvg() function, 178
  - getSum() function, 178
  - PlotResultsofTestsByBrowser() function, 181
  - simpleMath function, 178
  - test page, 179–181
  - unwoundfunction() function, 177
  - usingfunctions() function, 178
  - usingobjects function, 179
- Session/site abandonment, 8
- SpiderMonkey, 6
- src attribute, 136

statusCode node, 48

■ T

Test lab benchmark
- Android SDK
  - Device Manager, 198–200
  - download page, 196, 197
  - emulator, 200, 201
  - Manager, 197, 198
- browser support matrix, 193, 194
- iOS simulator, 196
- Keynote Device Anywhere, 196
- Virtual Box
  - download page, 195
  - homepage, 194, 195
  - with multiple VMs, 195, 196
Threads, 3
Transmission Control Protocol (TCP), 3
Trident, 6

■ U, V

useAppendChild function, 166

■ W, X

W3C Web Performance, 83
Webkit, 6
WebPagetest
- Auth tab, 20
- Block tab, 21
- code repository, 19
- document.onload event, 19
- performance optimization checklist, 22
- pie charts, 22
- Preserve original User Agent string option, 20
- public web site, 19
- results page, 21
- Script tab, 20
- setUserAgent command, 21
- SSL certification errors, 19
- Video tab, 21
- waterfall charts, 22
Web performance
- definition, 1
- network transactions diagram, 2
- optimizations
  - lazy loading (*see* Lazy loading)
  - page render bottlenecks (*see* Page render bottlenecks)

■ Y, Z

CPSIA information can be obtained at www.ICGtesting.com
Printed in the USA
LVOW111506021112

305625LV00003B/1/P